LIVING WITH UNCERTAINTY

Every choice we make is set against a background of massive ignorance about our past, our future, our circumstances, and ourselves. Philosophers are divided on the moral significance of such ignorance. Some say that it has a direct impact on how we ought to behave – the question of what our moral obligations are; others deny this, claiming that it only affects how we ought to be judged in light of the behavior in which we choose to engage – the question of what responsibility we bear for our choices. Michael Zimmerman claims that our ignorance has an important bearing on both questions, and offers an account of moral obligation and moral responsibility that is sharply at odds with the prevailing wisdom. His book will be of interest to a wide range of readers in ethics.

MICHAEL J. ZIMMERMAN is Professor of Philosophy at the University of North Carolina at Greensboro. His publications include *The Concept of Moral Obligation* (1996, 2007), also in the Cambridge Studies in Philosophy series.

CAMBRIDGE STUDIES IN PHILOSOPHY

General Editors

JONATHAN LOWE *(University of Durham)*
WALTER SINNOTT-ARMSTRONG *(Dartmouth College)*

Advisory Editors

JONATHAN DANCY *(University of Reading)*
JOHN HALDANE *(University of St. Andrews)*
GILBERT HARMAN *(Princeton University)*
FRANK JACKSON *(Australian National University)*
WILLIAM G. LYCAN *(University of North Carolina at Chapel Hill)*
SYDNEY SHOEMAKER *(Cornell University)*
JUDITH J. THOMSON *(Massachusetts Institute of Technology)*

Recent Titles

DAVID LEWIS *Papers on Ethics and Social Philosophy*
FRED DRETSKE *Perception, Knowledge, and Belief*
LYNNE RUDDER BAKER *Persons and Bodies*
ROSANNA KEEFE *Theories of Vagueness*
JOHN GRECO *Putting Skeptics in Their Place*
RUTH GARRETT MILLIKAN *On Clear and Confused Ideas*
DERK PEREBOOM *Living Without Free Will*
BRIAN ELLIS *Scientific Essentialism*
ALAN H. GOLDMAN *Practical Rules*
CHRISTOPHER HILL *Thought and World*
ANDREW NEWMAN *The Correspondence Theory of Truth*
ISHTIYAQUE HAJI *Deontic Morality and Control*
WAYNE A. DAVIS *Meaning, Expression and Thought*
PETER RAILTON *Facts, Values, and Norms*
JANE HEAL *Mind, Reason and Imagination*
JONATHAN KVANVIG *The Value of Knowledge and the Pursuit of Understanding*
ANDREW MELNYK *A Physicalist Manifesto*
WILLIAM S. ROBINSON *Understanding Phenomenal Consciousness*
D. M. ARMSTRONG *Truth and Truthmakers*
KEITH FRANKISH *Mind and Supermind*
MICHAEL SMITH *Ethics and the A Priori*
NOAH LEMOS *Common Sense*
JOSHUA GERT *Brute Rationality*

ALEXANDER R. PRUSS *The Principle of Sufficient Reason*
FOLKE TERSMAN *Moral Disagreement*
JOSEPH MENDOLA *Goodness and Justice*
DAVID COPP *Morality in a Natural World*
LYNNE RUDDER BAKER *The Metaphysics of Everyday Life*
SANFORD GOLDBERG *Anti-Individualism*

Living with Uncertainty

The Moral Significance of Ignorance

by

Michael J. Zimmerman
University of North Carolina at Greensboro

CAMBRIDGE
UNIVERSITY PRESS

CAMBRIDGE UNIVERSITY PRESS
Cambridge, New York, Melbourne, Madrid, Cape Town, Singapore,
São Paulo, Delhi, Dubai, Tokyo

Cambridge University Press
The Edinburgh Building, Cambridge CB2 8RU, UK

Published in the United States of America by Cambridge University Press, New York

www.cambridge.org
Information on this title: www.cambridge.org/9780521171717

First published 2008
This digitally printed version 2010

A catalogue record for this publication is available from the British Library

Library of Congress Cataloguing in Publication data

Zimmerman, Michael J., 1951-
Living with uncertainty : the moral significance of ignorance /
by Michael J. Zimmerman.
p.   cm. – (Cambridge studies in philosophy)
Includes bibliographical references and index.
ISBN 978-0-521-89491-3 (hardback)
1. Ethics. 2. Ignorance (Theory of knowledge) 3. Uncertainty.
I. Title. II. Series.
BJ37.Z49   2008
170'.42–dc22
2008019564

ISBN 978-0-521-89491-3 Hardback
ISBN 978-0-521-17171-7 Paperback

Contents

Preface   page ix
Acknowledgments   xv

1 Ignorance and obligation   1
   1.1   Three views of moral obligation   2
   1.2   Ross on moral obligation   8
   1.3   Against the Subjective View   13
   1.4   Against the Objective View   17
   1.5   The Prospective View refined   33
   1.6   Objections to the Prospective View   42
   1.7   Risking wrongdoing   57
2 Risk and rights   72
   2.1   Prima facie moral obligation   73
   2.2   Moral rights   78
   2.3   Test case: fidelity   87
   2.4   Test case: self-defense   97
3 Prospective possibilism   118
   3.1   Actualism vs. Possibilism   119
   3.2   A holistic approach   126
   3.3   Intentional action   132
   3.4   Extension of the account   138
   3.5   Obligation and control   146
   3.6   Shifts in obligation   151
4 Ignorance and responsibility   169
   4.1   Moral obligation vs. moral responsibility   171
   4.2   Ignorance as an excuse   173

Contents

4.3 Accuses 193
4.4 A cautionary conclusion 205

References 206
Index of names 214
Index of subjects 216

Preface

Ours is an uncertain world. Every choice we make, every decision we reach, is set against a background of massive ignorance about our past, our future, our circumstances, ourselves. This, ironically, is something that we know all too well.

Ignorance is ignorance of facts. It is a failure to know what is true. To know what is true, one must believe it (something that involves having a certain level or degree of confidence in it) and do so with adequate justification. Thus ignorance can come about in one of two ways: either by way of failure to believe the truth or by way of believing it without adequate justification. There are two corresponding kinds of uncertainty: doxastic uncertainty, which consists in one's lacking full confidence in a proposition, and epistemic uncertainty, which consists in one's lacking justification in having full confidence in a proposition. Although not all uncertainty entails ignorance – one can know a proposition regarding which one is either not fully confident or not justified in being fully confident – all ignorance entails uncertainty of one or both kinds.

Philosophers are divided on the moral significance of the ignorance that besets us. Some say that it has a direct impact on how we ought to behave; others deny this, claiming that it only affects how we ought to be judged in light of the behavior in which we choose to engage. Until recently, I sided with the latter. I now side with the former. My thinking was changed by a simple thought-experiment proposed by Frank Jackson. It involves a physician, Jill, and her patient, John. (To be honest, I had been familiar with the case for quite some time – several years, in fact – before its insight and power dawned on me. My hope is that readers of this book will be considerably less obtuse.) John is suffering from a minor but not trivial skin complaint. Jill has three drugs with which she might treat him: A, B, and C. All the evidence at her disposal indicates, in keeping with what is in fact the case, that giving John drug B would cure him partially and that giving him no drug would leave him permanently incurable; it also indicates that one of drugs A and C would cure him completely while the other would kill him, but it leaves completely open which of them would cure and which kill.[1] What ought Jill to do?

You are supposed to answer: "She ought to give him drug B."

Jackson says that this answer is obvious, and I think he's right. (That is, it's obvious, given the proviso that "all else is equal." This is just a thought-experiment, after all. As such, it is of course idealized and simplistic, but that is precisely what makes it so instructive. As John Fischer has observed, such "streamlining," such abstraction and schematization in moral reflection, is the analogue of conducting a controlled experiment in science: in holding all other factors fixed, one can test a particular factor for its moral significance.[2] The factor tested here is Jill's ignorance regarding the outcome of giving John either drug A or drug C.) I strongly suspect that you think that Jackson is right, too. However, some people I know, including some friends whose judgment I normally hold in high regard, claim that he's not right about this. They say that what Jill ought to do is give John whichever of drugs A and C would cure him completely. I don't believe they mean what they say. Under the circumstances, giving John either of these drugs would surely be far too risky. And my friends know this. Being conscientious people, they would not run such a risk, were they to find themselves in Jill's position. They would give John drug B without hesitation. Their behavior would betray what they really thought, namely, that it would be wrong to treat him in any other way.

That it would be wrong to run the sort of risk associated with not giving John drug B has profound implications. This book explores some of these implications. I begin in chapter 1 by distinguishing, in section 1.1, three views regarding the general nature of overall moral obligation: the Objective View, the Subjective View, and the Prospective View. According to the Objective View, our overall moral obligation is always to choose that option that would *in fact* be best under the circumstances. In the case of Jill and John, that would mean that Jill ought to give John whichever of drugs A and C would cure him completely; she ought *not* to give him drug B. According to the Subjective View, our overall moral obligation is always to choose that option that we *believe* would be best

---

[1] Jackson 1991, pp. 462–3. Some details of Jackson's original case have been slightly altered. A case with similar features may be found on pp. 264–5 of Regan 1980. I am embarrassed to report that I read these pages long before I read Jackson's article, and yet their import was entirely lost on me.

[2] Fischer 1995, p. 10.

under the circumstances. In the case of Jill and John, that would mean that Jill ought to give John whichever of drugs A, B, and C she happens to believe would be best for him. Some philosophers (notably H. A. Prichard and W. D. Ross) have defended the Subjective View. I discuss and argue against this view in sections 1.2 and 1.3. Many philosophers have defended the Objective View, but I argue against it in section 1.4 because of its verdict in Jackson's case. In place of the Objective and Subjective Views I propose that we accept the Prospective View, according to which our overall moral obligation is always to choose that option that is *prospectively* best under the circumstances. I point out that this doesn't mean that we ought to choose that option that is *probably* best; after all, in Jackson's case giving John drug B is *certainly not* best, and yet that is what Jill ought to do. Rather, the prospectively best option is that which, from the moral point of view, it is *most reasonable* for the agent to choose – which is precisely what Jill's giving John drug B would be, since her giving him either drug A or drug C would be *too* risky. (Under other circumstances, of course, running a risk can be perfectly reasonable. Indeed, not running a risk can be unreasonable.) In sections 1.5 and 1.6 I develop and defend the Prospective View. I note that what constitutes the best prospect for an agent is determined by the evidence available to him or her at the time; it is a function of the epistemic uncertainty with which the agent is confronted. I note, too, that such uncertainty can extend not just to empirical matters, such as what the effects of giving John a certain drug would be, but also to evaluative matters, such as how to evaluate the effects of giving John a certain drug. Thus the best prospect is not necessarily that option that maximizes expected value (in that common sense of "expected value" which is a function only of uncertainty regarding empirical and not also of evaluative matters). Rather, what constitutes the best prospect is a question of what maximizes what I call "expectable value." This point has some important implications, among which is the fact that, due to badly distorted evaluative evidence (the product, perhaps, of a skewed upbringing), a person could be overall morally obligated to commit great evil. I end the chapter in section 1.7 by distinguishing the matter of risking doing *harm* from that of risking doing *wrong*, and I address the issue of how best to respond to the worry captured in the question "What ought I to do when I don't know what I ought to do?"

I turn in chapter 2 to the matter of prima facie moral obligation and the related issue of moral rights. In section 2.1 I provide a formulation of the Prospective View that accommodates both prima facie and overall obligation, and then, in section 2.2, I discuss how rights are to be accounted for in light of this formulation. Given that our overall moral obligation is to choose that option that is the best prospect under the circumstances, which is itself in part a function of the evidence that is available to us; and given that this overall obligation is determined by the relative weights of the various prima facie obligations that we have; and given, finally, that whatever rights others hold against us are correlative to at least some of these prima facie obligations, it follows that the rights that others hold against us are themselves in part a function of the evidence available *to us*. This fact has far-reaching and, in some ways, subversive implications. I explore some of these implications in sections 2.3 and 2.4, in which I discuss, respectively, the question of what rights people hold against us when we borrow something from them and the question of whether and when it is justifiable to kill someone in self-defense. Tracing these implications is a way of testing the credentials of the Prospective View. I claim that, although some of the implications may be somewhat surprising, the Prospective View nonetheless passes the tests. I also claim that the commonly accepted judgment that killing in self-defense can be justifiable in certain circumstances in which one's life is imperiled by another lends further support to the Prospective View, independently of that provided by Jackson's case.

In chapter 3 I attend to the matter of developing the Prospective View in detail. I begin in section 3.1 by rehearsing a debate that has taken place recently within the camp of those who subscribe to the Objective View. This debate has to do with the implications of future failings for present obligation. Should we accept or reject the thesis that what we ought now to do is determined in part by whether we will in fact fail to do what is best, when it is in our power to avoid such failure? Actualists say that we should accept the thesis, whereas Possibilists say that we should reject it. Many accept the Actualists' verdict, but I point out that it is in some ways objectionable and is, furthermore, based on a rationale that is deeply flawed. Possibilism, by contrast, is very attractive; it has a structure that permits the resolution of many so-called deontic paradoxes. Yet the verdict regarding future failings that unqualified Possibilism furnishes is in some cases unreasonable. In sections 3.2 and 3.3 I develop a qualified version of Possibilism that preserves its attractions while avoiding this troublesome verdict; this version is, of course, given in terms of the Prospective View, and what emerges is a precise formulation of that view. In section 3.4 I extend this formulation to cover conditional as well as unconditional obligation, prima facie as well as overall obligation, and yet other modes of obligation. So formulated, the Prospective View implies, among other things, that "ought" implies "can." In section 3.5 I discuss the relation between obligation and control (the sort of control that, in the present context, "can" expresses), and in section 3.6 I defend the thesis that "ought" implies "can" against what I take to be the most serious charge against it: that it lets people off the hook in cases in which they render themselves unable to fulfill their obligations. I argue that, by attending to the way in which obligations can shift over time, this charge can be defused. Not only that, but accounting for such shifts affords us a deeper understanding of the nature of moral obligation. For example, it turns out, perhaps surprisingly, that we can fail to fulfill an obligation without infringing it, that is, without doing wrong by virtue of failing to fulfill it. It also turns out, really quite surprisingly, that we can infringe an obligation and yet fulfill it.

Finally, in chapter 4, I turn from a discussion of moral obligation to a discussion of moral responsibility. The term "responsibility" can be used in a forward-looking sense, in which case it is synonymous with "obligation," but it can also be used in a backward-looking sense to refer to our present responsibility for things that have happened in the past. It is with this backward-looking sense of the term that I am concerned. It seems often to be assumed that one is morally responsible for having done something if and only if one had a moral obligation not to do it that one did not fulfill. This thesis, which I discuss in section 4.1, is false. It overlooks excuses, which involve wrongdoing without responsibility, and it also overlooks what I call "accuses," which involve responsibility without wrongdoing. The possibility of excuses is commonly recognized, that of accuses not so commonly recognized. In section 4.2 I investigate the conditions under which ignorance affords an excuse. I focus on that sort of ignorance that is constituted by the failure to believe that what one is doing is wrong. (The emphasis has thus shifted from epistemic uncertainty in the first three chapters to doxastic uncertainty in this chapter.) I argue that such ignorance affords an excuse far more often than is commonly supposed, and that this has important implications for our reaction to wrongdoing – in particular, for our practice of punishment. In section 4.3 I argue that accuses are indeed possible and that this, too, has important implications for our reaction to the absence of wrongdoing – in particular, for our habit of terminating our moral inquiries when we discover that no wrong has been done. I end with a cautionary note: we should be skeptical of the accuracy of our everyday ascriptions of responsibility.

The upshot of my investigation is that a wholly "objective," actual-outcome oriented approach, of the sort advocated by many philosophers, to either moral obligation or moral responsibility is badly misguided. The correct approach to moral obligation is captured by the Prospective View. The correct approach to moral responsibility is captured by the strongly "subjective" view that such responsibility turns at bottom, not on whether we have actually done right or wrong, but on whether we believed we were doing right or wrong. The rejection of a wholly objective approach to either obligation or responsibility has, I think, profound implications for the way in which we lead – or, rather, should lead – our lives. I have in mind the ways in which we deal with and react to others both in informal social settings and through the formal mechanisms of the law. I pursue some of these implications in the pages that follow, but providing a comprehensive account of them is the subject of at least one other book and is thus a task that I do not undertake in this one.

Acknowledgments

I am very grateful to the following people for help and advice on precursors of various portions of this book: Robert Adams, Gustaf Arrhenius, Simon Blackburn, Johan Brännmark, John Broome, Krister Bykvist, Åsa Carlson, Erik Carlson, Sara Rachel Chant, Randy Clarke, Roger Crisp, Sven Danielsson, Julia Driver, Daniel Elstein, Fred Feldman, John Fischer, Rick Gallimore, Pieranna Garavaso, Heather Gert, Jonas Gren, Ish Haji, Ross Harrison, Tom Hill, Brad Hooker, Magnus Jiborn, Jens Johansson, Janine Jones, Niklas Juth, John King, Andreas Lind, Ruth Lucier, Doug MacLean, Hans Mathlein, Terry McConnell, Matt McGrath, David McNaughton, Joseph Mendola, Jim Montmarquet, Ragnar Ohlsson, Jan Österberg, Ingmar Persson, Tomasz Pol, Jerry Postema, Robert Pulvertaft, Wlodek Rabinowicz, Toni Rønnow-Rasmussen, Gary Rosenkrantz, Joakim Sandberg, Julian Savulescu, Geoff Sayre-McCord, Walter Sinnott-Armstrong, Torbjörn Tännsjö, Peter Vallentyne, Rebecca Walker, Ralph Wedgwood, Paul Weirich, Susan Wolf, and David Wong.

During the writing of this book I received financial support, for which I am also very grateful, from the National Endowment for the Humanities.

Finally, I am grateful for permission to draw upon portions of the following articles of mine, recorded in the list of references as Zimmerman 1995 (© 1995 the University of Notre Dame Press), 1997a (© 1997 The University of Chicago), 1997b, 2002a (© Blackwell Publishing Inc.), 2006a (© 2006 Cambridge University Press), 2006b, 2006c (© Springer Science and Business Media), 2006d (© 2006 Ashgate Publishing Ltd.), 2006e (© Springer Science and Business Media), and 2006f.

1

Ignorance and obligation

"Ought" is ambiguous. Few deny this fact.[1] It straddles several distinctions. One such distinction is that between what is counseled by morality and that which is counseled, not by morality, but by reason, or prudence, or aesthetics, or the law, and so on. Within the broad category of morality, there is another distinction between that which is required or obligatory and that which is merely recommended. Within the category of moral obligation, there is still another distinction between that which is overall obligatory and that which is merely prima facie obligatory. "Ought" may be properly used in all such contexts.

So much I presume. In this chapter I will focus on the concept of overall moral obligation, and I will address yet another alleged distinction: that between what are often called objective and subjective obligation. It is frequently claimed that "ought" (together with associated terms, such as "right" and "wrong") may be, and is, used to express both forms of obligation, and that as a result people sometimes find themselves talking at cross-purposes. Consider what W.D. Ross has to say on the matter:

[W]hen people express different opinions about the rightness or wrongness of an act, the difference is often due to the fact that one of them is thinking of objective and the other of subjective rightness. The recognition of the difference between the two is therefore in itself important as tending to reconcile what might otherwise seem irreconcilable differences of opinion.[2]

This may seem sensible, but I think it is mistaken.

---

[1] One of the few: Judith Jarvis Thomson, who in Thomson 2001, pp. 44 ff., insists that there is only one "advice" sense of "ought." (She does, however, acknowledge another, "expectation" sense of "ought," as in: "The train ought to arrive by 3:00.")
[2] Ross 1939, p. 147.

1.1 THREE VIEWS OF MORAL OBLIGATION

It is with overall moral obligation that the *morally conscientious* person is primarily concerned. When one wonders what to do in a particular situation and asks, out of conscientiousness, "What ought I to do?," the "ought" expresses overall moral obligation. "Ought" here is a contrary of "wrong." Conscientiousness precludes deliberately doing what one believes to be overall morally wrong.[3]

There is disagreement about the general conditions of overall moral obligation. Here is one view (where "ought" is of course intended to express overall moral obligation):

The Objective View (first formulation):
An agent ought to perform an act if and only if it is the best option that he (or she) has.

This formulation is extremely rough, but it will do for present purposes. Let me just note a few points.

First, by an "option" I mean something that the agent can do, where "can" expresses some form of personal control. Thus the Objective View presupposes that the "ought" of moral obligation implies the "can" of personal control – an issue that I will discuss further in chapter 3.

Second, this account of overall moral obligation may be straightforwardly extended to cover overall moral rightness and wrongness. Thus: it is overall morally right for an agent to perform an act if and only if he has no better option; and it is overall morally wrong for an agent to perform an act if and only if he has a better option. In what follows, I will assume that the Objective View includes this extension.

Finally, I intend "best" to be very elastic. In this way, I believe, the Objective View can be applied to any substantive theory of moral obligation. Since it may not be obvious that the Objective View is generally applicable in this way, let me explain.

It is clear that the Objective View can be applied to the theory of obligation advocated by G.E. Moore.[4] According to this theory, which is a version of what has come to be called consequentialism, what we *ought* to do is a function of the *value* of what we can do, which is itself a function

---

[3] This is not to say that conscientiousness requires deliberately doing, or trying to do, only what one believes to be overall morally right, since on occasion one may find oneself forced to act while lacking any belief about the overall moral status of one's act.
[4] Moore 1912, chs. 1–2.

of some non-evaluative *"stuff."* The kind of value in question is instrumental value, the value that an act has in virtue of the intrinsic value of its consequences. Consequentialists differ among themselves as to what the stuff of intrinsic value is. For some the list is very short: pleasure is the only intrinsic good, and pain is the only intrinsic evil. For others (including Moore) the list is longer: also among the intrinsic goods are love, knowledge, and various virtues such as compassion and conscientiousness; and among the intrinsic evils are hatred, ignorance, and various vices such as cruelty and callousness. Despite these differences, consequentialists of this stripe are united in saying that, whatever the stuff of intrinsic value – that is, whatever in the end should be said to have intrinsic value – what we ought to do is that act which, among our alternatives, is to be ranked first in terms of the promotion of this stuff. When coupled with the Objective View, this yields the claim that what we ought to do is that act which is *actually* instrumentally best, that is, *actually* best in terms of the promotion of this stuff, relative to the other acts that we are in a position to perform.

What is perhaps not so clear is that this "ought"-value-stuff framework can be applied to other substantive theories of obligation, too, and hence that the Objective View can likewise be applied to them. The type of value at issue may vary, as may the stuff that is ultimately at stake or the relation between value and stuff. Nonetheless, the framework fits. Consider, for example, not Moore's type of consequentialism – act-consequentialism, as it is often called – but instead a version of rule-consequentialism, according to which what we ought to do is that act which, among our alternatives, is to be ranked first in terms, not of its own promotion of the stuff of intrinsic value, but rather in terms of conforming to a rule, the general adherence to which promotes the stuff of intrinsic value. Here the stuff that is ultimately at stake is the same as with act-consequentialism: pleasure, pain, or whatever else should be said to be of intrinsic (dis)value. However, the relevant value to be ascribed to acts has changed. Now one act is to be deemed better than another, not if the former is itself instrumentally better than the latter, but rather if the rule that covers the former is such that general adherence to it is instrumentally better than general adherence to the rule that covers the latter. (Of course, there may be differences among rule-consequentialists concerning just what general adherence to a rule consists in.) Let us call the former act "rule-better," for short. When coupled with the Objective View, rule-consequentialism thus issues in the claim that we ought to do that act which is *actually* rule-best, relative to the other acts that we are in a position to perform.

3

Or consider the sort of virtue-theoretical, non-consequentialist theory according to which what we ought to do is a matter, not of promoting virtue or vice, but of displaying virtue or vice. Virtue-theorists differ among themselves as to what the stuff of virtue and vice should be said to be. For some, the list will be short: compassion, cruelty, conscientiousness, and callousness, for example. For others the list will be longer. But again, despite these differences, such theorists are united in saying that acts may be assigned a kind of value – that is, they may be ranked relative to one another – in terms of how they succeed or fail in displaying the various virtues and vices; and they agree that what we ought to do is that act which, among our alternatives, is to be ranked first in terms of such a display. (Of course, there may be differences between virtue-theorists concerning just what the display of a virtue or vice consists in and just what determines whether one display is to be ranked higher than another with respect to the determination of obligation.) When coupled with the Objective View, this yields the claim that what we ought to do is that act which is *actually* best in terms of the display of compassion, cruelty, and the like.

Or consider the theory that our obligations have essentially to do with respecting people's rights. Rights-theorists differ among themselves as to what it is that people's rights concern: life, liberty, privacy, medical care, rest and leisure, periodic holidays with pay...[5] But, again, they are united in saying that, whatever the stuff of rights, what we ought to do is that act which, among our alternatives, is to be ranked first in terms of according people the stuff of rights. (Again, though, differences may remain concerning just what "according" someone the stuff of rights consists in.) When coupled with the Objective View, this issues in the claim that what we ought to do is that which is *actually* best in these terms.

Or consider, as a final example, the view that our obligations turn on whether our actions are rationally defensible. Proponents of this view differ among themselves as to the stuff of rational defensibility. Some cash this idea out in terms of the universalizability of the maxim of one's action; others in terms of whether one's action complies with the terms of some contract; and so on. But such theorists are united in saying that what we ought to do is that act which, among our alternatives, is to be ranked first in terms of the relevant stuff. When coupled with the Objective View, this yields the claim that what we ought to do is that act which is *actually* best in terms of universalizability, or compliance with some contract, and so on.

[5] See the 1948 *Universal Declaration of Human Rights*, cited in Feinberg 1973, pp. 94–5.

4

The foregoing remarks are sketchy, but they should suffice to show the general applicability of the "ought"-value-stuff framework. The underlying idea is straightforward. Any substantive theory of obligation can be cast as one according to which what one ought to do is ranked higher than any alternative.[6] These theories will differ as to the principle of ranking. According to some, that which is to be ranked first is that which is instrumentally best; according to others, it is that which is rule-best; according to others, it is that which is best in terms of the display of compassion, cruelty, and so on; or best in terms of protecting people's lives, property, and so on; or best in terms of universalizability; and so on and so forth. When coupled with the Objective View, these theories declare that what we ought to do is that which is *actually* instrumentally best, rule-best, and so on. But when coupled with something other than the Objective View, they will have a different implication.

As an alternative to the Objective View, consider this view about the general conditions of overall moral obligation:

The Subjective View (first and only formulation):
An agent ought to perform an act if and only if he believes that it is the best option that he has.

This view, too, can be supplemented with clauses pertaining to overall moral rightness and wrongness. Thus: it is overall morally right for an agent to perform an act if and only if he believes that he has no better option; and similarly for wrongness. And this view, too, is applicable to any substantive theory of moral obligation. For example, an act-consequentialist who subscribes to the Subjective View would say that what we ought to do is that act which we *believe* to be instrumentally best; the rule-consequentialist would say that what we ought to do is that act which we *believe* to be rule-best; a virtue-theorist would say that what we ought to do is that act which we *believe* to be best in terms of the display of the various virtues and vices; and so on.

It is obvious that the Objective View and the Subjective View do not exhaust the views that one might hold about the conditions of overall moral obligation. Here is yet another view:

[6] This is true even of so-called "satisficing," rather than "maximizing," theories. (Cf. Slote 1989.) And it is true, by default, of those theories that rank obligatory actions first and all non-obligatory alternatives equally last.

The Prospective View (first formulation):
An agent ought to perform an act if and only if it is probably the best option that
he has.

Like the Objective and Subjective Views, the Prospective View can be
supplemented with clauses pertaining to overall moral rightness and wrongness and can be applied to any substantive theory of moral obligation.

Let me stress again that these formulations of the Objective, Subjective,
and Prospective Views are all extremely rough. I will make adjustments if
and when the need arises.

The three views just mentioned clearly conflict. By this I mean, not that
their verdicts must diverge in every case, but that their verdicts do diverge
in some cases. Here is one such case, inspired by a case given by Frank
Jackson:[7]

Case 1:
Jill, a physician, has a patient, John, who is suffering from a minor but not trivial
skin complaint. In order to treat him, she has three drugs from which to choose:
A, B, and C. Drug A would in fact be best for John. However, Jill believes that B
would be best for him, whereas the available evidence indicates that C would be
best for him.

In this case, the Objective View implies that, all else being equal, Jill ought
to give John drug A, the Subjective View that she ought to give him drug
B, and the Prospective View (given that "probably" expresses epistemic
probability) that she ought to give him drug C.[8]

I have said that the three views conflict, but of course this is true only if
"ought" is used univocally in the statement of these views. One could
reconcile the views by claiming that, in the Objective View, "ought"
expresses objective obligation, whereas, in the Subjective View, it expresses
subjective obligation, and, in the Prospective View, it expresses prospective
obligation. This would be in keeping with the suggestion, recorded at the
outset of this chapter, that "ought" is ambiguous even when restricted to
the context of overall moral obligation. I said that this may seem a sensible
suggestion, but is it really plausible? I think not. First, it is clear that still

---

[7] This is the first of several cases modeled on a case provided in Jackson 1991, pp. 462–3.
[8] Note: *all else being equal*. This simplifying assumption is intended to allow us to bracket
concerns with such matters as patient autonomy, financial costs, and the like. We may
assume that John has consented to Jill's treating him however she chooses, that each drug
costs the same as the others, and so on.

further views are possible.[9] Should we really expect "ought" to be so adaptable that, for each such view, there is a distinct sense of the term that validates the view? This strains credulity. But, if not all such views capture a legitimate sense of "ought," how are we to discriminate between those that do and those that don't? Second, there is good reason to insist that "ought" is *not* equivocal in the manner just indicated – to insist, that is, that there is only *one* kind of overall moral obligation, and thus only *one* corresponding "ought." Let me explain.

I have said that it is with overall moral obligation that the morally conscientious person is primarily concerned. Let us assume that Jill is such a person. Being conscientious, she wants to make sure that she does no moral wrong in her treatment of John. She seeks your advice, telling you that she believes that drug B would be best for John but that she isn't sure of this.

"So," she says, "what ought I to do?"

You are very well informed. You know that A would be best for John, that Jill believes that B would be best for him, and that the evidence available to Jill (evidence of which she is apparently not fully availing herself, since her belief does not comport with it) indicates that C would be best for him. You therefore reply, "Well, Jill, objectively you ought to give John drug A, subjectively you ought to give him B, and prospectively you ought to give him C."

This is of no help to Jill. It is not the sort of answer she's looking for. She replies, "You're prevaricating. Which of the 'oughts' that you've mentioned is the one that *really* counts? Which 'ought' *ought* I to act on? I want to know which drug I am morally obligated to give John, *period*. Is it A, B, or C? It can only be one of them. It can't be all three."

Jill's demand for an *unequivocal* answer to her question is surely reasonable. There is a *unique* sense of "ought" with which she, as a conscientious person, is concerned; it is with what she ought to do in *this* sense that she seeks guidance. Unless and until you single out one of the drugs as being the one that she ought to give John, you will not have answered her question.

---

[9] For example, the view that an agent ought to perform an act if and only if he believes that it is probably the best option that he has.

Ross is himself well aware of this fact. I noted above that he distinguishes between what he calls objective and subjective rightness. However, having done so, he immediately goes on to add:

> But the question remains, which of the characteristics – objective or subjective rightness – is ethically the more important, which of the two acts is that which we ought to do.[10]

It is curious that Ross is prepared to declare "right" ambiguous between objective and subjective senses but not to declare "ought" similarly ambiguous. I can find no justification for such discrimination. Just as Jill wants to know what she really ought to do, so too she wants to know what drug it would really be right for her to give John. Once again, it would be of no help to her – you would not be addressing the question she raises – if you were to say, "Well, Jill, it would be objectively right for you to give John drug A, subjectively right to give him B, and prospectively right to give him C." Even if we were to countenance a proliferation of senses of "right" in the present context, we would need to single out that one sense with which Jill is concerned and focus on it. So too with senses of "ought." But I see no need to countenance any such proliferation. When it comes to the question of what Jill is overall morally obligated to do, only one sense of "ought" and only one sense of "right" count. Let us therefore repudiate any other putative senses. Case 1 gives us all the information we need: A would in fact be best for John; Jill believes that B would be best; the available evidence indicates that C would be best. Under these circumstances, which drug *ought* Jill to give John?

I.2 ROSS ON MORAL OBLIGATION

Ross was one of the first philosophers to address at any length the question which of the Objective, Subjective, and Prospective Views (if any) is correct. In his most famous work, *The Right and the Good*, he implicitly embraces the Objective View.[11] In a later book, *Foundations of Ethics*, in which he explicitly discusses each of the Objective, Subjective, and Prospective Views (although he appears to think that the third of these reduces to the second), he rejects the Objective View in favor of the Subjective View.[12] Ross attributes his conversion to H.A. Prichard, whose article "Duty and Ignorance of Fact" he deemed to make a

---

[10] Ross 1939, p. 147.   [11] Ross 1930, ch. 2.   [12] Ross 1939, ch. 7.

conclusive case for such a conversion.[13] In this section, I will examine the arguments that Ross gives against the Objective View and in favor of the Subjective View. In the next section, I will discuss some arguments against the Subjective View.

One argument that Ross gives is this.[14] An act cannot be right or obligatory unless it is reasonable to do it. Doing that which is in fact best can be unreasonable. (For example, if Jill is utterly careless regarding how she treats John – she throws a cloth over drugs A, B, and C, say, and then reaches underneath to pick at random one of the drugs with which to treat John – then, even if she manages to give John the best treatment, she will have acted unreasonably.) Doing that which one believes to be best is always reasonable. (For example, if Jill gives John drug B, believing this to constitute the best treatment, she will have acted reasonably.)

This is a poor argument. Note, first, that it is at best an argument against the Objective View; it does not establish the Subjective View. Even if we accept that carelessly doing what is in fact best is not reasonable, this suffices only to preclude the Objective View. We would arrive at the Subjective View only if it were added that only doing that which one believes best is reasonable.[15] A second problem concerns what counts as reasonable. A proponent of the Objective View is likely to insist that there always *is* a reason to do that which is best. Whether he would go on to say that one always *has* a reason to do that which is best is less clear. Whether he would go still further and say that it is always *reasonable* to do that which is best is even less clear. But what does seem clear is that an appeal to reasons or what is reasonable by itself provides insufficient reason to abandon the Objective View.[16] (Having said this, I should add that I think Ross is in fact on to something very important here. I will return to this point in section 1.4.)

A second argument that Ross suggests is this.[17] One is blameworthy if and only if one fails to fulfill one's obligation. It is not the case that one is blameworthy if and only if one fails to do what is best. (For example, Jill may unluckily fail to treat John successfully; but if she has been as careful as possible in her effort to treat him, then she is not to blame for her lack of success.) One is blameworthy if and only if one fails to do what one believes to be best. (For example, if Jill fails to do what she believes to be best, then she is to blame, whether or not she thereby treats John successfully.) Hence

[13] Prichard 1932.   [14] Ross 1939, p. 157.   [15] Cf. McConnell 1988, p. 85.
[16] Cf. McConnell 1988, pp. 85–6.   [17] Ross 1939, pp. 163–4.

one's obligation is to do that which one believes to be best rather than that which is best.

This argument, too, is unconvincing. Even Ross himself does not wholeheartedly endorse it. He says that "[t]he notion of obligation carries with it very strongly the notion that the non-discharge of an obligation is blameworthy,"[18] but he goes on to claim that an act done from kindness may have "some moral goodness" even if it "does not harmonize with [the agent's] thought about his duty, and is not [subjectively] right."[19] But even without such a concession, the argument would be unpersuasive, since it wholly overlooks the possibility of excuses for – of being blameless for – behavior that is overall morally wrong. Almost all moral philosophers acknowledge (and, as I will argue in chapter 4, quite correctly acknowledge) that the conditions for an act's being overall morally wrong are distinct from the conditions for its agent's being morally blameworthy. Ross's argument thus presumes a drastic revision of our moral categories, a presumption that is itself in dire need of defense. (In this respect, Ross is much more sensitive in *The Right and the Good* than he is in *Foundations of Ethics*.)

A third argument that Ross suggests in connection with the Subjective View is this.[20] One cannot know whether one is performing an act that is in fact the best that one can do. (For example, Jill cannot know whether, in treating John as she deems best, she is doing what will in fact result in his recovery. Perhaps he will have an adverse reaction, and so on.) However, one can always know whether one is doing what one believes is best. (In attempting to cure John by giving him drug B, Jill knows that she is doing what she believes is best.) Furthermore, one can always know whether one is fulfilling one's obligation. Hence the Subjective View is to be favored over the Objective View.

This argument is fraught with problems. For one thing, like the first argument, it is at best an argument against the Objective View; it does not establish the Subjective View. Second, the claim that one can always know whether one is fulfilling an obligation is highly controversial; surely such a bold claim itself requires argument. Third, this claim, even if accepted, is not suitable as a premise in an argument for some particular view about the nature of moral obligation, since its employment *presupposes* some such view. Jill might have known, for example, that she was doing what she believed to be best; but, unless she already knew that the Subjective View

[18] Ross 1939, p. 163.   [19] Ross 1939, p. 167.   [20] Ross 1939, p. 163.

(or something close to it) was true, she would *not* have known that she was thereby fulfilling an obligation. Finally, the claim that one can always know whether one is doing what one believes to be best is false. We may assume that Jill believes it best to cure John, but, as noted, she doesn't know whether, in giving him drug B, she is doing this. We may also assume – indeed, Case 1 stipulates – that Jill believes it best to give John drug B, but it is again perfectly possible that she doesn't know whether she is doing this. She may give him one of the other drugs instead, mistaking it for drug B. It can thus easily happen that one does not know whether one is doing what one believes to be best.

The last point is obvious, but it may have been obscured by my illustration, which I put in terms of Jill's *attempting* to cure John. Even if one can fail to know whether one is succeeding in doing something, such as curing a patient or giving him a certain drug, one can always know (it seems plausible to suppose – but the matter is controversial) whether one is attempting to do something. It is partly in virtue of this supposition, I think, that Ross believes that one can always know whether one is fulfilling an obligation; for he believes that one's obligations are restricted to what one can attempt (or set oneself, or exert oneself) to do – let us call this the Attempt Thesis. It seems that Ross (following Prichard) thinks that the Subjective View and the Attempt Thesis are natural allies, but the fact is that they are strictly independent of one another.[21] Ross does propose one argument for the Attempt Thesis. It is grounded in an account according to which human action consists of a certain kind of mental activity (to which Ross and others variously refer as willing, trying, attempting, aiming, exerting oneself, or setting oneself) having a certain effect. For example, moving one's hand will typically consist of setting oneself to move it in such a way that, as a consequence, it moves as one intends.[22] Ross next observes that whether one's hand does indeed move as one intends is not in one's control, except in so far as one's self-exertion is. (In moving his hand, an able-bodied person is strictly no more active than a paralyzed person who, unaware of her paralysis, attempts to move hers. The fact that nature co-operates in the former case but not the latter is in neither agent's

---

[21] In Ross 1939, pp. 155–6, Ross quotes approvingly and at length from a passage in Prichard 1932 in which Prichard maintains that obligation is a characteristic of agents rather than acts. Both Prichard and Ross appear to believe that this claim somehow favors both the Subjective View and the Attempt Thesis. I have not managed to find a plausible reconstruction of the reasoning so that either thesis results, let alone both.

[22] Ross 1939, p. 153.

control.) Ross then argues as follows. On the assumption that what we are obligated to do must be within our control, it follows that our obligations range only over our self-exertions and not, beyond them, to include the effects of these exertions.[23] Hence, in the present case, Jill cannot be obligated to cure John, where "cure" covers both her self-exertion (her attempt to see to it that he recovers) and its intended effect (his recovery). She can at best be obligated to aim at his recovery.

This argument founders on the failure to distinguish two distinctions concerning the sort of personal control that we all hope we have over our actions (the sort of control that many believe to be threatened by causal determinism).[24] The first distinction is between what I will call *direct* and *indirect* control. One has indirect control over something just in case one has control over it by way of having control over something else; one has direct control over something just in case one has control over it that is not indirect. Let us suppose that the general account of human action to which Ross subscribes, according to which such action consists of a self-exertion having a certain effect or effects, is correct. Then, if the agent has control over his action, we may say that he has direct control over his self-exertion and, by virtue of this, indirect control over its effect or effects. Thus, if I move my hand and thereby flip a switch, turn on a light, alert a prowler, and so on,[25] and I have control over what occurs, then I have direct control over my exerting myself to move my hand and, thereby, indirect control over my hand's movement, the switch's going up, the light's going on, the prowler's being alerted, and so on. The second distinction is between what I will call *complete* and *partial* control. One has complete control over something only if its occurrence is not contingent on anything else that is beyond one's control; otherwise, any control one has over it is merely partial.

Ross appears to think that one is obligated to do something only if one has complete control over doing it, and that one has complete control over all and only one's self-exertions. He says:

[I]f a man had, without knowing it, become paralysed since the last time he had tried to effect [a] given type of [bodily] change, his self-exertion, though it would not produce the effect, would obviously be of exactly the same character as it

---

[23] Ross 1939, p. 160.

[24] This confusion is also evident in Broad 1985, pp. 133–4. See section 3.5 below for a fuller discussion of this issue.

[25] This illustration is borrowed from Davidson 1980, p. 4.

would have been if he had remained unparalysed and it had therefore produced the effect. The exertion is all that is his and therefore all that he can be morally obliged to; whether the result follows is due to certain causal laws which he can perhaps know but certainly cannot control, and to a circumstance, viz. his being or not being paralysed, which he cannot control, and cannot know until he performs the exertion.[26]

But this is misguided. It is clear that no one ever has complete control over anything, including any and all self-exertions. (If you doubt this, consider the simple fact that whatever control you enjoy over anything depends on your having been born – something that we may hope was in someone's control, but not yours. Succeeding in exerting oneself, just like succeeding in doing that to which one exerts oneself, requires the co operation of all sorts of factors, both past and present, over which one lacks control.) If obligation required complete control, nothing would be obligatory. Since (I assume) some things are obligatory, we may conclude that obligation does not require complete control. It remains possible, of course, that obligation requires partial control, and I believe that this is indeed the case. But self-exertions are not the only things over which we have partial control, even if they are the only things over which we have direct control. The effects of self-exertions, such as hands moving, switches going up, and so on, can equally be within our partial control. The upshot is that no good reason has been given to think that Jill's obligation regarding John's recovery covers only her aiming at this result and not also her accomplishing it.[27]

1.3 AGAINST THE SUBJECTIVE VIEW

Not only do Ross's arguments fail to establish the Subjective View, but there are also compelling reasons to reject this view. In tying one's obligations so tightly to one's thoughts about one's situation, the view is subject to a host of closely related difficulties. Since most of these difficulties are well documented in the literature, my examination of them can be brief.[28]

First, the Subjective View implies that all moral agents possess a certain kind of moral infallibility. For if (as seems plausible) we always know, whenever we have a belief about what it would be best to do, what it is that we believe, then, if the Subjective View were true and we knew this (that

---

[26] Ross 1939, p. 160.   [27] For a related criticism, see Dancy 2002, pp. 233–4.
[28] A particularly useful discussion is to be found in McConnell 1988.

is, we knew that an agent ought to perform an act if and only if he believes that it is the best option that he has[29]), we would always know (unless we made some kind of inferential mistake) what we ought to do. But this makes a mockery of the conscientious person's inquiry into what he ought to do, implying that such an inquiry can be successfully accomplished simply by way of introspection.[30]

Second, the Subjective View implies that the failure to believe that any act is best would make it the case that one has no obligations. But it is absurd to think that, for example, simply failing to attend to one's situation (and, as a result, failing to have any beliefs about what it would be best to do) should suffice to free one from obligation.

Third, the Subjective View implies that, on the assumption that he was doing what he believed to be best, Hitler did no wrong. But it is grotesque to think that such a perverse belief could render mass murder morally permissible.

Fourth, the Subjective View violates the principle that "ought" implies "can."[31] This is ironic, since Ross appeals directly to this principle when arguing that one's obligations range only over self-exertions. But, as pointed out in the last section, it is not the case that anything, including our self-exertions, is in our complete control. We should now note further that some self-exertions may not even be in our partial control. Just as I may lack the control I believe I have over my hand's moving, due to paralysis of which I am unaware, so too I may lack the control I believe I have over my exerting myself to move my hand, due to an impending fainting spell of which I am unaware. The Subjective View implies that some activity (whether a full-fledged act or merely a self-exertion) is obligatory if I believe it to be the best that I can do. In holding this belief I presuppose that the activity is in my control, but the presupposition may be false.

---

[29] It is of course possible to know that some view is true without knowing what that view says. (For example, someone might know, on the basis of some authority, that Einstein's Special Theory of Relativity is true and yet not have a clue as to its content.) The present argument concerns knowing the proposition that constitutes the content of the Subjective View.

[30] Someone sympathetic to the Subjective approach might hope that a different formulation of the Subjective View – perhaps something along the lines of the view mentioned in n. 9 above – would escape this objection and the other objections to follow. Not so. The underlying problem is that the Subjective View, however exactly it is to be formulated, holds that an agent's obligations are a function of his beliefs. As long as this feature of the view is retained, some version of the objections will apply.

[31] This point is not so frequently noted. But cf. Frankena 1963, p. 161.

The four points just made suffice, I believe, to show that the Subjective View is false; that is, they show that it is not the case that an agent ought to perform an act if and only if he believes that it is the best option that he has, *when (a) "ought" is taken to express overall moral obligation and (b) doing what is overall morally obligatory is taken to be the primary concern of the morally conscientious person.* I stress both (a) and (b), because they are crucial to my rejection of the Subjective View. I have no wish to deny that, if either (a) or (b) fails to apply, then the Subjective View, or something like it, is acceptable.

Consider what A. C. Ewing says:

> We may believe... that the soldiers who fight against us in a war are acting wrongly in fighting, yet every reasonable person will admit that, as long as they really think they ought to fight, they ought "to obey their consciences" and fight.[32]

There is clearly a tension in what Ewing says, something that he himself is quick to recognize. How can it be that our enemies are acting wrongly if, in doing so, they are obeying their consciences and they ought to obey their consciences? Ewing's answer is that "ought" is ambiguous, so that the sense in which our enemies "ought" to obey their consciences is different from the sense in which they "ought not" to fight us.

I do not deny Ewing's thesis. I have denied that the Subjective View is true, *in so far as both (a) and (b) apply*, but it is consistent with this to claim that one ought, in some sense of "ought" *not* governed by both (a) and (b), to do what one believes to be best. Ewing's remark may seem to suggest that he accepts this claim. In fact, he does not, and for good reason. What he does accept is the related but importantly different claim that one ought (in some sense not governed by both (a) and (b)) to do what one believes one ought (in the sense governed by both (a) and (b)) to do; or equivalently, that it is wrong (in the former sense) to do what one believes to be wrong (in the latter sense).[33] I would in fact advise against putting matters in this way; such a double use of "ought" (or "wrong") courts confusion. Much better to say that one is *blameworthy* if and only if one does what one believes to be wrong (in the sense governed by both (a) and (b) – in the

---

[32] Ewing 1948, pp. 120–1.

[33] Note that, just as "ought" and "wrong" can be used to do double duty in this way, so too can "expect." In one sense, all that can be expected of someone is that he do what he *is* obligated to do. In another sense, all that can be expected is that he do what he *believes* he is obligated to do.

There is a complication: Ewing 1948, pp. 132–3, reserves the term "moral obligation" for a sense of "ought" *not* governed by (b). There is a sense of "ought" according to which the primary concern of the conscientious person is to discover and do what he ought to do. I have used the term "overall moral obligation" for *this* sense of "ought." Ewing, however, says that

15

sense, that is, in which the primary concern of the conscientious person is to discover and avoid doing what is wrong).[34] This acknowledges and preserves the distinction, noted earlier, between the blameworthiness of agents and the wrongness of actions.

It may seem that I have been inconsistent in what I have said about conscientiousness. I have said that, if one acts conscientiously, one is not to blame.[35] But I have also said that, if one acts conscientiously, one may nonetheless act wrongly; that is, one may nonetheless fail to do what one is in fact overall morally obligated to do. Yet I have characterized overall moral obligation itself in terms of conscientiousness; I have said that doing what is overall morally obligatory is the primary concern of the conscientious person.

There is no contradiction. In his concern for doing what he ought – that is, is overall morally obligated – to do, the conscientious person is not concerned simply with escaping blame. That would be sheer self-indulgence.[36] Nor is he concerned simply with doing what his conscience dictates – that, too, would be a form of self-indulgence – for he may well worry whether what his conscience (his set of beliefs about what he morally ought to do) presently dictates is accurate. Thus he will not rest content with letting his conscience be his guide; for acting conscientiously does not guarantee that one will avoid doing wrong. This is something that the conscientious person recognizes; it is precisely his fallibility with respect to what his overall moral obligation is that drives his conscientious inquiries. However, when it comes to judging, not people's *actions* (in terms of moral obligation), but *people* (in terms of praise- and blameworthiness) in light of their actions, then we should look to whether they have acted as their consciences dictate. As long as the two types of judgment are kept distinct, there should be no suspicion of inconsistency.

one's "moral obligation" is not to do what one ought, in this sense, to do, but rather to do what one *believes* one ought, in this sense, to do. This seems to me to constitute a serious misapplication of the term "moral obligation," but the dispute is merely verbal.

[34] Actually, this is only roughly correct. The conditions of blameworthiness – at least when "blameworthy" expresses moral culpability, the "negative" side of moral responsibility – are more complex. In particular, a freedom condition must be satisfied. In addition, one can be blameworthy, even if one acts conscientiously, if one is to be blamed for one's conscience. (Cf. Brandt 1959, p. 363.) See Zimmerman 1988, pp. 40 ff. for a general treatment of the conditions of blameworthiness. See also chapter 4 below.

[35] See the last note for a qualification.

[36] Cf. Broad 1934, p. xxiv: "A healthy appetite for righteousness, kept in due control by good manners, is an excellent thing; but to 'hunger and thirst after' it is often merely a symptom of spiritual diabetes." Actually, I do not know whether by "righteousness" Broad has in mind avoidance of blameworthiness (in which case he could be construed as endorsing my point here) or avoidance of wrongdoing (in which case he could be construed as making a Wolf 1982-like point about moral saints). But the opportunity to quote this passage was too good to pass up.

16

1.4 AGAINST THE OBJECTIVE VIEW

The rejection of the Subjective View leaves open the question whether to accept either the Objective or the Prospective View.

To answer this question, let us now consider two variations on the case involving Jill and John. In each variation the following facts obtain: drug A would in fact completely cure John; drug B would relieve his condition but not cure him completely; drug C would kill him; and giving John no drug at all would leave him permanently incurable. Also, however, in each variation Jill is confronted with defective evidence regarding some of these facts. Consider first this case:

Case 2:
All the evidence at Jill's disposal indicates (in keeping with the facts) that giving John drug B would cure him partially and giving him no drug would render him permanently incurable, but it also indicates (in contrast to the facts) that giving him drug C would cure him completely and giving him drug A would kill him.

Suppose that, acting on the basis of the evidence, Jill gives John drug C and thereby kills him. Should we say that she has acted as she ought to have done, which is what, all else being equal,[37] the Prospective View implies, or should we deny this, as the Objective View implies?

Many would deny it. Moore, one of the chief proponents of the Objective View,[38] is a prime example. He would simply invoke once again the distinction between wrongdoing and blameworthiness. He would say that, although Jill did wrong in giving John drug C, she is not to blame for doing so.[39]

For many years I thought that this was the proper assessment of such a case. I no longer think this, for Jackson's own version of his case undermines the assessment.[40] That version may be put as follows:

Case 3:
All the evidence at Jill's disposal indicates (in keeping with the facts) that giving John drug B would cure him partially and giving him no drug would render him permanently incurable, but (despite the facts) it leaves completely open whether

---

[37] See n. 8 above. I won't keep repeating this qualification; it will be implicit throughout the discussion that follows.

[38] See n. 4 above.   [39] Cf. Moore 1912, pp. 81–2. Cf. Ross 1930, p. 32.

[40] See the reference to Jackson in n. 7 above. As Jackson formulates his case, it is drug A that promises the partial cure and drugs B and C that offer the choice between a complete cure and death. I have changed the labeling in order to render my discussion consistent with what has gone before.

it is giving him drug A or giving him drug C that would cure him completely and whether it is giving him drug A or giving him drug C that would kill him.

Suppose that, acting on the basis of the evidence, Jill gives John drug B and thereby partially cures him. Should we say that she has acted as she ought to have done? Moore and others are once again committed to denying this, but here their position is decidedly implausible. My argument for this claim is an *ad hominem* one. (We have all been taught that such arguments are to be avoided, but here it seems to me just the right type of argument to use.) Put Moore in Jill's place in Case 2. Surely, as a conscientious person, he would decide to act as Jill did and so give John drug C. He could later say, "Unfortunately, it turns out that what I did was wrong. However, since I was trying to do what was best for John, and all the evidence at the time indicated that that was indeed what I was doing, I cannot be blamed for what I did." But now put Moore in Jill's place in Case 3. Surely, *as a conscientious person*, he would once again decide to act as Jill did and so give John drug B. But he could *not* later say, "Unfortunately, it turns out that what I did was wrong. However, since I was trying to do what was best for John, and all the evidence at the time indicated that that was indeed what I was doing, I cannot be blamed for what I did." He could not say this precisely because he *knew* at the time that he was *not* doing what was best for John.[41] Hence Moore could *not* justify his action by appealing to the Objective View – the view that he ought to do that which is in fact best – even though this is his official position. On the contrary, since conscientiousness precludes deliberately doing what one believes to be overall morally wrong, his giving John drug B would appear to betray the fact that he actually subscribed to something like the Prospective View.

But here I need to make an adjustment; for the Prospective View, in its first formulation, does *not* imply that, in Case 3, Jill ought to give John drug B. This is because, as just noted, it is *not* the case that giving John drug B is probably best; on the contrary, Jill knows that giving it is only second best, since she knows that either giving him drug A or giving him drug C would be better.[42] Nonetheless it is obvious that, under the circumstances, giving John drug B is what I will call *prospectively* best, in that it provides Jill with a better prospect of achieving what is of value in the situation (namely, the

---

[41] This renders what is said at Moore 1912, p. 82, inadequate; so too with what is said at Brandt 1959, p. 367.

[42] Jackson is clear on this point. See Jackson 1991, p. 468. Others are not. See, for example, Russell 1966, pp. 31–2; Kagan 1998, pp. 65–6.

restoration of John's health) than giving him either drug A or drug C or no drug at all does; for, given the epistemic uncertainty that encumbers her, Jill's giving John either drug A or drug C would be far too risky, whereas her giving him no drug at all would certainly leave him worse off than he would be if she were to give him drug B.

Let us therefore reformulate the Prospective View as follows:

The Prospective View (second formulation):
An agent ought to perform an act if and only if it is the prospectively best option that he has.

Once again, this is just a very rough formulation of the view, although not as rough as the first formulation; further adjustments will be made when the need arises. Also, once again, I intend "best" to be very elastic. Thus an act-consequentialist who subscribes to the Prospective View would say that what we ought to do is that act which is *prospectively* instrumentally best; a rule-consequentialist would say that what we ought to do is that act which is *prospectively* rule best; and so on.

It is controversial precisely what "prospectively best" comes to. One obvious proposal (which for the time being I will assume to be correct) is to construe it in terms of the maximization of *expected value*. That giving John drug B in Case 3 would maximize expected value seems clear.[43] The expected value of an act is a function of the probabilities of its possible outcomes and the actual values associated with these outcomes. Suppose we stipulate that the actual value of providing a complete cure is 50, that of providing a partial cure is 40, that of killing John is −100, and that of rendering John permanently incurable is 0. Let us further stipulate in Case 3 that, in light of the evidence available to Jill, the probability that drug B will provide a partial cure is (for simplicity's sake) 1, that the probability that giving him no drug (call this option D) will render him permanently incurable is also 1, and that for each of drugs A and C the probability that it will provide a complete cure is 0.5 and the probability that it will kill John is also 0.5. (I will have more to say about the relevant notion of probability

---

[43] Since in Case 3 all else is being held equal, this claim is plausible, no matter what kind of obligation-relevant value is presupposed. Any plausible substantive theory of obligation would place actual value on the restoration of John's health, where "actual value" refers to whatever it is that, according to the theory in question, underwrites the relevant ranking of one's alternatives (whether in terms of actual value, expected value, or something else), such that what is obligatory is ranked first relative to all alternatives.

19

in the next section.) Then the expected values of Jill's alternatives are as follows:

$$EV(A) = [(50 \times 0.5) + (-100 \times 0.5)] = -25$$
$$EV(B) = (40 \times 1) = 40$$
$$EV(C) = [(50 \times 0.5) + (-100 \times 0.5)] = -25$$
$$EV(D) = (0 \times 1) = 0$$

Clearly, then, giving John drug B would maximize expected value. Of course, there is reason to doubt that such exact assignments of values and probabilities can ever be given, but the beauty and power of Jackson's case is that we apparently need no such exact assignments to be confident that Jill's giving John drug B would fail to be best, that is, would fail to maximize actual value, and yet would maximize expected value. If it is agreed that she ought to give John drug B, then, this would seem to suffice to disprove the Objective View while tending to confirm the Prospective View.

There are of course responses that might be made on behalf of the Objective View. Let me now attend to some.

A

One response that might be made on behalf of the Objective View is this. It is true that, if Moore were put in Jill's place in Case 3, as a conscientious person he would choose to give John drug B. But this choice would be perfectly in keeping with his adherence to the Objective View, for it would simply constitute an attempt on his part to minimize the risk of doing wrong.

This response is unacceptable. I have stipulated (unrealistically, to be sure, but nonetheless perfectly legitimately) that the probability that giving John drug B will cure him only partially is 1. From the perspective of the Objective View, then, the probability that giving him this drug is wrong is 1, whereas, for each of drugs A and C, the probability that giving him the drug is wrong is less than 1. Hence, according to the Objective View, giving John drug B does *not* minimize the risk of doing wrong; on the contrary, it is *guaranteed* to be wrong. (I will return to the issue of risking wrongdoing in section 1.7.) What giving John drug B does do, of course, is to minimize the risk of doing *harm* – which is precisely what the Prospective View, in contrast to the Objective View, mandates in this case.

This is not to say that the Prospective View mandates minimizing the risk of harm in every case. On the contrary, what it mandates is choosing that option that is prospectively best, which is a matter not only of the prospect of costs, such as harms, but also of the prospects of benefits. In Case 3, it happens that the prospectively best option is the one that minimizes the risk of harm. That is why any other option is *too* risky.[44] But in other cases it may be that the prospectively best option does not minimize the risk of doing harm. For example, if the risk of harm associated with either drug A or drug C were not very grave – not death, say, but rather a partial cure slightly less satisfactory than the partial cure guaranteed by drug B – then it might be that the prospectively best option for Jill would be to give John either drug A or drug C, even though giving him drug B would minimize the risk of his being harmed. If so, then her giving John drug B would be too *cautious*.

It is not clear just what the relation between risk and the prospectively best option should be said to be. This is because the concept of risk itself is difficult to pin down. Consider this account given by Nicholas Rescher:

Risk is the chancing of negativity – of some loss or harm. To take a risk is to resolve one's act-choices in a way that creates or enhances the chance of an unfortunate eventuation, rendering the occurrence of something unwanted more likely. And to be at risk is to be so circumstanced that something unpleasant might happen, some misfortune occur. Risk ... exists whenever there are probabilistically indeterminate outcomes some of which are of negative character.[45]

I take this to be a common construal of risk,[46] but note the following. First, consider the notion of harm. Should this be understood in absolute or relative terms? That is, is it the case that whether someone is harmed turns on what kind of state he *is* in, independently of what precedes his being in this state, or does it turn on what kind of state he *was* in? Either answer

---

[44] This claim may be too broad. Perhaps taking a risk regarding a certain outcome implies that that outcome is not certain. If so, then Jill's choosing to give John no drug should not be said to be (too) risky, since it is certain to render him permanently incurable.

[45] Rescher 1983, p. 5.

[46] Social scientists frequently, and philosophers sometimes, restrict use of the term "risk" to (idealized) situations in which the risk-taker has full information about the probabilities of the outcomes of alternative courses of action, and they use the term "uncertainty" for situations in which such information is lacking. (See, e.g., Knight 1921, pp. 19 f., 233 f.; Luce and Raiffa 1957; Kahneman and Tversky 1979.) This practice can be useful, but it runs counter to the more common, liberal use of "risk" according to which all decisions made in conditions of uncertainty involve taking a risk (as long as a "negative" outcome is in the offing). In this work, I employ "risk" in this more common sense.

21

poses problems. Consider the former. Suppose we undertake to draw up a list of harms in absolute terms. On this list we might well be tempted to put the following: being in excruciating pain, being in great pain, being in considerable pain, being in moderate pain, and so on; for it does seem plausible to maintain that any painful state is one in which one suffers some degree of harm. But now imagine that John is in excruciating pain and Jill has a choice between doing nothing for him and giving him a drug that will partially alleviate his pain. If she gives him the drug, shouldn't we say that he has been helped rather than harmed, even though he continues to be in pain? Suppose, now, that the drug is only likely, and not certain, to alleviate the pain, whereas it is certain that John's agony will persist if he doesn't receive it. If Jill gives him the drug, should we say that she has thereby exposed John to a risk of harm? That seems odd.

It may therefore be tempting to adopt a relative rather than absolute conception of harm and to understand risk accordingly. But now consider Jill's reducing John from a state of bliss to a state of intense but not blissful pleasure. Presumably such an "eventuation" is "unwanted," to use Rescher's terms, and John thereby undergoes a certain kind of "loss," yet it seems misleading to say that he has been harmed. Similarly, it seems odd to say that Jill's chancing such a loss is tantamount to her exposing John to some risk – unless we talk in terms of her exposing him to a risk of "losing out" on continued bliss, but that seems at best an attenuated sense of "risk."

Perhaps, then, some hybrid absolute-cum-relative conception of harm and of risk is called for: someone is harmed only if he is transferred to one of the states on the original "absolute" list of harms from a state that is relevantly superior to it, and someone is exposed to risk only if he is subjected to the chance of being harmed. But that doesn't seem quite right, either. Suppose that John is in agony and that Jill has two – and only two – drugs with which she might treat him, the first guaranteeing partial alleviation of his pain, the second being such that it might relieve his pain entirely but also might relieve it not at all. In such a case, Jill's giving John the second drug is surely risky (whether it is *too* risky depends on a number of factors: the actual values to be attributed to agony, partial alleviation, and complete relief, and the probabilities of each of these outcomes), even though there is no danger of John's condition deteriorating. What is more, her giving John the second drug is risky only because the first drug has different prospects. If the first drug were just like the second in terms of the relevant prospects (same chance of complete relief, same chance of no relief), then *neither* drug would be risky (on the condition that the only alternative were to give John no drug, guaranteeing no relief).

Just how risk is to be understood, then, is a difficult question. I have no precise account to offer. Fortunately for my purposes in this book, I need offer no such account. This is because, although risk is highly relevant to much of what I will have to say, a precise understanding of it is not crucial to the development and defense of the Prospective View. Granted, it is the verdict that, in Case 3, Jill's opting for something other than drug B would be too risky that provides the initial impetus for rejecting the Objective View in favor of the Prospective View, but that doesn't mean that the Prospective View must be formulated in terms of risk. On the contrary, if risk is somehow to be defined in terms of the chancing of "negativity," as Rescher plausibly claims, then any such formulation would be at best incomplete, since the chancing of "positivity" is clearly also relevant to determining what one ought to do. What one ought to do is choose that option that is prospectively best. On the present understanding of what this comes to (some adjustments will be made later), the prospectively best option is the one with the highest expected value. As noted, the expected value of an act is a function of the probabilities of its possible outcomes and *all* the actual values associated with these outcomes, regardless of whether these outcomes are to be characterized as positive or negative in either absolute or relative terms. Moreover, as is not the case with risk, the expected value of an act is a function only of *its* prospects and not also of the prospects of its alternatives.

B

A second response that might be made on behalf of the Objective View is to claim that the ranking of Jill's alternatives in Case 3 in terms of their actual values has been misrepresented and her giving John drug B would actually be best after all, despite the fact that it would only lead to a partial cure. This claim might be based either on the allegation that Jill's alternatives have been misdescribed or on the allegation that the actual values of her alternatives have been miscalculated.

As to the first allegation: I have said that an alternative, or option, is something that the agent can do, where "can" expresses some form of personal control. But this is pretty meager. We can and should distinguish between (at least) two senses of "can" that express a form of personal control. Although there is certainly a sense in which Jill can cure John completely by giving him drug A, there is also a sense in which she cannot do so; for she cannot *intentionally* cure him completely by giving him drug A.[47] However, not only can she cure him partially by giving him drug B, she can *intentionally* do so. It might then be argued that, if we count among an agent's options only those things that he can intentionally do, giving John drug B would turn out to be Jill's best option after all; thus the Objective View can be reconciled with the intuitively correct verdict that this is what she ought to do, and the Prospective View enjoys no advantage over it.

This argument is unacceptable. Let us grant that Jill cannot intentionally cure John completely by giving him drug A (or in any other way). Nonetheless, she presumably can intentionally give him drug A. Thus, even were we to count only those things she can intentionally do as being among her options, her giving John drug A would be an option of hers. Since it would actually be her best option, the Objective View would still prescribe that Jill give John drug A rather than drug B.

It may be retorted that we still have not isolated the relevant sense of "option," and that we should focus on those *outcomes* that an agent can intentionally achieve, regardless of the means of achieving them. The relevant outcomes in Case 3 are those of a complete cure, a partial cure, death, and permanent incurability. Given her evidential circumstances, only the second and fourth of these are ones that Jill can intentionally achieve. Clearly, a partial cure is actually better than permanent incurability. Thus, it may be argued, the Objective View, properly understood, does indeed mandate achieving a partial cure, and, since this can be accomplished only by means of giving John drug B, it mandates giving John drug B.

This argument is also unacceptable. The claim that our obligations are restricted to those outcomes that we can intentionally achieve is false. Consider the variation on the present case mentioned a short while ago, in which it is not death that drugs A and C risk but rather a partial cure slightly less satisfactory than the partial cure guaranteed by drug B. In this variation, I suggested, it is plausible to claim (depending on just how the details are filled in) that giving John drug B would be too cautious and that Jill ought therefore to give him either drug A or drug C. Yet neither of the

---

[47] Cf. Mele 2003, pp. 448–9, on the distinction between having a "simple" ability and being able to do something "intentionally." Cf. Goldman 1970, p. 203; Mason 2003, p. 321; Wiland 2005, p. 355.

possible outcomes of doing so (namely, a complete cure and an inferior partial cure) is something that, given her evidential circumstances, Jill can intentionally achieve. Or consider another variation of the case in which the probabilities associated with giving John drug B and with giving him no drug are reduced to the point (whatever this point is, exactly) that renders *none* of the outcomes that Jill can achieve something that she can intentionally achieve. In such a case, the present proposal implies that Jill has no obligation at all, which is surely false.

It might again be retorted that I have been presupposing a mistaken construal of the relevant notion of an outcome. In Case 3, as originally formulated, although neither a complete cure nor death is (individually) something that Jill can intentionally achieve, she can intentionally achieve either-a-complete-cure-or-death. *This* outcome, it may be said, is actually worse than a partial cure, and thus once again the claim that Jill ought to give John drug B can be reconciled with the Objective View.

This argument, too, is flawed. First, the claim that either-a-complete-cure-or-death is itself an outcome, in the relevant sense, let alone one that is actually better than a partial cure, is not at all straightforward. That disjunctive states should count as outcomes, in the relevant sense, is not obvious; nor is it obvious how such states are to be evaluated.[48] But, second, there is no need to pursue this point, because we can imagine a variation on Case 3 in which each of a complete cure, a partial cure, death, and permanent incurability is (as I would put it) a possible outcome of each of Jill's options, but they are such that none of them is, individually, something that Jill can intentionally achieve and are also such that none of the disjunctive states composed of them, even if intentionally achievable, indicates what it is that Jill ought to do. Consider, for example, this variation: the probability that giving John drug A will result in a complete cure is 0.4 and, for each of the alternative outcomes, the probability that giving him drug A will result in it is 0.2; for each of drugs B and C, the probability that giving John the drug will result in a partial cure is 0.4 and, for each of the alternative outcomes, the probability that giving him the drug will result in it is 0.2; and, for each of the outcomes, the probability that giving John no drug will result in it is 0.25. On this variation, it is clear

---

[48] If the evaluation is to be done in terms of intrinsic value, as act-consequentialists, for example, contend, the assignment of such value to disjunctive states is a highly controversial matter. See, e.g., Quinn 1974; Chisholm 1975; Oldfield 1977; Carlson 1997; and Zimmerman 2001, sect. 5.5.

that Jill ought to choose drug A. Yet she cannot intentionally achieve a complete cure thereby. Moreover, if any of the relevant disjunctive states is intentionally achievable (and I'm not sure whether any of them is), none of them warrants the conclusion that Jill ought to choose drug A.

As I will explain in chapter 3, specifying what counts as an agent's alternatives is crucial to developing an adequate account of obligation. Moreover, I will argue that the notion of what an agent can intentionally do is also crucial to such an account. Nonetheless, as far as I can tell, neither of these facts can serve to reconcile the Objective View with the verdict that, in Case 3 as originally formulated, Jill ought to give John drug B. Certainly the various attempts just considered do not succeed in achieving such reconciliation.

Consider, now, the second allegation that the actual values of Jill's alternatives (understood, as originally conceived, as those of giving John drug A, drug B, drug C, and no drug) have been miscalculated. It might be claimed that we should assign a certain disvalue to the running of risks, regardless of whether these risks are realized (and however precisely the concept of risk is to be understood). It could then be argued that the extra risk associated with Jill's giving John drug A renders her doing so actually worse than her giving him drug B, even though the former would be medically superior.[49]

This argument is problematic, for three reasons. First, it seems that a Jackson-type case can be constructed that accommodates the (alleged) disvalue of risk.[50] Second, the argument presupposes that, from the point of view of what counts regarding the determination of Jill's obligation,

---

[49] Cf. Sosa 1993, pp. 109–10.

[50] Recall the actual values assigned: a complete cure, 50; a partial cure, 40; death, −100; no cure, 0. Suppose that the (dis)value associated with the risk in giving either drug A or drug C is −15. Then, if we simply add in the value of risk-taking, the actual values of Jill's alternatives would be as follows: A, 35; B, 40; C, −115; D, 0. Even on the Objective View, then, Jill ought to give John drug B. But now suppose that Jill's evidence is such that it is not death but rather a less serious deterioration in John's health that she risks if she gives John either drug A or drug C. Let the actual value of such a deterioration be −50. Presumably, the actual (dis)value associated with risking such a deterioration will be less than that associated with risking death. Let us stipulate that this value is −8. Then the actual values of Jill's alternatives would be as follows: A, 42; B, 40; C, −58; D, 0. The Objective View would then imply that Jill ought to give John drug A after all. But this is highly dubious. Note that the expected values of Jill's alternatives (when no actual value is assigned to the taking of risks) would be as follows: A, 0; B, 40; C, 0; D, 0. The Prospective View would thus imply that Jill still ought to give John drug B. Although the numbers just used, and the method of aggregation, are of course spurious, their being so in no way undermines the general point that they serve to illustrate.

26

giving John drug A is vastly preferable to giving him drug C.[51] This seems wrong; since they are equally risky, these alternatives would seem to be on a par with one another from the point of view in question. Third, assigning a general disvalue to risk seems misguided anyway, since, as noted above, under some circumstances choosing a certain option may be too cautious (and thus *insufficiently* risky) rather than too risky.

C

A third response on behalf of the Objective View is this. Case 3 indicates precisely why we must distinguish between different "oughts" even within the context of overall moral obligation. As the Objective View implies, Jill ought objectively to give John drug A, since this is what would in fact maximize actual value. However, we can also say with perfect consistency that she ought prospectively to give John drug B, since this is what would maximize expected value. The Objective and Prospective Views are thus not rivals and can both be accepted.

This, too, is problematic. The Objective and Prospective Views, like the Subjective View, are intended to account for what an agent ought to do, *when (a) "ought" is taken to express overall moral obligation and (b) doing what is overall morally obligatory is taken to be the primary concern of the morally conscientious person.* I have argued that the Subjective View cannot be accepted under this dual condition, although it might be accepted if "ought" is construed differently. I advised against using "ought" in such a way, since there is alternative terminology available that is less confusing. So, too, my present use of Case 3 is intended as an argument against the Objective View, *under the condition that both (a) and (b) apply.* I concede that the Objective View might be accepted if "ought" is construed differently. But I would once again advise against using "ought" in such a way; we can simply say that Jill's giving John drug A would be *actually best* and leave it at that, avoiding any hint of confusion with the "ought" of overall moral obligation (the "ought" with which proponents of the Objective View such as Moore have traditionally been concerned).

---

[51] Compare the values of 35 and −115 assigned to A and C, respectively, in the last note.

D

But, it may be retorted, surely the conscientious person is concerned with the actual values of his alternatives, and so it would be a mistake to say that the "ought" of overall moral obligation is not to be understood in terms of such values. Jill, for example, will surely regret both the fact that she does not know what is best for John and the fact that, in giving him drug B, she is not doing what is best. What cause for regret could there be, though, if she were doing what she ought? Her regret indicates that she herself takes her obligation to be to do what is actually best for John.

We may agree that any morally sensitive person will be concerned with the actual values of his alternatives – indeed, more broadly, with how well the world is faring generally. Such a person will indeed regret not knowing what is best and will also regret that the world is not faring as well as it might. But this does not favor the Objective View over the Prospective View. Let us assume that Jill is very much concerned – quite correctly – with the actual values of a complete cure, a partial cure, no cure, and death. Despite this, she quite deliberately – and again quite correctly – chooses an alternative that she knows is not actually best. That is precisely how any clear-headed conscientious agent would act under the circumstances. It would be appalling, morally speaking, if Jill were to give John drug A; taking such a risk would be *unconscionable*.[52] Jill's concern with the actual values of her alternatives doesn't indicate that she believes that she ought to do what is actually best. (After all, since expected value is in part a function of actual value, anyone who is concerned with the former will be concerned with the latter, and so anyone who believes that his obligation is to maximize expected value rather than actual value will still be concerned with actual value.) So, too, Jill's regretting both that she doesn't know what is in fact best and that she is doing what is not best is no indication that she believes that she ought to do what is actually best. On the contrary, her giving John drug B indicates that she takes her obligation in this instance to be to do something that is not best; and that this is her obligation is yet another fact that she will presumably, and appropriately, regret.

I noted in section 1.2 that Ross claims that an act is morally right only if it is reasonable to do it. He uses this claim in an argument against the Objective View. I said at the time that the claim was inadequate to the task. Nonetheless, Ross does have a point, which we may adapt to the present

---

[52] Cf. Gibbard 1990, p. 43, n. 7.

case. In light of the risk of harm associated with each of drugs A and C, Jill's giving John either drug would surely be *unreasonable* (regardless of whether there *is* a reason, in some sense, to give him drug A, due to its in fact providing the most effective treatment). There is, then, a link after all between what is right and what is reasonable, and between what is wrong and what is unreasonable. Note, however, that unlike Ross I am not relying on this link in order to overturn the Objective View. On the contrary, I am relying on Jackson's case for this purpose, and it is this case that reveals the link.

E

But, it may again be retorted, consider Gladstone Gander, one of Donald Duck's associates. Gladstone is invariably lucky; acting on his hunches, he always manages to choose that alternative which is actually best, despite being no less ignorant than the common person about the details of the situations in which he finds himself. Suppose that Gladstone were to find himself in Jill's situation in Case 3. Acting on his hunch in this case, he would give John drug A. Surely, if someone invariably maximizes actual value, then he always acts as he ought. If so, Gladstone not only would but ought to choose drug A rather than drug B. We who are not so lucky ought to choose drug B, since in choosing A we would run an unreasonable risk of harm to John. But it is implausible to say that the correct moral theory should have radically different implications for lucky and unlucky (that is, normal) agents. Rather, we should recognize that all agents have a *fundamental* obligation to maximize actual value, as the Objective View declares. Moreover, all agents have a *derivative* obligation to act responsibly with respect to the production of actual value. We act responsibly in this regard when we do not run unreasonable risks with respect to the production of actual value. Gladstone would act responsibly if and only if he chose drug A, but a normal agent such as Jill would act responsibly if and only if she chose drug B. Hence Gladstone's derivative obligation coincides with his fundamental obligation, whereas there is no such coincidence in Jill's case. But Jill's fundamental obligation does coincide with Gladstone's: fundamentally, she ought to give John drug A.

I find the proposed distinction between fundamental and derivative obligation obscure, confounding, and unmotivated. It is obscure in that it is hard to see how one obligation can be "derived" from another when the two conflict. It is confounding in that it raises once again the

29

question which "ought" one ought to act on.[53] It is unmotivated in that there would appear to be no good reason to say that Gladstone has any obligation to give John drug A. His being invariably lucky diminishes neither the degree nor the unreasonableness of the risk that he runs in giving John drug A. His giving John this drug would be just as unconscionable as Jill's doing so.

It could of course happen that, at some point, Gladstone's unbroken string of lucky successes entitles him to rely on hunches that, up to that point, he was not entitled to rely on. But it is precisely at that point that he is no longer lucky when he manages to do what is actually best, in that his choosing that act which in fact maximizes actual value would no longer constitute running an unreasonable risk.[54] And it is at that point that his obligations would part way with those of normal agents such as Jill.

But does this not give rise to a paradox? Suppose that Gladstone is faced with a series of situations of the sort described in Case 3. Right from the start, he relies on his hunch and chooses drug A. Doing so invariably turns out best. At some point, his string of successes entitles him to rely on his hunch. At that point, I have said, his obligation is indeed to choose drug A, whereas previously his obligation was to choose drug B. But how can it be that, by consistently making a choice of the sort that he ought *not* to make, Gladstone manages to make it the case that he ought to make a choice of this very sort?

I find no paradox here. It frequently happens that one ought not to make a choice of some sort under one set of circumstances but ought to make a choice of that same sort under another set of circumstances. (Consider the choice to tell a lie, for example.) As the string of successes unfolds, Gladstone's circumstances change. True, his being faced with a choice between drugs A, B, and C is constant; but there is a dramatic change in his evidence with respect to the efficacy of choosing drug A.

---

[53] Note that, like "ought," the term "responsible" is treacherous. In one sense, one acts responsibly just in case one fulfills one's obligations (that is, one avoids wrongdoing). This is the sense at issue here. In another sense, one acts responsibly just in case one acts blamelessly (that is, one avoids blameworthiness). This is not the sense at issue here. Compare the remarks in sections 1.2 and 1.3 above concerning the distinction between wrongdoing and blameworthiness. See also chapter 4 below.

[54] He would remain lucky in another sense: he would be fortunate to have hunches whose promptings invariably coincide with the maximization of actual value.

F

In a final effort to defend the Objective View, one might propose the following. Suppose that Jill later comes into possession of new evidence that strongly indicates that drug A would indeed have cured John completely. Even if we understand and condone her having given John drug B, should we not nonetheless say now that she ought instead to have given him drug A? Indeed, is this not what she herself is likely ruefully to admit? If so, the Objective View is reinstated.

There are two main ways in which the claim that Jill ought to have given John drug A may be understood: (i) she was obligated to give him drug A; (ii) she is obligated to have given him drug A. The second reading may be dismissed, for obligations cannot be retrospective (contrary to what some philosophers maintain[55]). The first reading may seem to presuppose the Objective View, but in fact it does not; accepting the claim on that reading, therefore, does *not* provide an adequate defense of that view. On the contrary, one could say, in the spirit of the Prospective View, that in giving John drug B Jill acted as she ought, relative to her earlier evidence, to have done but that she did not act as she ought, relative to her later evidence, to have done. Some authors are willing to countenance both claims. (Jackson is one.[56]) Note, however, that this position does *not* serve to reinstate the Objective View, since it does *not* imply that Jill's obligation is ever simply to maximize actual value. On the contrary, it declares Jill's obligation always to be a function not directly of the facts, but of the evidence available to her, concerning the actual values of her alternatives.

Although the position just outlined is perfectly consistent with the general theme underlying the Prospective View, I see no reason to embrace it. I think it is a mistake to multiply "oughts" in the proposed way. Certainly Jill would be justified in saying later that it would have been *better* to give John drug A rather than drug B, but there is no need also to say that she *ought* to have given John drug A. (That, to paraphrase Bernard Williams, is to provide the agent with one "ought" too many.[57]) It is the

---

[55] See, for example, Castañeda 1981, p. 61; Feldman 1986, p. 43. This issue is briefly discussed in Zimmerman 1996, p. 37.
[56] See Jackson 1991, p. 471. Cf. Oddie and Menzies 1992, p. 521.
[57] Cf. Williams 1981, p. 18.

evidence available to an agent *at the time* that determines what he ought *at that time* to do.[58] Later evidence is irrelevant.[59]

This dismissal of extra "oughts" may seem too hasty, though. For the issue just raised occurs not only across times but also across agents. Consider a variation on Case 3 in which Jill's evidence is as stipulated, but Jack's evidence outstrips Jill's and strongly indicates that drug A would cure John completely. And suppose that Jill asks Jack whether she ought to give John drug A. What should Jack say?

If the "should" in the question just raised expresses overall moral obligation, it could be that the Prospective View itself would imply that Jack should advise Jill to give John drug A; for that may be what would maximize expected value *for Jack*, that is, relative to Jack's epistemic position. But the more important question here is whether Jack's telling Jill that she ought to give John drug A would be *truthful*.

If the evidence available to Jack is also available to Jill, then Case 3 has in fact been misdescribed. But if Case 3 has not been misdescribed, then the Prospective View implies that Jack's telling Jill that she ought (that is, is *overall morally obligated*) to give John drug A would *not* be truthful.[60] This seems to me the correct verdict.[61] Jill *ought* not to give John drug A but to give him drug B instead. (It would of course remain the case that, if Jack were to tell her that she would do *best* to give John drug A, he would be speaking both truly and justifiably.) As confirmation of this verdict, consider a variation on the present situation, one in which Jack is inaccessible to Jill – he's out of town, say. Jill wishes that he was available for consultation, because she knows that he would be in a position to tell her which of drugs A and C would cure John completely and which would kill him. She thus knows that he would advise her not to give John drug B. Yet she also knows that, under the circumstances, she nonetheless ought to give him

---

[58] Cf. Gruzalski 1981, pp. 168–9. Contrast Ross 1930, p. 32.

[59] As confirmation of this, consider the matter from *John's* perspective. Suppose that Jill had ignored the risk to John, tossed a coin ("Heads, A; tails, C!"), and the coin had come up heads. Although John would no doubt be relieved to have been completely cured, it would surely be reasonable for him also to be very angry with Jill for having gambled so recklessly with his life. He would think, correctly, that she had seriously wronged him in doing so. I will return to the issue of what it is to wrong someone in the next chapter.

[60] Unless Jack possesses an authority such that his very pronouncements have special evidential weight for Jill. In such a case, his telling Jill that she ought to give John drug A might suffice under the circumstances to make it the case that she ought.

[61] On p. 184 of Thomson 1986, Thomson wavers on this point, although that may in part be because she construes "ought" differently.

drug B. So, too, even if Jack *is* in a position to assess Jill's situation but she is not in a position to receive any advice from him. This is not surprising. After all, Jill knows that drug B is not best, and she knows that, even if someone else knows what is best, still she ought to give John drug B unless she can come to know what this other person knows. The mere fact that A is best does not imply that Jill ought to give John drug A. The mere fact that Jack knows that A is best does not imply that Jill ought to give John drug A. The mere fact that Jack knows that A is best and can communicate with Jill does not imply that Jill ought to give John drug A. It is only when the *grounds* for Jack's knowledge can in some way be imparted to Jill that it becomes true that she ought to give John drug A.

1.5 THE PROSPECTIVE VIEW REFINED

I have argued that both the Objective and the Subjective Views are false. This of course does not imply that the Prospective View is true, let alone that, if it is true, "prospectively best" is to be understood in terms of the maximization of expected value. Nonetheless, I propose that we now take the further step of assuming that the Prospective View is true, since it provides such a straightforward explanation of what drives our judgment that in Jackson's case – Case 3 – Jill ought to give John drug B, while allowing for the possibility that in other cases certain options can be too cautious rather than too risky. I propose, therefore, that we accept that what a conscientious person would strive to do, and what any person ought to do, is whatever is his prospectively best option. I want now to refine this claim. In order to do so, I will for the time being continue to understand "prospectively best" in terms of the maximization of expected value. (Adjustments to this conception will be made in due course.) Thus, for the time being, the Prospective View is to be understood as follows:

The Prospective View (third formulation):
An agent ought to perform an act if and only if it is the option that has the greatest expected value for the agent.

As noted earlier, the expected value of an action is a function of the probabilities of its possible outcomes and the actual values associated with these outcomes. I have already said that I will leave open precisely what sort of value is at stake, so that my development of the Prospective View can remain compatible with all substantive accounts of moral obligation, such as those proposed by act-consequentialists, rule-consequentialists, virtue-theorists, rights-theorists, and so on. But I must now say something more about the kind of probability at issue.

It is common to distinguish three kinds of probability: objective, subjective, and epistemic. The exact nature of each is controversial.[62] Objective probability has to do with the chances that exist "in nature," such as the chance that a one-pack-a-day smoker will contract lung cancer. Subjective probability has to do with the degree of belief – the confidence – that people have in certain propositions, such as the confidence that a one-pack-a-day smoker has that he will not contract lung cancer. Epistemic probability has to do with the degree of belief in certain propositions that is warranted or justified by a certain body of evidence, such as evidence concerning the link between smoking one pack of cigarettes a day and contracting lung cancer.

As the previous sections indicate, it is with *epistemic* probability that the Prospective View is concerned. Consider Case 3. I stipulated that in this case giving John drug A would in fact cure him completely, giving him drug B would cure him partially, giving him drug C would kill him, and giving him no drug would render him permanently incurable. I could have made the case more complicated. For example, I could have stipulated that there is a 0.9 objective probability that giving John drug A would cure him completely, a 0.7 objective probability that giving him drug B would cure him partially, a 0.8 objective probability that giving him no drug would kill him, and a 0.75678213 objective probability that giving him no drug would render him permanently incurable. Such a stipulation would leave entirely unaffected the verdict that Jill ought to give John drug B, as long as it is also stipulated that her evidence concerning her alternatives remains unaffected (that is, as long as it continues to be the case that, despite the objective probabilities at issue, all the evidence at Jill's disposal indicates that giving John drug B would cure him partially and that giving him no drug would render him permanently incurable, while leaving completely open which of drugs A and C would provide the complete cure and which of them would be lethal). Any objective probabilities pertaining to the case are therefore irrelevant to the question of what Jill's overall moral obligation is.

So, too, with any subjective probabilities pertaining to the case. I could have stipulated that Jill was (unwarrantedly) highly confident that giving John drug C would cure him completely and that giving him drug A

---

[62] For a helpful recent discussion, see Mellor 2005.

would kill him. As the discussion of the Subjective View in section 1.3 shows, though, this would also have been irrelevant to the question of what Jill ought, as a matter of overall moral obligation, to do. This is something that Jill herself, as a conscientious person, would acknowledge. As noted above, no such person is content simply with acting on the beliefs she happens to have regarding the values of her alternatives (although it is of course the case that, when the time comes to act, it is these beliefs that will inform her decision regarding what to do; for, as also noted above, conscientiousness precludes deliberately doing what one believes to be overall morally wrong). On the contrary, the conscientious person is concerned with whether her beliefs in this respect are *accurate* and recognizes that the best and only guide she has on this score is the *evidence* that is available to her. She recognizes, furthermore, that it is this evidence that determines what it is she ought to do. In Case 3, when choosing to give John drug B, Jill, as a conscientious person, acts on the basis of her evidence and chooses that option that (she believes) has the highest expected value. In so doing, she is acting as (she believes) she ought. It is the epistemic probabilities that (she believes) attach to her alternatives, not the subjective probabilities that (she believes) attach to them, that dictate her choice.[63]

The notion of evidence thus plays a central role in the account of obligation that I wish to develop and defend. It is with considerable chagrin, therefore, that I concede that I have little to say by way of clarifying this crucial concept. What follows is very meager, although I hope it will be of some use and that it is consistent with the best theory of evidence that epistemologists have to offer.

Evidence that is available to one person may not be available to another. (Remember Jack, whose epistemic position was superior to Jill's.) It is the evidence that is immediately available to the agent that determines that agent's obligation. We must distinguish between evidence that is *available* to someone and evidence of which that person in fact *avails* himself.

---

[63] In Jackson 1986, pp. 358 ff., and 1991, pp. 464 f., Jackson argues that epistemic probabilities are reducible to subjective probabilities. His argument concerns the blame that attaches to the failure to undertake further investigation concerning (the values of) one's alternatives when one believes that such investigation is itself likely to be of value. I believe the argument fails. Jackson appears to ignore the distinction between blameworthiness and wrongdoing (regarding which see section 1.3 above and chapter 4 below). There is clearly a difference between *believing* that further investigation will or might bear fruit and being *justified* in believing this. It is the latter, not the former, that is relevant to whether one does wrong in failing to undertake such investigation; it is the former, not the latter, that is relevant to whether one is to blame for such a failure.

Available evidence is evidence of which someone *can*, in some sense, and *ought*, in some sense, to avail himself. I confess that the exact senses of this "can" and "ought" elude me.[64] Still, I should add that, whatever exactly the sense of "ought" at issue is, it is an epistemic one. It should *not* be understood in terms of moral obligation, for that would introduce a circularity into the Prospective View.[65]

Assignments of epistemic probability may be understood as follows. If a proposition, p, is certain for someone, S (that is, if S is justified, epistemically, in having full confidence in p), then the probability of p for S is 1. If p is certain for S, then its negation, $\sim p$, is certainly false for S; in this case, the probability of $\sim p$ for S is 0. If p and $\sim p$ are counterbalanced for S (that is, S is justified in having some confidence in each of p and $\sim p$, but no more confidence in one than in the other), then the probability of each of p and $\sim p$ for S is 0.5.[66] If S is justified in having greater confidence in p than in $\sim p$, then the probability of p for S is greater than 0.5 and the probability of $\sim p$ for S is less than 0.5; in such a case, p may simply be said to be probable for S, and $\sim p$ improbable.[67] I will not try to explicate the notion of confidence (or degree of belief, or subjective probability). Perhaps it can be construed in terms of certain kinds of betting behavior under certain conditions, but I will leave the matter open. I will use the term "evidence" to refer to whatever it is that justifies someone's being more or less confident in a proposition. (I will not inquire into the nature of evidence.) The stronger S's *total* evidence for p, the greater the confidence that S is justified in having in p. (Presumably, in order for S to *know* p, p must be probable for S, but more than that I will not venture to say – not only because of Gettier-type concerns having to do with misleading evidence, but also because of

---

[64] For a valuable discussion of this issue, see Richard Feldman 1988.

[65] I do not mean to deny that there is a moral question about what evidence to seek, use, and so on. Of course there is. (For a brief discussion of this question, see subsection A of section 1.7 below.) My point is that the notion of available evidence is itself not a moral one but an epistemic one. The "-able" indicates not simply evidence that can be accessed but evidence that is in some sense epistemically worthy of access, so that, if one's beliefs do not comport with one's evidence, one has made an epistemic mistake, whether or not one has made a moral mistake.

[66] The stipulation that S is justified in having some confidence in each of p and $\sim p$ ensures that the equal probabilities of these propositions are not derived simply from S's being wholly ignorant about them. Cf. Mellor 2005, pp. 27–9, on the principle of indifference.

[67] Cf. Chisholm 1989, ch. 2, who gives a similar account, but one that is couched in terms of degrees or levels of justification rather than, as here, in terms of the justification of degrees of belief. Also, Chisholm does not tie degrees of justification with attributions of probability as I have done.

36

lottery-paradox-type concerns having to do with very high probabilities that seem nonetheless insufficient for knowledge.)

It may frequently be the case that S's situation is such that the probability of p for S cannot even in principle be assigned a precise number between 0 and 1 (although for the sake of illustration I will often assume otherwise). There is, in addition, the question of how epistemic probability of the sort outlined here relates to the standard probability calculus. Certain of the standard axioms appear not to apply in the present context. Consider, for example, the thesis that no proposition is more probable than any proposition that it entails. When it comes to epistemic probability, this thesis is to be rejected, I believe. (It may be that p entails q but that S has no evidence of this entailment.) Or consider the thesis that all necessary propositions have probability 1. When it comes to epistemic probability, this thesis is also to be rejected, I believe. (It may be that S's evidence regarding p is defective, even though p is necessarily true.)[68] It would of course be helpful if some positive account were given of how epistemic probability operates beyond the merely negative observation that it appears to violate some of the standard axioms. Again, though, I am afraid that I have nothing useful to offer. Some may choose to say that any conception of probability that is non-standard in this way forfeits its claim to the name "probability."[69] Perhaps so, although I am inclined to disagree; for talk of probabilities (or chances, or likelihoods, and so on) in the present epistemic sense is both very common and very natural, even if it should turn out that they do not conform to the standard probability calculus.

Let us now return to Case 3. There the verdict was that Jill ought to give John drug B, because doing so would maximize expected value – any other choice would be unacceptably risky. But this verdict may have been too hasty. It may seem obviously correct, because it may seem obvious what the actual values at stake are. Yet it could be that it is *not* obvious to Jill what these values are; it could be that her evidence is defective in *this* regard, too. If so, this would make a difference to what she ought to do. Let me explain.

In the last section I stipulated, for the sake of illustration, the following actual values: providing a complete cure, 50; providing a partial cure, 40; killing John, – 100; rendering John permanently incurable, 0. On this basis, the following expected values were assigned:

---

[68] Cf. Mellor 2005, pp. 16–17. Mellor, however, argues that the standard axioms apply to all kinds of probability, including epistemic probability.
[69] Cf. Huemer 2007, pp. 126–7.

$$EV(A) = [(50 \times 0.5) + (-100 \times 0.5)] = -25$$
$$EV(B) = (40 \times 1) = 40$$
$$EV(C) = [(50 \times 0.5) + (-100 \times 0.5)] = -25$$
$$EV(D) = (0 \times 1) = 0$$

These calculations reflect the (unrealistic) presupposition that the evidence available to Jill is such that it is certain for her that giving John drug B will partially cure him and that giving him no drug will render him permanently incurable, while, for each of drugs A and C, she is justified in having no more confidence in the proposition that giving John the drug will cure him completely than in the proposition that it will kill him. Note that, although the calculations are sensitive to deficiencies in Jill's evidence regarding the possible outcomes of her options, they are not sensitive to deficiencies in her evidence regarding the possible values of these outcomes. It is as if all the relevant values are being treated as being certain for her, even if some of the relevant outcomes are not. But this could well be false. It could happen, for instance, that all the relevant outcomes are certain while some of the relevant values are not. For example, suppose that Jill has a pill that she can dispense to either John (act E) or to Jane (act F), but not to both. The pill is certain to induce a partial recovery in John but a complete recovery in Jane. The problem is that, although John is a human being, Jane is not – she is a hamster (Jill is both a physician and a vet) – and Jill's evidence concerning the relative values of the lives of humans and hamsters is equivocal. It is certain for her that the value of a partial recovery in John is 100, but her evidence concerning the value of a complete recovery in Jane is divided. She is justified in having some confidence in the proposition that hamsters' lives are considerably less valuable than humans', such that the value of a complete recovery in Jane is only 20. But she is justified in having equal confidence in the proposition that such an assignment of value is merely speciesist and that the value of a complete recovery in Jane is actually 120. Let us suppose that these are the only possible values in contention. Under the circumstances, what I will call the *expectable values* of Jane's alternatives may then be computed as follows:

$$E*V(E) = (100 \times 1) = 100$$
$$E*V(F) = [(20 \times 0.5) + (120 \times 0.5)] = 70$$

(Whereas the expected value, EV, of an act is a function of the probabilities of its possible outcomes and the *actual* values associated with these outcomes, the expectable value, $E*V$, of an act is a function of the probabilities

of its possible outcomes and the *probable* values associated with these outcomes.[70]) The general lesson of Case 3 is that an agent's overall moral
obligation is a function, not directly of the outcomes of his options, but of
the evidence available to him concerning these outcomes. Such evidence
may be empirical (as in Case 3, in which the relevant evaluative facts are
implicitly taken as certain) or evaluative (as in the present case of John and
Jane, in which the relevant empirical facts are implicitly taken as certain). In
his own discussion of his case, Jackson pays attention only to empirical
probabilities and ignores evaluative probabilities. This is unwarrantedly
one-sided. We should take both kinds of probabilities into account.[71]
Doing so requires that we reformulate the Prospective View once again:

The Prospective View (fourth formulation):
An agent ought to perform an act if and only if it is the option that has the greatest
expectable value for the agent.

Unfortunately, this reformulation does not suffice, I think, to accommodate all ways in which defective evidence may affect one's obligations.
Regardless of whether we make the move (as I have just argued we should)
from expected to expectable value, there is the possibility that one's
evidence *concerning one's evidence* be defective. (This possibility might be
resisted by appealing to the thesis that, if one is justified in believing a
proposition, then one is justified in believing that one is so justified. But this
thesis is implausible.[72]) Thus the evidence pertaining to the expectable (or
expected) value of one's alternatives could be just as defective as the
evidence pertaining to their actual values. Case 3 (in conjunction with

---

[70] The usual calculation for expected value goes as follows: for each possible outcome, O_i, of
an act, A, multiply its probability, given A, by its (actual) value, V, and then sum these
products. The resulting formula for the expected value of A is this: $\Sigma_i \text{prob} (O_i/A) \times V(O_i)$.
The calculation for expectable value introduces a further variable, in that each possible
outcome has a number of possible values, V_j, whose probabilities must be accommodated.
The resulting formula for the expectable value of A is this: $\Sigma_i \text{prob} (O_i/A) \times \Sigma_j \text{prob} (O_i$ has
$V_j) \times V_j$. (For this formula to be applicable, it must be assumed that, if V_j is infinite, then
prob (O_i has V_j) = 0. Also, its applicability, just like the applicability of the formula for
expected value, is restricted to those cases in which the probabilities and values can in
principle be assigned a precise number – unless fuzzy measurements of the sort described in
n. 75 below are admitted.)

[71] In Smith 2006 and in press, Smith notes that there is no good reason to claim that overall
moral obligation is a function of empirical but not of evaluative probabilities. However, he
concludes that neither kind of probability is relevant, rather than that both kinds are. In
doing so, he appears not to recognize that the Moore-type move of (correctly) distinguishing between wrongdoing and blameworthiness is not an adequate response to Case 3.

[72] Cf. Feldman 1981, pp. 277–8.

the "further step" mentioned in the first paragraph of this section) shows us, I believe, that, when one's evidence is such that maximizing actual value conflicts with maximizing expectable value, we should sacrifice the former in favor of the latter. But surely a similar case can be constructed in which one's evidence is such that maximizing expectable value conflicts with maximizing expectable expectable value, in which case we should once again sacrifice the former in favor of the latter.

To see the problem, consider the original assignment of values to Case 3:

	Actual Value	Expected Value
A	50	−25
B	40	40
C	−100	−25
D	0	0

Let us assume, unrealistically but for the sake of simplicity, that it is certain for Jill that the value of providing a complete cure is 50, that of providing a partial cure is 40, that of killing John is −100, and that of rendering him permanently incurable is 0. Then the expectable values will match the expected values. That is:

	Actual Value	Expectable Value
A	50	−25
B	40	40
C	−100	−25
D	0	0

Let us further unrealistically assume not only that the values of providing a complete cure, and so on, are certain for Jill, but that it is certain for her that they are certain for her. But now let us suppose that the relevant empirical probabilities are *not* certain for her. For example, I have stipulated (unrealistically) that it is certain for Jill that giving John drug B will partially cure him; that is, that

$$\text{prob}(\text{partialcure}/B) = 1.$$

Suppose, however, that it is not the case that

$$\text{prob}[\text{prob}(\text{partialcure}/B) = 1] = 1.$$

Suppose instead that

$$\text{prob}[\text{prob}(\text{partialcure}/\text{B}) = 0.8] = 0.5, \text{and}$$
$$\text{prob}[\text{prob}(\text{partialcure}/\text{B}) = 0.4] = 0.5.$$

We could then say that

$$\text{prob}_2(\text{partialcure}/\text{B}) = [(0.8 \times 0.5) + (0.4 \times 0.5)] = 0.6.$$

Suppose further that

$$\text{prob}_2(\text{death}/\text{B}) = 0.4.$$

Then (given that there are no evaluative uncertainties and only empirical uncertainties), the expectable expectable value of Jill's giving John drug B is this: $[(40 \times 0.6) + (-100 \times 0.4)] = 16$. Suppose that similar calculations resulted in the following values for A, C, and D, respectively: -30, 10, and 5. The situation would then be this:

	Actual Value	*Expectable Value*	*Expectable Expectable Value*
A	50	−25	−30
B	40	40	16
C	−100	−25	10
D	0	0	5

And here is the point. The Objective View says that Jill ought to maximize actual value and so implies that she ought to give John drug A. I have argued that this is mistaken. The Prospective View, as currently formulated, says that Jill ought to maximize expectable value and so implies that she ought to give John drug B. But surely this is mistaken too. Ought she not rather to maximize expectable expectable value and so give John drug C?

But of course that cannot be the final move, either. What if maximizing expectable expectable value conflicts with maximizing expectable expectable expectable value? Clearly a regress threatens, and this is troubling. There is a solution, however. Let us call what I have so far called expectable value "expectable value at level 1." Let us call what I have called expectable expectable value "expectable value at level 2." And so on. Now, no human agent is such that there can ever be an infinite number of levels of evidence pertaining to expectable value; on the contrary, on any occasion the number of such levels is likely to be very small, due to the fact that one's being justified in having any degree of confidence in a proposition requires that one grasp that proposition,[73] and propositions involving more than

---

[73] Cf. Feldman 1981, p. 275; Chisholm 1989, p. 99.

just a few levels of such evidence are likely to be beyond anyone's grasp. Thus for every human agent there will always be a level of evidence, L, such that maximization of expectable value at that level does not on that occasion conflict with maximization of expectable value at any higher level, either because, due perhaps to the agent's cognitive limitations, there is no such higher level, or because, if there is such a level, any such level is one at which what maximizes expectable value at it also maximizes expectable value at level L. Let us call L the agent's "definitive" level of evidence on that occasion. I then propose that, instead of the fourth formulation, we now accept the following (still rough) formulation of the Prospective View:

The Prospective View (fifth formulation):
An agent ought to perform an act if and only if it is the option that has the greatest expectable value for the agent at his definitive level of evidence.[74]

Even though still rough, this formulation is unfortunately rather complicated.[75] I am afraid, though, that that just is the lesson of Jackson's case. Overall moral obligation is not as simple a matter as the Objective View would have it or as we might wish it to be.

I.6 OBJECTIONS TO THE PROSPECTIVE VIEW

In section 1.3 I leveled four charges against the Subjective View, claiming that that view (a) misattributes to all moral agents a certain kind of moral infallibility; (b) has the absurd implication that people can escape moral obligation through sheer inattention to their situation; (c) has grotesque implications regarding what it is morally permissible to do; and (d) violates the principle that "ought" implies "can." It is clear that the Prospective View, which implies that whatever an agent ought to do will be something that he has the option of doing, does not fall to the last of these objections,

---

[74] If, for some non-human agent in some situation, there is no definitive level of evidence, then that agent has no moral obligation in that situation.

[75] Calculation of expectable value at levels greater than 1 is a complex matter, especially since the relevant empirical and evaluative probabilities can vary independently of one another. The fact that evidence rarely if ever yields precise probabilities (see the discussion above of assignments of epistemic probability) simplifies the calculation in one way, since one need not worry about computing exact products and sums. But in another way it makes the calculation more complex, since in principle it involves the difficulty of making fuzzy measurements (by means, perhaps, of appealing to intervals rather than to determinate numbers).

but it may appear vulnerable to versions of the other objections. (It might be argued that it is a defect in the Prospective View that it *doesn't* violate the principle that "ought" implies "can." I will have more to say about, and in defense of, this principle in sections 3.5 and 3.6.)

A

Consider, first, the question of infallibility. The charge against the Subjective View was that, if that view were true and we knew this, then we would always know (unless we made some kind of inferential mistake) what we ought to do – something that would make a mockery of the conscientious person's inquiry into what he ought to do, since such an inquiry could then be successfully accomplished simply via introspection. The Prospective View clearly does *not* fall to the analogous objection that, if it were true and we knew this, then we would always know what we ought to do. It does not fall to this objection precisely because, unlike the Subjective View, it does not imply that there is some proposition such that merely believing it is sufficient to make some act morally obligatory. According to the Prospective View, whether an act is morally obligatory is determined by the agent's evidence and not by his beliefs. Thus, if his beliefs fail to comport with his evidence, it is perfectly possible that he should misidentify his obligation, even if he knows that the Prospective View is true. In this way, the Prospective View escapes the charge that all moral agents are infallible regarding what they are obligated to do.

It may seem, however, that the Prospective View does not escape a closely related objection. For, although it does not imply that, if we knew it to be true, we *would* always know what we ought to do, it may seem to imply that we *could* always know this. Thus it may seem to imply that all moral agents are *potentially*, if not actually, infallible regarding what they are obligated to do.

It is unclear to me whether the Prospective View has any such implication. Suppose that you knew that this view was true.[76] Would you then always be in a position to know what you ought to do? Well, suppose that some act *A* has greater expectable value for you at your definitive level of evidence than any other option that you have. Given your knowledge of the Prospective View, you would have the general knowledge that any such act is something that you ought to do. But, as just noted, you might

---

[76] That is, suppose that you knew the proposition that constitutes its content. See n. 29 above.

not know that A in particular is something that you ought to do, because (even if you were guilty of no inferential error) your beliefs with respect to A might not comport with your evidence with respect to A. But must it be that you *could* know that you ought to do A, in the sense that your present evidence suffices for your knowing this, if only you did believe it? I think not. Recall what it is for A to maximize expectable value for you at your definitive level of evidence. It is for it to be such that, for some level of evidence, A maximizes expectable value for you at that level, and there is no higher level of evidence such that A does not maximize expectable value at it. The absence of any such higher level of evidence may not itself be something about which you have evidence. If it is not, then surely you do not know that A maximizes expectable value for you at your definitive level of evidence. Your general knowledge of the Prospective View would then not suffice for your knowing that you ought to do A, even if you correctly believed that you ought to do A.

But suppose now that your total evidence *does* confirm the fact that A maximizes expectable value for you at your definitive level of evidence. If you correctly believe that you ought to do A, would it now be the case that you know that you ought to do A? This is unclear to me. I have not attempted, nor will I attempt, to specify just what kind of epistemic justification or what degree of confidence is required for knowledge. In the absence of any such specification, it seems to me that it would at best be premature to conclude that, under the circumstances envisaged, you know that you ought to do A.

It should be noted that, even if on some occasion you do know of some act that you ought to perform, it could still be the case that you don't know whether you are fulfilling an obligation in respect of it. Jill might know, for example, that she ought to give John drug B but absent-mindedly give him drug C instead. In so doing, she will falsely believe that she is doing what she ought and so not know whether she is fulfilling her obligation. What, though, of Ross's "bold" claim, recorded in section 1.2, that one *can* always know whether one is fulfilling an obligation? *Could* Jill know whether she was doing what she ought regarding her treatment of John? Perhaps so. If she knew the Prospective View to be true and, in light of this, knew that she ought to give John drug B, then presumably her evidence would suffice for her knowing whether she was giving John drug B and thus whether she was fulfilling her obligation, even if, due to absent-mindedness, she wasn't paying heed to this evidence. But, even if the Prospective View does thus imply that, under certain conditions, we can

44

know not only what we ought to do but whether we are doing it, such an implication does not seem objectionable. On the contrary, that the view holds out some hope of our sometimes knowing both what we ought to do and whether we are doing it is surely welcome. Conscientious inquiry would otherwise be doomed to failure, as on many versions of the Objective View it would seem to be. (Consider Moore's claim that propositions about the moral rightness of particular acts are incapable of proof or disproof.[77]) Even if we cannot realistically aspire to the kind of infallibility implied by the Subjective View, we can surely hope to avoid the sort of crippling moral ignorance that is apparently implied by theories such as Moore's.[78]

B

Consider, next, the question concerning the conditions under which one may escape moral obligation. The charge against the Subjective View was that it implies that one can escape such obligation through sheer inattention to one's situation, since such inattention can result in one's failing to have any beliefs about what it would be best to do. The Prospective View does not of course imply that inattention alone can have any such effect. For, unlike the Subjective View, it ties one's obligations to one's evidence – to the beliefs that one would be *justified* in having – and not to one's actual beliefs. But the Prospective View does have an analogous implication, namely, that failing to have any evidence regarding the actual values of one's alternatives suffices to free one from moral obligation. Isn't this just as objectionable?

On the contrary, the implication seems to me to be a decided advantage for the Prospective View over the Objective View. A common complaint about the Objective View is that it is hard to see how it could capture the *moral* aspect of moral obligation. Consider, for example, Moore's own version of the view, according to which an agent ought to perform an action if and only if that action would have a higher instrumental value than the instrumental value of any alternative. Moore restricts his theory to actions that he calls "voluntary," apparently taking these to form a proper subset of actions that he calls "human." Voluntary actions are, he says, those which the agent could have prevented if, immediately beforehand, he had

---

[77] Moore 1903, p. x.
[78] On whether Moore's theory actually has this implication, see Lemos 2004, pp. 171 ff.

so chosen.[79] As far as I can tell, though, such actions are regularly performed by individuals other than human beings. Grizzly bears, for instance, apparently have a choice whether to attack or retreat. Should we therefore say that a grizzly does *moral wrong* when it makes a picnic of a picnicker? This seems absurd.

One advantage of the Prospective View is that it restricts the ascription of overall moral obligation to individuals for whom there is some epistemic probability that certain actual values pertain to certain actions; for only under such circumstances can actions have expectable values, that is, values that are expectable for or relative to those individuals. As noted earlier, a proposition can have an epistemic probability for someone only if that person grasps the proposition. It follows that only those who have a grasp of the concept of actual value can be morally obligated to perform some action. Presumably grizzly bears won't qualify. I leave open how firm the grasp must be; certainly, though, it should not be said to be so firm that few people qualify. Anyone, for example, who understands the point of Jackson's original case about Jill and John will qualify, regardless of whether he can specify precisely the actual values associated with Jill's options.

C

Consider now the question concerning grotesque implications regarding what it is morally permissible to do. Above, I rejected the Subjective View on the grounds that it implies that a false belief can justify murder. A similar charge may be brought against the Prospective View. Consider again Case 2:

Case 2:
All the evidence at Jill's disposal indicates (in keeping with the facts) that giving John drug B would cure him partially and giving him no drug would render him permanently incurable, but it also indicates (in contrast to the facts) that giving him drug C would cure him completely and giving him drug A would kill him.

As noted earlier, the Prospective View implies that Jill may, indeed ought to, give John drug C. If she does this, though, she will kill him. Although it may be an exaggeration to say that her killing him would be tantamount to murder, isn't it nonetheless plainly a mistake to say that Jill may, let alone ought to, kill John?

---

[79] Moore 1912, pp. 5 ff.

A proponent of the Objective View would of course say that in this case it would be wrong for Jill to give John drug C (and that she ought to give him drug A instead). But this is unacceptable, as I hope I have shown. One could, however, agree with my verdict and yet resist inferring from it that Jill may, let alone ought to, kill John. Judith Thomson advocates such resistance. She notes that such an inference presupposes the truth of some kind of "inheritance principle." The basic principle she has in mind is in essence this (where "*P*" ranges over persons and "*A*" and "*B*" over acts):

The First Inheritance Principle (IP1):
If *P* ought not to do *A*, then if it is the case that if *P* does *B*, he will thereby do *A*, then *P* ought not to do *B*.[80]

In Case 2, if Jill gives John drug C, she will thereby kill him. Suppose that she ought not to kill him. It follows from IP1 that she ought not to give him drug C. But, if we reject IP1, we might then hold on both to the claim that Jill ought not to kill John and to the claim that she may nonetheless give him drug C. Thomson endorses rejecting IP1 for just this kind of reason.[81]

I will discuss inheritance principles further in section 3.2. Let me simply state here that I think Thomson is quite correct to reject IP1, but that that does not warrant our saying in Case 2 both that Jill may give John drug C and that she ought not to kill him. This is because, although IP1 is false, the following related principle is true:

The Second Inheritance Principle (IP2):
If *P* ought not to do *A*, then if *P* cannot avoid its being the case that if he does *B*, he will thereby do *A*, then *P* ought not to do *B*.

(This is actually only a rough version of the relevant principle, but it will do for present purposes.) Notice that this principle also implies in Case 2 that, if Jill ought not to kill John, then she ought not to give him drug C; for (we may assume) she cannot avoid its being the case that, if she gives him this drug, she will thereby kill him. But then, if we say that she may give him the drug, we must infer that she may kill him after all.

Here, though, you may think that the Prospective View runs into a problem. I have said that, in Case 2, Jill may, indeed ought to, give John drug C. Why? Because all the evidence at her disposal indicates that giving

---

[80] Thomson 1986, p. 186. In her article, Thomson uses the label "(IP₁)" to refer a different principle.
[81] Thomson 1986, pp. 186 and 188.

him this drug would cure him completely; thus her giving him this drug maximizes expectable value (for her, at her definitive level of evidence). But, you may say, even if giving John drug C maximizes expectable value, surely it doesn't follow that killing John also maximizes expectable value. On the contrary, the expectable value of her killing him will presumably be very low, and so she ought not to kill him after all. Thomson's approach to this sort of question is thus vindicated, and we should reject IP2 as well as IP1.

I cannot yet deal fully with this matter; I must postpone doing so to chapter 3. At this point, let me simply beg your indulgence and reiterate that I take IP2 to be true. From the claim that, in Case 2, Jill may give John drug C it thus follows that she may kill him. Indeed, I think that she *ought* to kill him! This may seem outrageous, but I will defend the claim later. In the meantime, let me just add that I take it also to be the case that Jill ought *not* to kill John *intentionally*.

Even though I will wait until chapter 3 to give a full defense of my position, I should still say something further here in response to the charge that the Prospective View has grotesque implications with respect to what it is morally permissible to do. For it is clear that it implies not only that it can happen that one ought to kill someone, when doing so would actually constitute committing great evil, but that it can happen that one ought *intentionally* to kill someone, when doing so would actually constitute committing great evil. This is because expectable value is in part a function of the evidence that one has concerning what is evil, and, even if (as I assume) it is not true of Jill in Case 2, it can surely happen that one's evidence on this score is grossly defective. Suppose, then, that one is faced with the choice between causing great pain to some innocent people or refraining from doing so, and suppose that it would actually be best to refrain from doing so, but that, due to deficiencies in one's evaluative evidence, it would maximize expectable value (for one, at one's definitive level of evidence) to cause the pain (intentionally). Is it not grotesque to think that under such circumstances one's overall moral obligation is to cause the pain?

I believe not. I grant again that this implication may initially appear unpalatable, but the fact is that any plausible moral view will have some such implications. For example, a proponent of the Objective View should recognize, as Moore himself does, the distinction between wrongdoing and blameworthiness. In acknowledging the possibility of excuses, one is acknowledging the possibility of *blameless wrongdoing*. Hitler committed enormous evil. An application of the Objective View will likely yield the conclusion that he therefore did great wrong. (Whether it does yield this conclusion depends on just how the view is developed.) But even on the Objective View it could be that Hitler was blameless. This perhaps unwelcome possibility should not be dismissed lightly. (On my view, whether Hitler was to blame depends in part on whether he non-culpably believed that he was doing no wrong. I will pursue this issue in chapter 4.) An application of the Prospective View might yield the conclusion that Hitler did no wrong. (Whether he did so would depend in part on the evidence available to him concerning the relative values of sparing and taking the lives of millions of innocents. I see no reason to believe that his evidence differed significantly from ours in this regard, but the possibility cannot be dismissed out of hand.) The Prospective View thus opens up the perhaps unwelcome possibility of *wrongless evil-doing* in a way that the Objective View does not. Note, though, that this possibility does nothing to diminish the evil in question and should not be dismissed as grotesque, any more than the possibility of blameless wrongdoing should be dismissed as grotesque.

There are, of course, other positions that one might adopt on this issue. One could insist that it just is grotesque to think that humans can perpetrate great evil (while having the option not to, and without any compensating benefit) and yet do no wrong, and hence that the Prospective View (as currently formulated) must be rejected. But what, then, should be accepted in its place. The Objective View? No. Jackson's case shows otherwise. *No one* in Jill's place in Case 3 could conscientiously do other than give John drug B (assuming the he or she has an adequate appreciation of the actual values at stake). The Subjective View? No. That is grotesque in its own way and has other problems besides. The Prospective View on its third formulation, according to which what one ought to do is a matter of maximizing expected and not expectable value? But even this view entails the possibility of wrongless evil-doing (although admittedly not in the way that the fifth formulation does, since it takes only empirical and not also evaluative evidence into consideration). Consider again Case 2. If Jill gives John drug C in this case, she will maximize expected value and yet do great evil. To repeat, then: any plausible moral view will have some implications that may initially appear unpalatable. What one must do is "pick one's poison," that is, choose that view whose implications appear least unpalatable. As I see it, that means (as far as our discussion up to this point reveals) that we should choose the Prospective View on its current, fifth formulation, according to which what one ought to do is maximize expectable value.

It is important to note that the allegation that the Subjective View has grotesque implications is rooted in the fact that it implies that whether one does wrong is a function, in part, of what one *does* believe, as opposed to what one is *justified* in believing, whereas the Prospective View has the converse implication. There is a sense, then, in which moral obligation is, according to the Prospective View, an "objective" matter, even though this view is of course distinct from the so-called Objective View. (This issue is closely related to the question of fallibility, discussed above.) The sense at issue is this: obligation is objective if one's obligations are not even in part determined by the beliefs that one happens to have about one's situation, and subjective otherwise. It is the Prospective View's implication that obligation is objective in this sense that shields it from the charge that its implications are grotesque in the manner in which the implications of the Subjective View are.

Of course, the term "objective" may be understood differently. In another common sense, obligation may be said to be objective if one's obligations are not even in part determined by one's mental state, and subjective otherwise. On this understanding, the Prospective View implies that obligation is subjective. (Note that, even though the Prospective View implies that what one ought to do is in part a function of what one is *justified* in believing rather than of what one *does* believe, still what one is justified in believing is a function of what one *does* grasp or understand.) Lest this be thought objectionable, it is worth pointing out that even adherents of the Objective View are likely to take obligation to be subjective, in the present sense. (Whether this is in fact so will depend on how exactly they develop their view.) As noted earlier, Moore himself takes obligation to be restricted to those acts that he calls "voluntary" (in the sense that one would perform them if one chose). Moreover, it seems clear that any plausible view of obligation must take it to be subjective, in the present sense. This is because whether one is a moral agent (in the sense of being capable of having moral obligations) is, as just mentioned, surely in part a function of one's mental capacities. Normal adults are moral agents, whereas infants and grizzly bears are not, and this has at least in part to do with the difference in their mental capacities.

The Objective and Prospective Views would thus appear to be on a par with respect to whether moral obligation is objective or subjective, in the two senses just discussed. Perhaps there is a third sense that would serve to

50

distinguish these views in this regard. For example, one might claim that, although the Objective View should be understood to imply, as the Prospective View does, that one's state of mind is an "enabling condition" of one's being obligated to perform some act,[82] it does not imply, as the Prospective View does, that that act's being obligatory "supervenes" at all on one's mental state. But this is a matter that I will not pursue here.

D

Consider, finally, an objection to the Prospective View that is clearly inapplicable to the Subjective View. According to the Prospective View, one ought to choose that option that is prospectively best. The prospectively best option is the one that it is most reasonable to choose, in light of the costs and benefits that are evidently at stake. Some options may not be prospectively best because they are too risky, others because they are too cautious. In its current formulation, the Prospective View says this:

The Prospective View (fifth formulation):
An agent ought to perform an act if and only if it is the option that has the greatest expectable value for the agent at his definitive level of evidence.

As noted in the last section, the expectable value of an act is a function of the possible values of its possible outcomes and the epistemic probabilities of these values and outcomes. Now, it is certainly plausible to maintain that the prospectively best option has *some* close relation to the maximization of expectable value, but it may be doubted whether what is prospectively best just *is* what maximizes expectable value. I will briefly discuss six reasons for doubting the equivalence. I find the first reason inadequate. I'm not sure what to say about the next two. The final three, though, seem to me to succeed in showing that the prospectively best option is *not* necessarily one that maximizes expectable value. Thus I believe that the Prospective View on its current formulation is indeed false.

The first consideration is this. It may be that there is an asymmetry between costs and benefits, such that the former are to be weighted more heavily than the latter in the determination of the value of an outcome and hence of what it is one ought to do. (For example, it may be that suffering is to be weighted more heavily than happiness.[83]) I grant this, but I think it

---

[82] Compare Dancy 2004, pp. 38 ff.   [83] Cf. Mayerfeld 1999, ch. 6.

poses no problem for the current formulation of the Prospective View. There is no need to think that, in calculating the actual values of outcomes, all component values, whether positive or negative, must be weighted equally. Thus there is no need to think that the calculation of the expect-able values of acts presupposes the equal weighting of these component values.

A second consideration has to do with the possibility that some prospects are negligible, the probabilities involved being so low as to constitute possibilities that are not "real" and thus ones that it is not reasonable to take into account, even though, being greater than 0, they do figure into the calculation of expectable value.[84] (Consider the possibility that you will be struck by lightning if you take a walk on a cloudless day.) I'm not sure that there is a problem here. Why not say that the probabilities in question are so small that in almost all cases they will not affect the ranking of one's alternatives in terms of expectable value and hence will not affect what it is most reasonable to do, but that in those rare cases in which the ranking is affected then what it is most reasonable to do is likewise affected? This strikes me as plausible, although there may be situations in which such an approach proves misguided.

A third, contrary consideration has to do with the possibility that some prospects are so momentous in terms of their evident value that they should be pursued (if good) and avoided (if bad) no matter how low the prob-ability of their attainment. For example, in some cases a possible outcome may be so bad as to constitute a "catastrophe" and to warrant avoidance even when strict adherence to the prescription to maximize expectable value would require courting the catastrophe.[85] Again, I'm not sure that there is a problem here, although I am more sympathetic to this suggestion than the last. It might be contended, for example, that in Case 3 what is really driving the judgment that Jill ought to give John drug B is the idea that John's dying would be a catastrophe. It's not because giving him drug B would maximize expectable value that Jill ought to choose this option; it's rather that any risk of death, however small, is in this case to be avoided. In support of this contention, consider a variation on the case in which the probability of death on either drug A or drug C is 0.05 (rather than 0.5) and the probability of a complete cure is 0.95 (rather than 0.5). Then, given the original actual values assigned, the expected (and, let's assume, the

[84] Cf. Rescher 1983, pp. 35 ff.   [85] Cf. Rescher 1983, pp. 70 ff.

expectable) value of giving John either drug A or drug C will be 42.5, *higher* than that of giving him drug B. Still, it might be contended, Jill ought to give him drug B – any other action would be unreasonable – and hence what it is reasonable to do in this case does not match up with what would maximize expectable value.

I'm not sure what to make of this argument. My difficulty has to do with the initial assignment of actual values. I am prepared to grant (although some who are less risk-averse may not) that, in the modified case in which the probability of death is greatly reduced and that of a complete cure is greatly enhanced, it would still be unreasonable of Jill to do other than give John drug B. But what is not clear to me is that her giving John drug B would fail to maximize expectable value. The original numbers were, after all, pulled out of thin air, merely for the sake of illustrating a point. Perhaps they don't accurately represent the actual values at stake, in which case the present consideration is at best inconclusive.

A fourth consideration concerns the well-documented fact that the average person's choices do not always conform to expected utility theory. Consider this case (which constitutes a version of what is known as Allais's paradox[86]):

Case 4:
Jill has two patients, Jim and Joe, who suffer from paraplegia and for each of whom there is a choice of two treatments, A and B. With regard to Jim, the pertinent facts are these.

A:	recovery of the ability to walk (but not run)	probability 1
B:	recovery of the ability to run	probability 0.09
	recovery of the ability to walk (but not run)	probability 0.89
	no recovery	probability 0.02

With regard to Joe, the pertinent facts are these:

A:	recovery of the ability to walk (but not run)	probability 0.11
	no recovery	probability 0.89
B:	recovery of the ability to run	probability 0.09
	no recovery	probability 0.91

It is certain for Jill that these are the pertinent probabilities and also that, for each of Jim and Joe, the recovery of the ability to run is better than the recovery of the ability merely to walk, which is itself far better than no recovery, and that the pertinent values are the same in Jim's case as in Joe's.

---

[86] Cf. Savage 1953.

53

What treatment ought Jill to administer to Jim? What treatment ought she to administer to Joe? Consistency of a certain sort would require her to choose the same treatment in each case; which treatment to choose would depend on just what values are to be assigned to the possible outcomes.[87] However, I think that, if I myself were in Jim's shoes, I would probably choose treatment A, whereas if I were in Joe's shoes I would probably choose treatment B. The fact that I could be certain of a considerable, even if only partial, recovery in the first case, and that I could be almost certain of no recovery in the second case, would weigh heavily with me. Apparently, I am not alone in this.[88] Let us suppose that Jill would choose as I would and that therefore, putting herself in her patients' shoes, she chooses treatment A for Jim and treatment B for Joe. Is such a departure from expected utility theory unreasonable? I believe not. Is it morally wrong?[89] Again, I believe not. If I am right, then the Prospective View cannot be accepted on its current formulation.

A fifth consideration concerns the fact that two options may involve equally probable outcomes of equal probable value and hence appear to be prospectively equal, and yet one option may be due greater regard than the other because the evidence in the one case is more reliable than that in the other. An alternative and, I think, better way to construe such a situation is to say that the options would *not* be prospectively equal precisely *because* of the disparity in evidence. On this view, prospective value is a function not just of the probable values of probable outcomes, but also of the reliability of the evidence that yields the probabilities. Since expectable value is not a function of the reliability of such evidence, we see once again that the Prospective View on its current formulation won't do. Consider, by way of illustration, this case:

---

[87] Let the values (common to both cases) of a full recovery (the ability to run), a partial recovery (the ability to walk but not run), and no recovery be a, b, and c, respectively. Suppose that, in the case of Jim, A is to be preferred to B. Where the probabilities are put in terms of percentages, this would seem to imply:

$$100b > (9a + 89b + 2c); \text{i.e.,} 11b > (9a + 2c).$$

Suppose that, in the case of Joe, B is to be preferred to A. This would seem to imply:

$$(11b + 89c) < (9a + 91c); \text{i.e.,} 11b < (9a + 2c).$$

These implications are of course inconsistent.

[88] See the discussions in Savage 1953, Kahneman and Tversky 1979, and McClennen 1983.

[89] Recall the implicit proviso "all else being equal." See n. 8 above.

Ignorance and obligation

Case 5:
Jill has a choice between two drugs, A and B, for John. For each drug the probability for Jill of its curing John completely is 0.7, and the probability of its being ineffective but harmless is 0.3. It is certain for Jill that these are the pertinent probabilities and also that curing John is better than leaving him in his current state. Drug A has been widely researched; the data are plentiful. Drug B has hardly been researched at all; the data are very meager indeed.

It is surely plausible to maintain that in this case Jill ought to give John drug A, not drug B, even though the expectable value of giving him A is equal to that of giving him B. Indeed, it seems that she would be obligated to give him A even if the expectable value of doing so were somewhat less than that of giving him B.[90] (In general, the more relevant data one possesses, the better. Of course, gathering further data and thereby reducing, if not eliminating, one's ignorance is itself an activity that can carry its own risk.[91] I will return to this point in the next section.)

A sixth and final consideration concerns the matter of supererogation. Two alternatives may have the same expectable value and yet the agent may be morally justified in treating them quite differently because of the (risk of) high personal cost associated with one of them and not the other. Consider this case:

Case 6:
Jill has a choice between two drugs, A and B, for John. The probability for her that drug A will cure John completely is 0.9, and the probability that it will be ineffective but harmless is 0.1. The probability for her that drug B will cure John completely is 0.8999, and the probability that it will be ineffective but harmless is 0.1001. It is certain for Jill that these are the pertinent probabilities and also that curing John is better than leaving him in his current state. Jill knows that giving John drug A will cost her $10,000, whereas giving him drug B will cost her nothing.

It is surely plausible to contend that Jill is not morally obligated to give John drug A, despite the fact that doing so would appear to have higher expectable value (for her, at her definitive level of evidence) than giving him drug B. It might be retorted that, given the personal cost to her of giving him drug A, it is in fact *not* the case that giving him this drug has higher expectable value than giving him drug B; for this personal cost should be counted among the obligation-relevant values that are at stake in

---

[90] Cf. Ellsberg 1961; Gärdenfors and Sahlin 1982; Weirich 2001.
[91] Cf. Russell 1966, pp. 31–2.

55

the situation. But such a retort won't do if, as is surely plausible, we want to declare Jill's giving John drug A supererogatory and thus say that she is not obligated *not* to give him this drug. For, if that is the case, then the cost to her of giving him the drug cannot simply be thrown into the "mix" with the other values that are at stake in order to determine what her obligation is.

There are, then, at least three good reasons, and maybe more, to think that what one ought to do does not necessarily match what would maximize expectable value. Thus, to repeat, the Prospective View on its current formulation is, I believe, unacceptable. But this does *not* mean that the Prospective View itself is dubious; it only means that prospective value is not to be understood wholly in terms of expectable value. Just how it is to be understood depends on just what adjustments to expectable value are required for the points just raised (and perhaps others too) to be adequately accommodated. I'm afraid that I have no precise formula to offer here.[92] Once again, then, there is a gap in my account which, with considerable chagrin, I am forced to leave it to others to fill; I hope nonetheless that the account in its present state, and as developed further in the next two chapters, will prove both fruitful and consistent with the best theory of reasonable decision-making that decision-theorists have to offer. At this point, I will simply revert to the second formulation of the Prospective View, *with the stipulation* that "prospectively best" is now to be understood in terms of the maximization of expectable value for the agent, at his definitive level of evidence, adjusted in whatever way is necessary for the points just mentioned to be adequately accommodated. To remind you of this stipulation, I will call the resulting formulation of the Prospective View not its second formulation but its sixth. Thus:

The Prospective View (sixth formulation):
An agent ought to perform an act if and only if it is the prospectively best option that he has.

Even with "prospectively best" understood as stipulated, this formulation of the Prospective View is still very rough. Further refinement will be provided in chapter 3.

---

[92] Regarding the matter of supererogation in particular, however, cf. Zimmerman 1996, ch. 8, on how to reconcile the possibility of supererogation with a maximizing theory of obligation.

Recall Case 3:

Case 3:
All the evidence at Jill's disposal indicates (in keeping with the facts) that giving John drug B would cure him partially and giving him no drug would render him permanently incurable, but (despite the facts) it leaves completely open whether it is giving him drug A or giving him drug C that would cure him completely and whether it is giving him drug A or giving him drug C that would kill him.

This case is the linchpin in my argument against the Objective View and in favor of the Prospective View. Any conscientious person (with an adequate appreciation of the values at stake) would, I have contended, give John drug B in this case, were he in Jill's position. Even the self-avowed Objectivist would do this, thus indicating that he does not in fact subscribe to the Objective View after all. I noted in section 1.4 that someone might reply that giving John drug B would actually be consistent with subscribing to the Objective View, since so acting could be construed as an effort to minimize the risk of doing wrong. However, I explained how this response fails, since the Objective View does *not* imply that giving John drug B in Case 3 minimizes the risk of doing wrong, even though it does of course minimize the risk of doing harm.

To risk doing harm is one thing, then, while to risk doing wrong is another. So far, the cases that we have considered have been concerned either with risking harms (harms such as death, injury, and poor health) or with "risking" forgoing benefits. What, though, of risking wrongdoing? What are the implications of the Prospective View in this regard?

A

To take a risk of some "negativity" eventuating – whether the negativity is construed in absolute or relative terms – is to perform an act that has a probability greater than 0 (and perhaps less than 1^{93}) that the negativity will occur. Degree of risk is a function of the extent to which the outcome in question is negative, of the probabilities at issue, and also of at least some of the matters raised at the end of the last section. (Although how risky an act is does not depend on whether it is supererogatory, for example, it does

[93] See n. 44 above.

depend, I believe, on how reliable one's evidence is. Perhaps, too, such questions as whether the probabilities are negligible and whether the outcome would be catastrophic are pertinent to degree of risk.) The Prospective View requires that one do what is prospectively best, which on some occasions involves forgoing options that are too risky with respect to the actual values that are at stake. From the outset, I have left open the question what these values are, so that the Prospective View may be seen to be applicable to all substantive accounts of moral obligation, such as those provided by the act-consequentialist, the rule-consequentialist, the virtue-theorist, and so on. However, there is a limit to how elastic the construal of "negativity" can be. Although it can be understood in terms of deficiencies regarding the promotion of intrinsic value, the display of virtue, and so on, one interpretation that *cannot* be given to it is this: deficient regarding the fulfillment of obligation. For, although it is certainly true that an act that is wrong is deficient regarding the fulfillment of obligation (and that it can be deficient to a greater or lesser degree, depending on how seriously wrong it is), it cannot be that obligation and wrongdoing are themselves to be understood in terms of *such* deficiency; that would be viciously circular. Whether an act is actually right or wrong may be a function of the risk of doing harm, then, but it cannot itself be a function of the risk of doing wrong.

But then what are we to say about the risk of doing wrong? The conscientious person's goal is to avoid wrongdoing, and he is worried that he might fail to do so. That is, he is worried about the risk of doing wrong. Isn't it perfectly sensible, then, to ask whether it is right or wrong to risk doing wrong?

I think the best way to tackle this issue is to consider first what a proponent of the Objective View would say. On this view, an act is obligatory if it is in fact the best option that one has. In Case 3, Jill's best option is to give John drug A. Hence, according to the Objective View, that is what she ought to do. Of course, in so acting she risks doing what is not best, and so risks doing what, according to the Objective View, is wrong. Nonetheless, the view implies that that is what she ought to do, despite the risks involved. In general, the Objective View implies that one ought to do what is in fact best, regardless of whether, in so doing, one risks doing wrong.

The Prospective View is of course different from the Objective View. It does not imply that one ought to do what is in fact best, regardless of the risk of doing what is not best. According to this view, Jill ought in Case 3 to give John drug B rather than drug A, precisely because doing so is prospectively best *in terms of what is actually valuable*. However, even on the Prospective View, it could still be the case that Jill's giving John drug B is *not* prospectively best *in terms of the fulfillment of obligation.* (How so? Well, perhaps her evidence favors the Objective View and hence the judgment that she ought not to give John drug B.) Jill could thus be running a serious risk of doing wrong in giving John drug B, but that doesn't alter the Prospective View's verdict that she ought to give him this drug. Thus, although the Objective and Prospective Views certainly differ from one another in significant ways, they share this implication: whether an act is right or wrong has nothing to do with the risk of wrongdoing that an agent would run in performing that act.

This result is hardly surprising. No coherent view about the general conditions of overall moral obligation, rightness, and wrongness could fail to have the implication just mentioned. Consider any view that maintains, for example, that certain conditions are necessary and sufficient for an act's being morally wrong. Call these conditions *C.* Suppose that performing some act, *A,* would involve a risk of doing wrong. The question arises: would it be wrong to risk doing wrong by virtue of doing *A*? The answer: yes, if doing *A* satisfies *C*; otherwise, no. What else could the answer be?

The point that I have just made is an obvious one. Applied to the Prospective View in particular, it yields this result: it is wrong to perform an act that involves a risk of doing wrong if, but only if, performing that act is not among the agent's prospectively best options. End of story.

(It may be salutary briefly to apply the lesson of this story to another issue that some find puzzling. According to the Prospective View, right and wrong are in part a function of the evidence that is immediately available to the agent. But there may be evidence in the offing that is not immediately available. For instance, in Case 3 one option that Jill has is to conduct further research into drugs A and C, as a result of which she might acquire new evidence that indicates that it is drug A that would cure John completely and drug C that would kill him. Shouldn't someone who ties right and wrong to evidence say that there is in general an obligation to seek further relevant evidence, and hence that in particular Jill has an obligation to do the research rather than give John drug B forthwith? Not at all. Seeking further evidence is itself an activity that carries its own risk. As such, it is clear what the Prospective View has to say about it: one ought to seek further evidence if, but only if, doing so is prospectively best.[94] What else could it say? In Case 3, it is clearly *not* the case that Jill ought to do the

---

[94] Cf. Jackson 1991, p. 465. Jackson claims that epistemic probabilities reduce to subjective probabilities. I do not share this view.

research before choosing which drug to give to John; for all the evidence at her disposal indicates that doing so would come at far too high a cost – the cost of rendering him permanently incurable.)

B

The foregoing treatment of the question whether it is wrong to risk doing wrong may strike you as unsatisfactory, indeed superficial. "Of course," you may say, "any view that provides necessary and sufficient conditions for wrongdoing generally will imply that it is wrong to perform some particular act that involves the risk of doing wrong if and only if that act satisfies those conditions. That's a trivial point. Nonetheless the question remains how best to respond to the concern of a conscientious person who is uncertain about what he ought to do; for surely such a person is intent not only on avoiding wrongdoing but also on reducing the risk of doing wrong. Consider the plight of such a person who has searched in vain for an answer to the question 'What ought I to do?' and yet finds himself forced to make a decision. In such a case he might say: 'Well, I haven't managed to figure out what I ought to do. *Now* what ought I to do?'[95] If, as you have insisted, 'ought' is *un*ambiguous when it is taken to express overall moral obligation, this is an odd question. The only answer can be, 'You ought to do whatever it is that you ought to do, whether you know what that is or not.' But that is a singularly unhelpful response. If we do distinguish between senses of 'ought,' however, another answer can be given, one that invokes different *orders* of obligation: 'When you don't know what you ought$_1$ to do, you ought$_2$ to do such-and-such.' Depending on what 'ought$_2$' is said to consist in, this answer looks like it could be helpful in addressing the conscientious person's desire to reduce the risk of doing wrong."

I grant that the conscientious person, in wanting to avoid wrongdoing, is likely also to want to reduce the risk of wrongdoing. But it's not clear to me

---

[95] Note two points. First, the sort of situation I have in mind is one in which the person in question hasn't managed to arrive at a moral assessment of *all* his options. He may well have managed to rule out *some* of his options ("I ought not to steal my neighbor's car"; "I ought not to shoot my neighbor's cat"); it's just that he hasn't managed to determine, with respect to those options that remain, whether he ought to, may, or ought not to perform them. Second, the question that I am imagining the person to be asking himself is "What *ought* I to do?" and not "What would enable me to *escape blame?*" As noted in section 1.3, these are distinct questions. (Contrast Feldman 2006, sect. 6, in which the questions are conflated.)

whether the latter desire can properly be said to correspond to any kind of moral obligation, despite the admitted naturalness of the question *"Now what ought I to do?"* Let me explain.

To begin with, notice that the answer just given to the conscientious person's inquiry suggests the possibility of a further question, namely, "What ought I to do when I don't know what I ought$_2$ to do?" One might answer in turn, "When you don't know what you ought$_2$ to do, you ought$_3$ to do so-and-so." But this answer simply suggests yet another question, with yet another answer, and so on and on. Thus a regress looms, a series of obligations of different orders generated by repeated instances of moral ignorance. In light of this prospect, what are we to make of the present proposal?

One suggestion that might seem promising in this regard involves the distinction between unconditional and conditional obligation. For an illustration of this distinction, suppose that it is Matt's overall moral obligation (as determined by the account given in the Prospective View) to attend a meeting on the first floor of his office building.[96] This is to be understood as an unconditional obligation. Even though he has this obligation, it may nonetheless be the case that Matt also has an overall moral obligation (as determined by an extension of the account given in the Prospective View) to attend a meeting on the second floor (due to take place at the same time as the meeting on the first floor), *if* he fails to attend the meeting on the first floor. This would be a conditional obligation. It is commonplace to observe that a conditional obligation does not in general warrant the detachment of an unconditional obligation simply in virtue of its condition's being satisfied.[97] If it did, then, if Matt were in fact to be about to fail to attend the meeting on the first floor, he would have an unconditional obligation to attend the meeting on the second floor. But this obligation would conflict with his obligation to attend the meeting on the first floor, and hence Matt would be in a moral dilemma. But surely there is no dilemma. Matt's only unconditional obligation is to attend the meeting on the first floor. If he does that, then, even though he must of course thereby fail to attend the meeting on the second floor, he does no wrong whatsoever.

The commonplace observation just mentioned is simplistic. We can and should detach unconditional obligations from conditional obligations, while avoiding dilemmas, by invoking *levels* of obligation. We may say that Matt has a *primary* obligation to attend the meeting on the first floor;

---

[96] This example and the ensuing discussion derive from Zimmerman 1996, ch. 4.
[97] Such detachment was first given the useful label "factual detachment" in Greenspan 1975.

that he has a *secondary* obligation to attend the meeting on the second floor, if he fails to attend the meeting on the first floor; that he has a *tertiary* obligation to attend a meeting on the third floor, if he fails to attend either of the first two meetings; and so on. We can then say that, if Matt in fact fails to fulfill his primary obligation to attend the meeting on the first floor (that is, he fails to do what he ought[1] to do), then he has a *secondary* *un*conditional obligation (that is, he ought[2]) to attend the meeting on the second floor; and so on.[98] Suppose that Matt does not attend the meeting on the first floor. Then he does (unconditional) wrong. If he fails also to attend the meeting on the second floor, he *compounds* this (unconditional) wrongdoing; the seriousness of the wrongdoing is *amplified.* If he fails also to attend the meeting on the third floor, he compounds the wrongdoing still further; and so on. Notice, however, that the relevant unconditional subsidiary (that is, non-primary) obligations are detached if but *only* if the relevant conditions are satisfied. If Matt attends the meeting on the first floor, he does no unconditional wrong whatsoever. As it stands, the Prospective View implicitly concerns only primary unconditional obligation. It can be extended to cover subsidiary obligation. In that way levels of "ought" can easily be accommodated, and moreover, although a regress looms, there is no threat of its being vicious; for, like the number of floors in Matt's building, the number of levels of obligation will be finite.

There is an obvious similarity between the different levels of obligation just described and the different orders of obligation invoked a short while ago in an effort to provide a helpful response to the conscientious person's request for advice concerning what to do in situations of moral ignorance. Indeed, it is tempting to think that to say that someone has a first-order moral obligation to do something (that is, that he ought[1] to do it) *just is* to

---

[98] Factual detachment may in general be represented as follows:

$$O(q/p)\&p \vdash O(q).$$

My claim is this: such detachment is valid when, but only when, the obligations at issue are on the same level. Thus, whereas we should not endorse

$$O^2(q/p)\&p \vdash O^1(q),$$

we should endorse, for any n,

$$O^n(q/p)\&p \vdash O^n(q).$$

For further discussion, see Zimmerman 1996, ch. 4. (Note that I am here using "ought^n" or "O^n" to designate an obligation of *level n*, and "ought$_n$," to designate an obligation of *order n*.)

say that he has a primary obligation to do it (that is, that he ought[1] to do it); that to say that he has a second-order moral obligation to do something (that is, that he ought$_2$ to do it) *just is* to say that he has a secondary obligation to do it (that is, that he ought^2 to do it), given his ignorance about what he ought$_1$ to do; that to say that he has a third-order moral obligation to do something (that is, that he ought$_3$ to do it) *just is* to say that he has a tertiary obligation to do it (that is, that he ought^3 to do it), given his ignorance both about what he ought$_1$ to do and about what he ought$_2$ to do; and so on.

This temptation should be resisted. Although the Prospective View can and should indeed be extended to accommodate subsidiary obligation, both conditional and unconditional (concerning which see section 3.4), such an extension is *not* applicable to the present question of what to do in situations of moral ignorance. This is because ignorance of one's obligation, at whatever level, does *not* generate some further subsidiary obligation. Consider Matt. His primary obligation is to attend the meeting on the first floor; doing so is, we may say, "deontically supreme," in that it is to be ranked first (from the point of view of what determines obligation) relative to his other options. To say that he has a secondary obligation to attend the meeting on the second floor, if he fails to attend the meeting on the first floor, is to say that, if the option of attending the meeting on the first floor is abstracted from his range of options and thus discounted, then the option of attending the meeting on the second floor becomes deontically supreme. In order for this conditional obligation to be transformed into an unconditional obligation, it must be the case that the option that is abstracted does *not* occur. But then this approach cannot be applied to our present problem, precisely because ignorance of an act's being obligatory doesn't entail non-performance of that act. Matt may be ignorant of his obligation to attend the meeting on the first floor, but *that* doesn't trigger an obligation to attend the meeting on the second floor. Despite his ignorance, Matt might nonetheless attend the meeting on the first floor. If he does, then he does no wrong whatsoever. It is therefore *not* in general the case that, if you don't know what you ought[1] to do, then you ought[2] to do something else.[99] If it is held, then, that it *is* in general the case that, if you don't know what you ought$_1$ to do, then you ought$_2$ to do something

---

[99] More generally still, it is not the case that

$$O^n(p)\ \&\ \sim K[O^n(p)] \vdash O^{n+1}(\sim p).$$

else, this alleged fact about *orders* of obligation cannot be accounted for in terms of *levels* of obligation of the sort just noted.[100]

The different orders of obligation that have been proposed as a way of handling the conscientious person's plea for help must therefore be understood in other terms, if they are to be understood at all. But how? Here is one suggestion. According to the Prospective View, our overall moral obligation is to do that act which is the best prospect under the circumstances with respect to the actual values at stake. It seems reasonable to suppose that, when one knows what is actually best, what constitutes the best prospect with respect to what is actually valuable coincides with what is actually best (I will return to this point shortly); however, when one doesn't know what is actually best, then what constitutes the best prospect with respect to what is actually valuable may well diverge from what is actually best. We can say something analogous about the risk of doing wrong. When one knows what one ought to do, what constitutes the best prospect with respect to the fulfillment of one's obligation coincides with what is actually obligatory; however, when one doesn't know what one ought to do, then what constitutes the best prospect with respect to the fulfillment of one's obligation may well diverge from what is actually obligatory. In light of this, we may say that, just as one ought$_1$ to do that act which constitutes the best prospect with respect to what is actually valuable, so too one ought$_2$ to do that act which constitutes the best prospect with respect to the fulfillment of one's first-order obligation. If one knows what one ought$_1$ to do, then what one ought$_2$ to do will coincide with what one ought$_1$ to do, but otherwise the two may well

Again, the reason is that, even if you don't know that you ought^n so to act that p (i.e., $\sim K[O^n(p)]$), this is consistent with your nonetheless so acting that p and thus with your doing what you ought^n to do; and if you do do what you ought^n to do, then no unconditional obligation^{n+1} to act otherwise will arise.

100 Here is an alternative route to the same conclusion. The following principle is plausible:

$$O^n(p) \& O^{n+1}(\sim p/q) \vdash O^n(\sim q).$$

(For an account of moral obligation that sanctions this principle, see chapter 3 below.) Now suppose, for purposes of *reductio ad absurdum*, that (1) you ought$_1$ so to act that p and that (2) you ought$_2$ so to act that $\sim p$, given that you don't know that you ought$_1$ so to act that p. If orders of obligation were equivalent to levels of obligation of the sort at issue in the principle just mentioned, it would follow from this principle that (3) you ought$_1$ so to act that you know that you ought$_1$ so to act that p. But surely (3) is, as a general rule, false: we do not in general have an obligation to know what our obligations are; that is, we are sometimes justifiably ignorant of our obligations. Once again, then, we must conclude that levels of obligation of the sort just noted cannot account for orders of obligation of the sort alleged.

diverge. This treatment can of course be continued. Thus, what one ought$_3$ to do is that act which constitutes the best prospect with respect to the fulfillment of one's second-order obligation; and so on. In general: one ought$_{n+1}$ to do that act which constitutes the best prospect with respect to the fulfillment of one's nth-order obligation.[101]

How plausible is this proposal? I find little merit in it. It faces at least three problems. First, it's hard to see how the instruction "You ought$_{n+1}$ to do that act which constitutes the best prospect with respect to the fulfillment of your nth-order obligation" would be of any more help to the conscientious person than the banal advice "You ought to do whatever it is that you ought to do." For if, despite the evidence at his disposal – in light of which, according to the Prospective View, an agent's (first-order) obligation is to be determined – someone fails to know what he ought$_1$ to do, it's difficult to see how he might nonetheless know what he ought$_2$, or ought$_3$, or ought$_4$, etc., to do, since it is the same body of evidence that determines these obligations too. Thus the instruction just mentioned seems unlikely to provide him with any guidance.

(It is worth pausing here to ponder the implication of this point for so-called decision procedures. Such procedures are often distinguished from so-called criteria of obligation, such as those provided by the Objective and Prospective Views. The procedures are touted as ways of facilitating decision-making in conditions of moral uncertainty. But how they are supposed to do this is a mystery. First, any criterion will of course imply that one ought to follow a certain procedure if and only if doing so satisfies the conditions laid down by the criterion. If one is unsure whether these conditions are satisfied, how can one be any more sure that one ought to follow the procedure? If, in response to this, it is claimed that the "ought" that applies to following the procedure is of a different order from that contained in the criterion, still the question arises how one can be confident that this higher-order "ought" applies. Presumably it is supposed to apply in virtue of constituting the best prospect with respect to satisfying the lower-order obligation. But if one lacks, or is unaware of, the relevant evidence concerning the lower-order obligation, how is one's evidence regarding the higher-order obligation supposed to be any more satisfactory? Consider, for example, a proponent of the Objective View who concedes that it is often very difficult to determine how that view requires one to act and therefore proposes that one adopt the policy of maximizing

[101] Cf. Lockhart 2000, p. 95, for a related proposal.

expected value as a decision procedure. Even if this policy were easy to implement – a point to which I will return shortly – what possible evidence could the Objectivist have that deciding in accordance with this policy constitutes the best prospect with respect to fulfilling his first-order obligation, as determined by the Objective View, when he lacks evidence sufficient to determine directly what that first-order obligation is? In order to reach this judgment, he would have to have good reason to believe that implementing the policy will be better – on this occasion? on most occasions? – than not implementing it, and that requires that he have good evidence concerning the actual values of his alternatives, the very sort of evidence that he admits he lacks.[102])

A second problem with the present proposal is that there is no guarantee that the regress of "oughts" is finite. Indeed, in light of the problem with evidence just mentioned, it seems likely often to be infinite. That someone should ever be subject in this way to an infinite number of obligations, though, is highly implausible.

A third problem with the proposal is that it raises the specter of moral dilemmas. Recall from section 1.1 the question "Which of these 'oughts' is the one that *really* counts? Which 'ought' *ought* I to act on?" At that point, the question concerned the issue whether we should distinguish different kinds of overall moral obligation ("objective" obligation, "subjective" obligation, and so on). I have claimed that we should not, arguing that there is just one kind of overall moral obligation, and that the Prospective View gives the correct account of it. A proponent of the present proposal may agree with me about this but still contend that, *within* this one kind of obligation, a distinction is to be drawn between orders of obligation in the manner that he prescribes. But surely the question can be applied to this contention in turn: which of these various "oughts" is the one that counts? One answer, of course, is simply: the "ought" that counts is "$ought_1$." But in that case invoking different orders of obligation is superfluous; no higher-order obligations would carry any moral weight. A second answer is: the "ought" that counts is the first "ought" about which you are not ignorant. Thus, if you know what you $ought_1$ to do, then that is what you really ought to do. However, if you don't know what you $ought_1$ to do but do know what you $ought_2$ to do, then *that* is what you really ought to do.

---

[102] Cf. Bales 1971, pp. 263–4. Concerning the relation between criterion and decision procedure, see also Hare 1981, Norcross 1990, Frazier 1994, Lenman 2000, Chappell 2001, and Gren 2004.

And so on. But that cannot be right. Ignorance cannot be its own reward in this way, for that would render conscientious inquiry otiose. Why bother trying to find out what you ought$_{n-1}$ to do? Just do what you ought$_n$ to do, and all will be well. But if such complacency cannot be countenanced, that returns us to our original problem. If you shouldn't rest content with plumping for what you ought$_n$ to do but should instead (time and circumstances permitting) aim at discovering and doing what you ought$_{n-1}$ to do, then you shouldn't rest content with doing what you ought$_{n-1}$ to do but should instead aim at discovering and doing what you ought$_{n-2}$ to do – and so on, all the way back to what you ought$_1$ to do. But in that case invoking different orders of obligation is once again superfluous. A third answer is: all the "oughts" count. But then the agent would suffer an embarrassment of riches. Suppose that, because of the quandary you are in, various "oughts" are said to apply: you ought$_1$ to do A (even if you don't know this), ought$_2$ to do B (even if you don't know *this*), ought$_3$ to do C, and so on. If all these "oughts" counted, then, given that you could not do all of A, B, C, and so on, you would be in a moral dilemma. But, regardless of whether moral dilemmas should be said to be possible, surely the mere fact that you are in a quandary should not be thought sufficient to put you in a dilemma.[103] It might be countered that the sort of dilemma envisaged is not the sort usually discussed. Usually, when dilemmas are discussed, it is implicitly a conflict between two or more *first*-order obligations that is at issue. Here, though, it is a conflict between obligations of *different* orders that is at issue. I cannot see that that matters. If all the "oughts" at these different levels count – that is, they all carry some moral weight, such that a failure to fulfill them constitutes genuine wrongdoing of some sort – then the fact is that your being in a quandary would itself be sufficient to put you in a position in which you cannot avoid doing genuine wrong. Even if it were maintained that the significance of the wrongs diminishes as one ascends the orders of obligation, that would not placate those (such as myself) who insist that wrongdoing is in principle always avoidable.[104] On the contrary, if the regress of obligations is infinite – which, as I have just pointed out, it probably would be – then the agent could not avoid doing an infinite number of genuine wrongs. On any plausible aggregation principle, this would entail that the agent could not avoid doing serious wrong, simply by

---

[103] Cf. Conee 1989. [104] See section 3.6 for a qualification of this claim.

virtue of being ignorant of his first-order obligation. Again, this is highly implausible.[105]

Given these problems, I think we must reject the present proposal. And I'm afraid that I can find no better way to address the conscientious person's avowed concern with the risk of wrongdoing. Because of this, I am inclined to think that the question "What ought I to do when I don't know what I ought to do?" is, though quite natural, nonetheless incoherent, if it presupposes that there is some "ought" that expresses an order of overall moral obligation other than first-order obligation.[106]

C

It could be, though, that in some cases the question "What ought I to do when I don't know what I ought to do?" isn't really the question that the despairing conscientious person has in mind. To see this, consider, first, the "opposite" question, namely, "What ought I to do when I *do* know what I ought to do?" Everyone will agree that the answer to this question is "You ought to do that which (you know) you ought to do." Notice that the following question is different: "What ought I to do when I know what is actually best?" Here we cannot assume that everyone will agree what the answer is. We know what answer it is that the Objective View implies: "You ought to do that which (you know) is actually best." But what answer does the Prospective View imply?

Consider the following case:

Case 7:
Jill knows that giving John drug A will cure him completely, giving him drug B will cure him partially, giving him drug C will kill him, and giving him no drug will render him permanently incurable.

I suspect that there would be little hesitation on anyone's part in saying that, in this case, Jill ought to give John drug A, but in fact there is reason to doubt this verdict. For consider: even if Jill knows that giving John drug A will cure him completely and that giving him drug C will kill him, that by

---

[105] On pp. 240–1 of Dancy 2002, Dancy proposes a treatment of the present issue which avoids multiplying senses of "ought" but which commits him to accepting the possibility that dilemmas arise simply by virtue of moral ignorance. He appears happy to accept this possibility.

[106] Note that the various levels of subsidiary obligation discussed above are different levels of *first-order* obligation. The failure to satisfy a subsidiary obligation constitutes compounding the *first-order* wrong that is done when a primary obligation is not satisfied.

itself doesn't imply that she ought to give him drug A rather than drug C – not if, for example, her available evidence indicates that killing him is more valuable than curing him; under these circumstances, the Prospective View implies that Jill ought to give him drug C rather than drug A. But presumably these circumstances are ones under which Jill doesn't *know* what is actually best precisely because her available evidence concerning the relevant values is defective. What, though, if her evidence is not defective in this respect? Could there still be reason to deny that she ought to give John drug A?

Suppose that Jill's evidence concerning the relevant values is accurate and, moreover, that she is justified in having a high degree of confidence in the proposition that giving John drug A will cure him completely. But suppose that she also has some reason to suspect that giving him drug A will kill him, and thus that she cannot be certain that doing so will cure him completely. Under such circumstances, giving John drug A might be unacceptably risky, so that what Jill ought to do is give him drug B instead. Now consider this question: is it compatible with the circumstances just outlined that Jill *knows* that giving John drug A will cure him completely? (That is, could the high probability of this proposition suffice under the circumstances for her knowing it, despite the fact that she also has evidence against it?) If the answer to this question is "Yes," then the Prospective View does not in general imply, as the Objective View does, that the answer to the question "What ought I to do when I know what is actually best?" is "You ought to do that which is actually best." I suspect, however, that we should *not* say that, under the circumstances, Jill knows that giving John drug A is actually best. (I am in no position to insist on this, though, since I have not attempted to specify just what the relation is between epistemic justification and knowledge.) If this is right, then the answer that the Prospective View in general implies to the question "What ought I to do when I know what is actually best?" would seem to be the same as that implied by the Objective View: "You ought to do that which is actually best." This is because, under the circumstances envisaged, what is actually best apparently coincides with what is prospectively best.

Let us now return to the question with which we were originally concerned: "What ought I to do when I *don't* know what I ought to do?" It is clear that we should distinguish this question from the following: "What ought I to do when I don't know what is actually best?" Notice that the latter question doesn't even hint at a multiplicity of "oughts." Notice also that, while the answer that the Objective View provides ("You ought to do that which is actually best") is not at all helpful, the answer that the Prospective View provides ("You ought to do that which is prospectively best") could be more helpful. It is plausible to contend that it is often (and perhaps always) very difficult (and perhaps impossible) to determine what is actually best. (Whether this is indeed the case depends on what substantive account of the relevant actual values is presupposed. In keeping with my intention to accommodate all such accounts, I won't investigate this issue here.) But even if this is so, determining what is prospectively best could well be easier, since this only involves attending to the evidence that is available.

I say "only," but this must not be misconstrued. It could well be that on many occasions attending to the available evidence remains a difficult task. Indeed, contrary to what is sometimes maintained, it is likely to be very difficult to determine with any great precision the prospective values of one's alternatives.[107] (Again, just how difficult this is depends, in part, on what the relevant actual values are.) However, precision is not always necessary in order for one to be confident in one's judgment. (Consider Jackson's own case, that is, Case 3. There it is easy to figure out what is prospectively best, even if the relevant probabilities cannot be precisely determined. Hence the case's beauty and power. Still, it must also be admitted that the case is an artificially simple one.)

The point I want to make here is simply this. We should distinguish the following three questions: "What ought I to do when I don't know what I ought to do?"; "What ought I to do when I don't know what is actually best?"; "What ought I to do when I don't know what is prospectively best?" I have suggested that the first question is incoherent, if it presupposes "oughts" of different orders. (If it doesn't presuppose this, then it is perfectly coherent but can then only be given the trivial answer: "You ought to do whatever it is that you ought to do, whether you know what that is or not.") The second question is not incoherent. Moreover, the Prospective View provides a non-trivial answer to it: "You ought to do that act which is prospectively best." As I see it, this answer could be helpful in responding to the conscientious person's request for guidance. It would, for example, indicate to Jill that in Case 3 she ought to give Jack drug B.

---

[107] This is appropriately stressed in Feldman 2006, p. 56. Cf. Strasser 1989; Gren 2004. Cf. also n. 75 above. Contrast Ewing 1948, who declares (on p. 128) that "in the light of probabilities we can determine with relative ease and even sometimes with fair certainty what an agent ought to do…"

The third question is also not incoherent but, given the Prospective View, it can only be given the trivial answer: "You ought to do whatever it is that is prospectively best, whether you know what that is or not." The upshot is this. If someone has tried and failed to discover what he ought to do, and "crunch time" has come and he asks you what he ought *now* to do, the proper reply is this: "You ought to do that act which is prospectively best for you." If neither he nor you know which act is prospectively best for him, there is no further advice you can give. This may be a disappointing result, but at least you will have spoken truthfully, if not helpfully. Anyone who believes that there is a better answer, one that invokes some higher-order "ought," is simply deluding himself.

This treatment of the problem posed by the conscientious person's desire to reduce the risk of doing wrong is admittedly more a dissolution than a solution of it and may provoke the following objection. "If the unhelpfulness of the response 'You ought to do that act which is prospectively best' (made to someone who hasn't managed to figure out what is prospectively best) is not sufficient reason to reject the Prospective View, then the unhelpfulness of the response 'You ought to do that act which is actually best' (made to someone who hasn't managed to figure out what is actually best) is not sufficient reason to reject the Objective View. But in that case there is no need to move from the Objective View to the Prospective View in the first place." This, however, misrepresents the reason for rejecting the Objective View in favor of the Prospective View. That reason was *not* to find a helpful response to the question "What ought I to do when I don't know what is actually best?"[108] Rather, the move was dictated by the recognition that Jackson's case (Case 3) shows quite clearly that it is not in general the case that one ought, in the sense that expresses overall moral obligation, to do what is actually best. If the response "You ought to do that act which is prospectively best" is helpful to someone who has not been able to discover what is actually best, that is simply a bonus, and not the purpose, of the move from the Objective to the Prospective View. That the latter view does not itself furnish a helpful response to the further question "What ought I to do when I don't know what is prospectively best?" gives no reason to reject it in turn.

---

[108] Thus in my case, at least, Feldman mischaracterizes the motive underlying what he calls "the move to expected utility." See Feldman 2006, pp. 50, 62–3.

2

Risk and rights

In chapter 1, I compared and contrasted three accounts of the general conditions of overall moral obligation. The most recent formulations of these accounts are as follows:

The Objective View (first formulation):
An agent ought to perform an act if and only if it is the best option that he (or she) has.

The Subjective View (first and only formulation):
An agent ought to perform an act if and only if he believes that it is the best option that he has.

The Prospective View (sixth formulation):
An agent ought to perform an act if and only if it is the prospectively best option that he has.

I noted a number of points about these formulations. First, they are all very rough. Second, by an "option" I mean something that the agent can do, where "can" expresses some form of personal control. Third, the accounts may be extended to cover overall moral rightness and wrongness. Fourth, the accounts are intended to be applicable to any substantive theory of moral obligation, such as those proposed by the act-consequentialist, the rule-consequentialist, the virtue-theorist, and so on, in as much as "best" may be variously construed as "instrumentally best," "rule-best," "best in terms of the display of virtue," and so forth.

I argued that we should accept the Prospective View and reject the Objective and Subjective Views. My argument was based on a consideration of cases in which certain options were insufficiently good prospects, in light of the agent's evidence, to be morally permissible, despite the fact that these options were either actually best or believed to be best by the agent. In many of these cases, the options were insufficiently good prospects because they were too risky. This chapter broadens the discussion by showing how the Prospective View may be extended to provide an account first, in section 2.1, of prima facie moral obligation (in addition to overall moral obligation) and then, in section 2.2, of moral rights (which are plausibly taken to be correlative to prima facie moral obligations). When thus extended, the Prospective View implies that, contrary to what is often said, we do not in general have a right not to be harmed but rather have a right not to be put at risk of harm. I respond to some objections to this thesis and then, in sections 2.3 and 2.4, further investigate the Prospective View's position on rights by tracing its implications regarding rights held by individuals in two kinds of situation in particular: situations in which a promise has been made, and situations in which one person's life is imperiled by another. Some of these implications may be somewhat surprising, but I argue that they should be accepted. I argue further that the common and plausible judgment that killing in self-defense is typically justifiable when one's life is imperiled by another (and no other means of escape is available) provides a fresh reason, independent of the considerations presented in the last chapter, for embracing the Prospective View.

2.1 PRIMA FACIE MORAL OBLIGATION

The term "prima facie obligation" (or "prima facie duty") was coined by W. D. Ross to refer to a certain kind of moral reason that an agent may have to perform some act.[1] It is not very felicitous, as Ross himself acknowledges, since it may seem to suggest that the obligation in question is merely apparent, whereas Ross wants to insist – and rightly so – that that is not the case; on the contrary, prima facie obligations are genuine moral entities. "*Pro tanto* obligation" would be a more apt term,[2] but, since "prima facie obligation" is by now so well entrenched, this is the term that I will continue to use. It is to be contrasted with "overall obligation," which refers to what the agent has a conclusive or decisive moral reason to do.[3]

---

[1] Ross 1930, pp. 19–20. It should be noted that, although all prima facie moral obligations are a kind of moral reason, not all moral reasons constitute prima facie moral obligations. See Zimmerman 2001, pp. 95–6, and 2007, sect. II, for brief discussions of various kinds of reason. Cf. also Dancy 2004, ch. 2.

[2] This is the term used in Kagan 1989, p. 17.

[3] The term "overall obligation" is not Ross's. Instead he talks variously of "absolute obligation," "actual obligation," "duty proper," and "duty *sans phrase*." (See Ross 1930, pp. 18–20, 28, 30.) None of these terms is particularly apt and, since none of them enjoys the same currency as "prima facie obligation," we may safely dispense with them.

The distinction between prima facie and overall moral obligation is familiar. One can find oneself in a situation in which a variety of moral considerations pertain. What one ought to do in so far as some of these considerations are concerned may not be what one ought to do in so far as others of them are concerned. If so, one will be faced with a number of moral reasons to act, some that point in one "direction," others that point in others. Given such a conflict, the question arises which reason, or set of reasons, predominates – which, that is, constitutes a conclusive or decisive reason to act in one way rather than another. It is that reason, or set of reasons, that will settle what one's overall obligation is under the circumstances.

Each of the Objective, Subjective, and Prospective Views may be developed in such a way as to accommodate this account of the relation between prima facie and overall obligation. My concern in this section is of course with developing the Prospective View in this respect. I will begin, though, with the Objective View (the view that Ross implicitly embraces in *The Right and the Good* when he first presents his account of prima facie obligation). Even though I reject the Objective View, developing it in this way will facilitate development of the Prospective View. (There will be no need to undertake any further elaboration of the Subjective View.) In order now to develop the Objective View in a way that incorporates prima facie obligation, let me use terminology that Ross uses more frequently in *Foundations of Ethics*, in which he contrasts the Objective View with the Subjective and Prospective Views.

We can say that some acts are "objectively morally suitable" to the situation in which an agent finds himself.[4] Henceforth, I will simply use the term "suit" and its cognates to express this idea. To say that an act suits its agent's situation is to say that it serves some actual value that is at stake in that situation. ("Actual value" is here being used, as in the last chapter, to refer to whatever values are relevant to the determination of overall moral obligation, whether one takes such obligation to be a matter of maximizing actual value, of maximizing expectable value, or of something else.[5]) Such suitability comes in degrees. For example, suppose that you have

[4] Ross 1939, pp. 146 ff.
[5] Note that, just as "reason" can be used to refer to something other than prima facie moral obligation (see n. 1 above), so too "suit" can be used to refer to something other than serving that sort of actual value that is relevant to the determination of moral obligation. Ross's and my use of "suit" is, therefore, a decidedly restrictive one. When presenting his own substantive account of the nature of moral obligation, Ross lists the following actual values

gratuitously insulted Bert. Perhaps it would be most suitable (in so far as your having insulted him is concerned) for you to apologize to him in person. Or perhaps it would be equally suitable for you to send him flowers with a card expressing your remorse. It might be less suitable, but suitable nonetheless, if you left him a brief apology on his answering machine. However, you would be overdoing it if you bought him a new television, and it might be positively unsuitable if you bought him a new car. It would also be unsuitable (for reasons of gross deficiency rather than gross excess) if you wrote Bert a letter in which you repeated your insults. We thus get a sort of hierarchy of suitability and unsuitability.

Pertinent obligation-relevant values may of course conflict, so that an act may be (un)suitable with respect to one aspect of one's situation but not with respect to another. The illustration just given has to do with reparation for a previous wrongful act. Another kind of illustration may be given that has to do with fidelity to a previous commitment. For example, if on Monday you lend me a book that I promise to return to you by Friday, then it would seem that what fidelity requires is that I return the book as promised. Ross believes that each kind of response (reparation, fidelity) is suitable to that particular aspect of one's situation (previous wrongdoing, previous commitment) that has been specified. If one is so situated that one cannot both make reparation and keep a promise, then doing the former

(Ross 1930, p. 21): fidelity, reparation, gratitude, justice, beneficence, self-improvement, and non-maleficence. To all of these he ascribes the following two characteristics. First, the values apply to all agents in all situations; that is, if ever an agent has an opportunity, for example, to display fidelity to a commitment or make reparation for a mistake, then he has reason to do so and this will be relevant to determining his overall obligation. (This is implicit throughout ch. 2 of Ross 1930.) Second, that these values are relevant to determining the agent's overall obligation is self-evident. (This is stated explicitly on p. 29 of Ross 1930.) Ross also appears to ascribe to at least some of these values a third characteristic, namely, a certain kind of agent-relativity. Fidelity and reparation, for example, seem to be values of this sort. Ross seems clearly to think that for each of us there is special value in our keeping *our* promises and in our making reparation for *our* past mistakes. He may agree that there is value in our seeing to it that others keep *their* promises and make reparation for *their* past mistakes but, if so, this would seem to fall under the general heading of beneficence rather than the particular headings of fidelity and reparation. This third characteristic sets Ross's theory apart from a standard form of consequentialism, which takes only the *promotion* of values to be relevant to the determination of obligation. Ross seems clearly to think that, in some cases at least, it is the agent's own *exemplification* of values that is relevant to the determination of obligation. My talk of "serving" values is intended to cover both the promotion and the exemplification of values.

In what follows, I will employ certain of Ross's examples of obligation-relevant values, but solely for the purposes of illustration. I do not intend thereby to endorse any part of his substantive account of moral obligation. Of course, this disclaimer should not itself be construed as a repudiation of any part of his substantive account, either.

will suit one aspect of one's situation but not another, whereas doing the latter will suit the other aspect but not the one. Which act is more suitable to one's situation as a whole, taking all aspects of the situation into account, will vary from case to case. Sometimes making reparation will take precedence, sometimes keeping a promise will.

In light of the foregoing, the Objective View may now be reformulated as follows:

The Objective View (second formulation):
For any act, *A*,
(1) *A* is prima facie morally right if and only if there is some aspect, *S*, of the agent's situation such that no other option that he has more suits *S*;
(2) *A* is prima facie morally wrong if and only if there is some aspect, *S*, of the agent's situation such that some other option that he has more suits *S*;
(3) *A* is prima facie morally obligatory if and only if there is some aspect, *S*, of the agent's situation such that *A* suits *S* more than any other option that he has;
(4) *A* is overall morally right if and only if no other option that the agent has more suits his situation as a whole;
(5) *A* is overall morally wrong if and only if some other option that the agent has more suits his situation as a whole;
(6) *A* is overall morally obligatory if and only if *A* suits the agent's situation as a whole more than any other option that he has.

There are a number of points to note about this formulation of the Objective View. First, like the previous formulation it is designed to be adaptable to all substantive accounts of moral obligation, not just Ross's. (For example, it fits act-consequentialism, if suitability is cashed out in terms of the promotion of some intrinsic value; it fits rule-consequentialism, if suitability is cashed out in terms of conforming to some rule; it fits virtue-theory, if (un)suitability is cashed out in terms of the display of some virtue or vice; and so on.) Second, the term "more suits" or "suits more" is to be understood liberally. If two options, *A* and *B*, are positively unsuitable to some aspect, *S*, of the agent's situation, but *A* is less unsuitable than *B*, then *A* "suits *S* more" than *B*. (Compare the common liberal use of "better," according to which that term covers not only "more good" but also "less bad.") Third, this formulation draws a sharp distinction between "ought" (or "obligatory") and "right." Ross recognizes this distinction but then deliberately blurs it for stylistic reasons.[6] I find no reason to follow his lead in this regard. Fourth, an alternative formulation would tie *degrees* of

---

[6] Ross 1930, pp. 3–4.

rightness to degrees of suitability and degrees of wrongness to degrees of *un*suitability. As far as I know, Ross doesn't explicitly rule out this possibility for prima facie rightness and wrongness; but he does for overall rightness and wrongness,[7] and I think he is quite right to do so. More precisely, I think it makes no sense to talk of one option's being more right than another, whether prima facie or overall. Certainly, it makes sense to say that one option is more suitable than another, but, even if we were to adopt the Objective approach and maintain that right and wrong are a direct function of what is actually suitable, this would simply imply that the latter option is *not* right, and not that it is *less* right than the former. Certainly, too, it makes sense to say that one prima facie obligation is more stringent than another, but this simply implies that the latter is *not* overall right, and not that it is *less* overall right than the former. And certainly it makes sense to say that one option is more seriously wrong than another (as I did when discussing subsidiary obligation in the last chapter), but again, even if we were to adopt the Objective approach, this would simply imply that the latter is further removed from what is most suitable, and not that either of them is positively unsuitable. Finally, an alternative, more restrictive formulation of the Objective View would state that *A* is overall morally obligatory if and only if it suits some aspect of the agent's situation more than any other option suits any other aspect. (Similar accounts could be given of overall moral rightness and wrongness.) Ross seems sometimes to embrace this account.[8] However, at other times,[9] he suggests the more liberal formulation that I have given. The latter formulation seems wiser, since it accommodates the possibility that, by virtue of suiting more aspects of the agent's situation, *A* suits that situation as a whole more than any other option, even though some other option suits some aspect more than *A* suits any particular aspect.

With the second formulation of the Objective View as a guide, developing the Prospective View so that it accommodates prima face as well as overall obligation, right, and wrong is straightforward. Recall the understanding of "prospectively best" that is at issue in the most recent formulation of the Prospective View: an act is prospectively best for its agent just in case it has greatest adjusted expectable value for him, at his definitive level of evidence, where the adjustment in question reflects the various points mentioned (but not pursued) at the end of section 1.6. Instead of saying that an act is prospectively best for its agent, we can say that it provides its

---

[7] See Ross 1930, p. 41. [8] E.g., at Ross 1930, p. 19. [9] E.g., at Ross 1930, p. 41.

agent with the best prospect of doing what is actually valuable. Given that what is actually valuable is now being understood in terms of what suits the agent's situation, we can say in turn that such an act provides its agent with the best prospect of doing what suits his situation, whether as a whole or just with respect to some aspect of it. The following formulation of the Prospective View thus emerges:

The Prospective View (seventh formulation):
For any act, A,
(1) A is prima facie morally right if and only if there is some aspect, S, of the agent's situation such that no other option that he has provides him with a better prospect of doing what suits S;
(2) A is prima facie morally wrong if and only if there is some aspect, S, of the agent's situation such that some other option that he has provides him with a better prospect of doing what suits S;
(3) A is prima facie morally obligatory if and only if there is some aspect, S, of the agent's situation such that A provides him with a prospect of doing what suits S better than that provided by any other option that he has;
(4) A is overall morally right if and only if no other option that the agent has provides him with a better prospect of doing what suits his situation as a whole;
(5) A is overall morally wrong if and only if some other option that the agent has provides him with a better prospect of doing what suits his situation as a whole;
(6) A is overall morally obligatory if and only if A provides the agent with a prospect of doing what suits his situation as a whole better than that provided by any other option that he has.

2.2 MORAL RIGHTS

Many moral philosophers have applied Wesley Newcomb Hohfeld's seminal account of legal rights to moral rights.[10] At the heart of this account is a thesis that holds rights "in the strictest sense" – that is, claim-rights – to be correlative to duties or obligations. This thesis may be put as follows:

The Correlativity Thesis:
One person, Q, has a moral right against another person, P, that P perform some act, A, if and only if P has an obligation to Q to perform A.

For example: John has a moral right against Jill that she give him drug B if and only if Jill has a moral obligation to John to give him drug B.

It is important to note that the Correlativity Thesis does not assert that all moral rights are correlative to moral obligations; it says this only of

[10] Hohfeld 1919, pp. 35 ff.

claim-rights. Hohfeld identifies three kinds of rights other than claims: liberties, powers, and immunities. I think he is quite right to do so, and a full account of rights would therefore take these other kinds of rights into consideration. In this chapter, however, my focus will be almost exclusively on claim-rights, and when I talk of rights without qualification, it is always claim-rights in particular that I will mean.

It is also important to note that the Correlativity Thesis does not assert that all moral obligations are correlative to moral rights; it says this only of obligations that are *owed to* someone. We should distinguish between the person whom, if anyone, an obligation concerns and the person to whom, if anyone, that obligation is owed (even if, as is frequently the case, the same person satisfies both descriptions). Suppose, again, that you have lent me a book that I have promised to return to you by Friday, and let us for the moment assume that the promise generates an obligation on my part to return the book to you by then. This obligation certainly *concerns* you, for it is to you that I must return the book. Whether the obligation is one that I *owe to* you is not so clear. If the promise that I made was a promise to you, then we may presumably say that the obligation I have is one that I owe to you. However, if I made the promise to some third party – to your mother, say – then I owe it to her to return the book to you by Friday. (Whether I would still owe it to you to do so is not so clear.) Let us call an obligation that is owed to someone an *associative* obligation: it is one that involves a kind of association (or bond, or tie, or link, or ligation) between obligor and obligee. Etymologically, the term "obligation" invokes this idea of association, but its sense has broadened so that it expresses a contrary of wrongdoing generally; and it is certainly plausible to think that not all wrongdoing (whether prima facie or overall) need involve wronging someone, in the sense of failing to give someone his due. It is plausible, that is, to say that some obligations are not associative.[11] (Consider the matter of charity. It is plausible to say that those who are well-off have an obligation to donate some of their resources to charity, even if they don't owe it to anyone in particular to do so. Of course, once having made a pledge to some particular person to make a donation, one might well then owe it to that person to fulfill the pledge.) The Correlativity Thesis asserts that *associative* obligations are correlative to rights. It makes no such claim

---

[11] Plausible, but also debatable. Some substantive theories of moral obligation may claim that all obligations are associative. Even if this were correct, however, the conceptual distinction between associative and non-associative obligations would remain.

about non-associative obligations. (Thus, pointing out that the well-off have an obligation to give to charity but that no one has a right to their doing so provides no reason to doubt this thesis.)

I propose that we accept the Correlativity Thesis.[12] We may understand the sort of associative obligation it concerns to be *prima facie* obligation. Just as prima facie obligations are in principle subject to being overridden by countervailing considerations, so too, then, are rights; that is, it can happen that the infringement of a right is overall morally permissible or justifiable. In such a case, we may say that the right, though infringed, is not violated; only an infringement that is overall unjustifiable constitutes the violation of a right.[13] (The alternative construal of the Correlativity Thesis, according to which rights are correlative only to overall obligations, is not plausible. It would require that we radically revise our common way of talking about rights. For example, we could not talk of a homeowner's having a right to privacy under those exceptional circumstances in which it is overall justifiable to invade his privacy, even though he has done nothing to warrant the invasion. I will return to this point in section 2.4.)

In the last chapter I argued for the Prospective View. According to that view, the moral obligations one has (whether associative or otherwise) turn on the prospects of the costs and benefits associated with one's alternatives. Given the Correlativity Thesis, it follows that the moral rights that are held against one also turn on such prospects. This, though, is an idea that some writers have resisted.

Consider Judith Thomson, for example. I noted in section 1.6 that she accepts that it can be overall morally permissible to impose a minor risk of harm on someone, even when the risk is unfortunately realized.[14] She also accepts that it can be overall morally impermissible to impose a major risk of harm on someone, even when the risk is fortunately not realized.[15] I of course concur. However, when it comes to what rights we have in respect of harm, Thomson urges that we accept

The Harm Thesis:
We have moral rights against others that they not cause us harm,

while rejecting

---

[12] For fuller discussion, see Zimmerman 1996, pp. 176 ff.   [13] Cf. Thomson 1990, p. 122.
[14] Thomson 1986, pp. 177 ff.
[15] Thomson 1986, pp. 181 ff. See also Thomson 1990, pp. 243 ff.

The Risk Thesis (first formulation):
We have moral rights against others that they not impose risks of harm on us.[16]

Her reason is that she finds the Risk Thesis too prolific, yielding an unacceptable profusion of rights. She considers a case in which someone, D, throws a log onto a nearby highway while clearing his land, thereby imposing a risk of harm on anyone who might pass by. "[I]s it the case," she asks, "that for everyone in the universe who could have got to the highway and tripped over that log, D infringed a claim of his or hers? We might well prefer that our theory of rights avoid saying this."[17] She then considers replacing the Risk Thesis with

The High-Risk Thesis:
We have moral rights against others that they not impose high risks of harm on us,

but finds this unpromising, too. She finds "high" vague, and she also says that in many cases there is no such thing as *the* size of the risk of harm imposed, since a single act may impose a risk of various, and variously severe, harms on someone. She concludes that, although D may well have acted wrongly in risking harm to others when throwing the log onto the highway, he did not thereby infringe anyone's rights. So, too, for other such cases – for instance, a case in which one person plays Russian roulette on another without his knowledge; even if no bullet is fired, the first person does wrong but, given that no harm is caused, no right is infringed.[18]

I don't find Thomson's doubts about the Risk Thesis compelling. Why should we worry about the proliferation of rights? Thomson's own view

---

[16] Thomson 1990, pp. 229 ff. Thomson uses the term "claim" in her formulation of these theses. I have replaced it with the term "moral right," since, as noted at the outset of this section, it is only with claim–rights that I will be concerned in this chapter. (At Thomson 1990, pp. 70–6, Thomson expresses some doubts about the usefulness of classifying certain rights as *moral* rights in particular. I don't share these doubts. I will not pursue the issue here, however.) This point applies also to the Means Principle for Rights and the High-Risk Thesis below.

[17] Thomson 1990, p. 245.

[18] At Thomson 1990, p. 244, Thomson briefly considers the argument that imposing a risk of harm on someone is to put that person at a disadvantage, and that to put someone at a disadvantage is to cause him a kind of harm, so that imposing a risk of harm is itself a form of causing harm. In this way, the Risk Thesis would be true, because included in the Harm Thesis. She accepts the first premise of the argument but denies the second. This seems to me clearly correct. In saying so, I don't mean to deny that the *law* understands the imposition of a risk of harm sometimes to constitute a way of causing harm. There is reason to think that it does. (Cf. Finkelstein 2003.) I do think, though, that such an understanding is a distortion of the facts, and thus that, if the law does view matters in this way, it might be advisable to reform it.

implies that we have very many rights indeed. On her view, the following is true:

The Means Principle for Rights:
If (i) *Q* has a moral right against *P* that *P* not do *B*, and
  (ii) if *P* does *A* then he or she will thereby do *B*,
then *Q* has a moral right against *P* that *P* not do *A*, that right being at least as stringent as *Q*'s right that *P* not do *B*.[19]

Suppose, as she does, that I have a right against you that you not harm me. Given the Means Principle for Rights, it follows that I have a right (against you) that you not stick a knife one inch into my back, a right that you not stick a knife two inches into my back, indeed an infinite number of such rights, corresponding to the infinite number of distances between one and two inches, let alone yet other rights having to do with other weapons and other parts of my body. These rights that you not stick a knife into my back are in a sense incidental (in that they bear a merely contingent relation to the right not to be harmed), but they are genuine rights all the same; and anyway, the Means Principle for Rights yields an infinite number of non-incidental rights: the right not to be harmed to this degree, to that degree, to another degree…, in this way, in that way, in another way… The Risk Thesis involves proliferation of still another kind, of course, since it adds yet another dimension (degree or size of risk) that admits of infinite variation, but it is hard to see why this proliferation should bother Thomson when other types do not. I think that none of these proliferations should worry us; they all emanate in a systematic way from a single source, namely, the interest we have in not being harmed.

You might object that the Risk Thesis allows rights to be "lightweight," to "come too cheaply." Doesn't it imply that all of us are routinely violating the rights of others, given that just about any kind of activity involves imposing a risk of harm on someone? Shouldn't we, at best, be talking about the right that others have that we not impose a *high* risk of harm on them? But this would be a mistake. First, the problems that

---

[19] Thomson 1990, pp. 156–7. Again, I have substituted "(moral) right" for "claim" in both the title and the formulation of this principle. I have also substituted "*A*" for "alpha," "*B*" for "beta," "*Q*" for "*X*," and "*P*" for "*Y*." I think the principle is in fact false, but that we should accept a variation on it in which clause (ii) is modified as follows: *P* cannot avoid its being the case that if he does *A* then he will thereby do *B*. Compare the discussion of IP1 and IP2 in section 1.6 above.

Thomson notes with the High-Risk Thesis would once again come into play. Second, recall the distinction between the violation of a right and the mere infringement of it. The Risk Thesis may imply that we are all routinely infringing the rights of others, but it certainly doesn't imply that we are all routinely violating these rights. Third, given that rights are, in general, correlative to prima facie obligations, which can vary infinitely in stringency, and not only to overall obligations, it seems innocuous to say that, all else being equal, the lower the risk of harm, the less stringent the right in question, with very low risks simply involving very weak rights.[20] And finally, *any* plausible account of rights must allow for the possibility that rights be weak or lightweight. Consider, for example, my right to the two cents you owe me.

Another objection to the Risk Thesis is that, to be plausible, it must allow for rights sometimes to be overridden by considerations that are, from the duty-holder's perspective, self-centered, and that this is unacceptable; for example, my alleged right that you not impose a risk of harm on me must not be thought to imply that it is overall impermissible for you to drive your car past me while I am walking nearby on the sidewalk. But, again, this is unpersuasive, since on any plausible account rights just can be overridden by such considerations. Consider, for example, the permissibility of your breaking an appointment because you have a splitting headache.

A final objection to the Risk Thesis is this. If one person infringes another's right, then the former incurs an obligation to compensate the latter for the infringement; but there is no obligation to compensate someone for any alleged infringement of a right not to be put at risk of harm, if the risk isn't realized, precisely because no harm is done; hence there is no such right.

There are several problems with this objection. First, the first premise is suspect, in that whatever intuition it serves would seem to be just as well served by the following revised premise: if one person infringes another's right and thereby causes a harm or loss, then the former incurs an obligation to compensate the latter for the infringement. But, of course, this revised premise would not allow the argument to run through.

Second, the first premise is suspect for another reason, especially if the compensation that is allegedly owed is supposed to match whatever harm

---

[20] Innocuous, that is, apart from the difficulties involved in stating clearly *just* what constitutes either a harm or a risk of harm. See the discussion above in section 1.4, subsection A.

or loss may have been suffered by the right-holder. (This point would also apply to the revised premise just mentioned.) Let us agree that, when an innocent person suffers a loss, that person deserves to have that loss made whole. If this is true, it is true regardless of the cause of the loss. Consider Alf and Bert, both innocent people. Each has had a leg broken. Alf's was broken when a tornado struck his house; Bert's was broken when Charlie's car struck his car. A common reaction, in keeping with the first premise, is to say that Charlie owes Bert some form of compensation. Why should Bert suffer the loss that Charlie has imposed? Let Charlie suffer it instead; after all, he caused it. This natural reaction is problematic, however. First, it leaves Alf out in the cold (unless he has insurance), even though he is no less deserving of compensation than Bert. Second, it may be that Charlie is just as innocent as Bert; he may not have been at fault in any way when his car struck Bert's. Third, even if Charlie was at fault, the degree of fault may not match up with the degree of Bert's loss, so that, again, he (Charlie) is relatively innocent. (How to match fault with loss is of course a very difficult matter.) Fourth, Dave may have been driving just as faultily as Charlie and yet have luckily avoided causing any loss; if Charlie deserves to be made to make amends due to his having driven faultily, Dave would seem to be just as deserving. In my view, justice would be done in this case if Alf received compensation along with Bert, and if Dave were made to make amends along with Charlie in keeping with the degree of fault displayed, which in Charlie's case may or may not match up with the degree of loss caused to Bert by Charlie and in Dave's case clearly does not match up with the degree of any loss caused by Dave. The first premise of the objection would have Charlie make compensation in full to Bert. This may not be in keeping with the degree of fault (if any) displayed by Charlie, and it entirely overlooks both Alf and Dave. I therefore find it unacceptable.[21]

Finally, the second premise of the objection is suspect, if "compensate" is given a wide reading, so that it covers apologies and other (such) ways of making amends. For it seems plausible to say that, in many cases in which one person puts another at risk, the former at least owes the latter an apology, even if the risk isn't realized. Consider again, for example, the following case from chapter 1:

---

[21] See Zimmerman 1994 for a fuller discussion of this issue. The view that I have just outlined has much in common with the views presented in Schroeder 1995 and Waldron 1995.

Case 3:
All the evidence at Jill's disposal indicates (in keeping with the facts) that giving John drug B would cure him partially and giving him no drug would render him permanently incurable, but (despite the facts) it leaves completely open whether it is giving him drug A or giving him drug C that would cure him completely and whether it is giving him drug A or giving him drug C that would kill him.

Recall that, in this case, it is drug A that would in fact cure John completely and drug C that would kill him. Suppose now that Jill ignores the risk to John associated with giving him either of these drugs, that she tosses a coin ("Heads, A; tails, C!"), and that the coin comes up heads. Although John would no doubt be relieved to have been completely cured, it would surely be reasonable for him also to be very angry with Jill for having gambled so recklessly with his life. He would think, correctly, that she had seriously wronged him in doing so.[22] It is surely plausible to contend that Jill owes John an apology for this wrongdoing, even if she admittedly owes him no apology for curing him completely.

I think, therefore, that there is very good reason to say, in keeping with both the Prospective View and the Correlativity Thesis, that, just as moral obligations turn on the prospects of costs and benefits, so too do moral rights. I must immediately acknowledge, though, that the relation between such prospects and rights is not straightforward, for two reasons.

First, the Risk Thesis, as so far formulated, is severely restricted. It concerns only the risk of harm, whereas we presumably have rights concerning other matters as well. Consider again the example of the borrowed book. Even if my failing to return the book to you as promised would not cause you any harm, it is surely plausible to contend that you have a right against me concerning its return. (In the next section I will investigate exactly what the content of this right should be said to be.) It's not easy to say, though, just how the Risk Thesis is to be generalized. One proposal is this:

The Risk Thesis (second formulation):
We have moral rights against others that they not perform actions that risk adversely affecting us.

But I think this is both too broad and too narrow. It is too broad because, even if causing harm and breaking promises (at least in some cases) can be said to be ways of adversely affecting people in such a way that their rights

---

[22] This repeats a point made in n. 59 to chapter 1.

are infringed, it is plausible to contend that other ways of adversely affecting people do not infringe their rights. Suppose, for example, that the slogan emblazoned on my t-shirt offends you. It is plausible to maintain that I may be obligated not to offend you without being obligated *to you* not to offend you, and thus that you have no right against me that I not adversely affect you in this way. If so, only some ways of adversely affecting people infringe their rights. I am afraid, though, that I have no general account to offer of which ways of adversely affecting people do infringe their rights and which ways do not. The second formulation is also too narrow because it concerns only costs ("adverse effects") and not benefits, and people's rights are sometimes "positive," involving the gain of benefits, and not, or not only, "negative," involving the avoidance of harm and other costs. If I am designated as the beneficiary of some rich person's estate, am already well off, and am prevented from receiving my inheritance, my being so prevented may constitute an infringement of a right of mine but seems itself not to count as my being adversely affected in any way. (Of course, I may be angry or disappointed at being denied my inheritance, and such a reaction may count as my being adversely affected, but that is an incidental matter.) Once again, though, I am afraid that I have no general account to offer of which ways of being denied a benefit infringe people's rights and which do not. (It may be that positive rights arise only in the context of special relationships and commitments and are not held generally – that they are rights *in personam* and not *in rem* – but some would dispute this.[23])

Second, it is very important to note that the risk at issue in the Risk Thesis is a risk relative, not to the obligee's (the right-holder's) epistemic situation, but to the obligor's. Consider again what the Correlativity Thesis says:

The Correlativity Thesis:
One person, Q, has a moral right against another person, P, that P perform some act, A, if and only if P has a moral obligation to Q to perform A.

According to the Prospective View, P's obligation is in part a function of the evidence that is available to P. It thus follows that Q's right is likewise in part a function, not of the evidence available to Q, but *of the evidence available to P*. (As noted in the last chapter, this evidence has to do not only with empirical but also with evaluative matters.) This is important,

---

[23] Cf. Feinberg 1973, pp. 59–60.

because it is possible that the evidence available to *P* is defective and does not indicate, for example, that causing *Q* harm fails best to suit some aspect of *P*'s situation. If such were unfortunately the case, *Q* would *not* have a right against *P* that *P* not impose a risk of harm on him.

I propose, therefore, that we understand the Risk Thesis as follows:

The Risk Thesis (third formulation):
We have moral rights against others that they not impose on us any risk by virtue of their failing to do what is prospectively most suitable to some aspect of their situation, when such failure constitutes the failure to satisfy an associative obligation that they owe to us.

(Here, "risk" is being used broadly, so that it includes that attenuated sense in which someone who is exposed to the chance of forgoing a benefit is put at risk of forgoing the benefit.[24]) I have arrived at this formulation on the basis of the most recent (seventh) formulation of the Prospective View coupled with the Correlativity Thesis. It is of course my contention that we should accept the Risk Thesis on this formulation. I grant, though, that it may have implications that are somewhat surprising. I will now pursue some of these implications by means of a consideration of two examples, examples that can be construed as test cases for the present account of the relation between risk and rights. I believe that the account passes the tests, but of course you will have to make up your own mind about that. Indeed, as I see it, the second example not only vindicates the Risk Thesis but provides further support for the Prospective View independently of the considerations mustered in the last chapter.

For simplicity of exposition, I will assume, in both examples to be discussed, that no one is such that his or her *evaluative* evidence is defective. It is only with variations in *empirical* evidence that I will be concerned.

2.3 TEST CASE: FIDELITY

Let us return to the example in which on Monday you lend me a book that I promise to return to you by Friday. Ross employs this very sort of case to compare and contrast the Objective and Subjective Views. In *The Right and the Good*, in which he embraces the Objective View, he says that, given my promise, I have an obligation to return the book to you by Friday. This, he

---

[24] See again the discussion in section 1.4, subsection A.

claims, is what fidelity requires.[25] In *Foundations of Ethics*, in which he embraces the Subjective View, he says that what fidelity requires is merely that I aim at your receiving the book by Friday.[26] This is a view that he had explicitly repudiated in his earlier book, saying:

> [I]f I have promised to return the book to my friend, I obviously do not fulfil my promise and do my duty merely by aiming at his receiving the book; I must see that he actually receives it.[27]

Such a position certainly seems sensible and, in light of the arguments that I made in section 1.3 against the Subjective View, it may appear that it is the correct position. I reject it, however. I reject it because I reject the Objective View. For reasons given in the last chapter, I subscribe to the Prospective View, which in the present case implies that (given that my evidence concerning the actual values at stake is accurate) my obligation is to do that which will most probably result in your receiving the book by Friday, whether or not you in fact receive it.

Even though, in his earlier work, Ross endorses the claim that I will fulfill my obligation to you if and only if I return the book to you by Friday, he appears to be a little uneasy with it. He says:

> We get the curious consequence that however carelessly I pack or dispatch the book, if it comes to hand I have done my duty, and however carefully I have acted, if the book does not come to hand I have not done my duty. Success and failure are the only test, and a sufficient test, of the performance of duty.[28]

Despite acknowledging this consequence to be curious, he nonetheless goes on to defend it:

> [T]hat our conclusion is not as strange as at first sight it might seem is shown by the fact that if the carelessly dispatched book comes to hand, it is not my duty to send another copy, while if the carefully dispatched book does not come to hand I must send another copy to replace it. In the first case I have not my duty still to do, which shows that I have done it; in the second I have it still to do, which shows that I have not done it.[29]

On the assumption that my obligation to return the book is an obligation that I owe to you, and on the further assumption that the Correlativity Thesis is true, Ross's position may be captured in chart 2.1, in which the

[25] Ross 1930, pp. 21, 43.
[26] Ross 1939, p. 157. Here, rather than the term "aim at" (which he uses at Ross 1930, p. 43), Ross uses instead the phrase "set oneself to do that which one thinks likely to produce."
[27] Ross 1930, p. 43.   [28] Ross 1930, p. 45.   [29] Ross 1930, pp. 45–6.

Carefully dispatched	Book received	Associative obligation to resend – Right to resending
Yes	Yes	No
Yes	No	Yes
No	Yes	No
No	No	Yes

Chart 2.1

last column concerns whether I have an obligation to you to send either the book itself or a replacement, that is, whether you have a right against me that I do this.[30]

The Prospective View does not endorse Ross's position. The position it does endorse is somewhat more complicated. I said just now that the Prospective View implies that my original obligation is to do that which will most probably result in your receiving the book by Friday. This may seem a mistake, given the distinction, upon which I insisted in section 1.4, between that which is probably best (or most suitable) and that which is prospectively best. But this distinction is idle in the present case, which is a very simple one that concerns an all-or-nothing matter. You cannot more or less receive the book; you can only receive it or not. If you receive it, then I have done what is (most) suitable; if not, not. No degrees of suitability are in the offing and, under such circumstances, that act which provides the best prospect of doing what is suitable can only be that act which is probably most suitable. But we only have to complicate the illustration a little in order to see once again how these two characteristics can come apart. So let us now suppose (more realistically) that my promise carries with it the implicit commitment to return the book to you in as good condition as I can. On this supposition, a Jackson-type case is easily constructed. Here's one:

Case 8:
I have a choice between three delivery services, A, B, and C. I know that B will deliver the book in pretty good condition. I also know that either A or C will

---

[30] Ross in fact expresses doubts about the Correlativity Thesis at Ross 1930, pp. 48 ff. In particular, he doubts whether P's having an obligation to Q to do A implies that Q has a right against P that P do A. His reasons are not compelling. First, he appears to confuse what it is to have an obligation *concerning* someone or something and what it is to have an obligation *to* someone or something. (See my remarks on this in the last section. See also Zimmerman 1996, pp. 6–8.) Second, he implausibly holds that an individual, Q, can have a claim-right to something only if Q can make (that is, in some way give voice to) the claim.

89

deliver it in somewhat better condition, and that either A or C will deliver it mangled, but I have no idea which will provide the good service and which the bad (although it is in fact A that would provide the superior service).

In this case, the Prospective View implies that I ought to use service B, since doing so provides me with the best prospect of keeping my promise and returning the book to you in as good condition as possible, even though it is certain that some other service would return it to you in better condition.

There is a complication. I have just said that *using service B* provides me with the best prospect of keeping my promise, but surely *keeping my promise* provides me with an even better, indeed the best possible, prospect of keeping my promise. Doesn't the Prospective View therefore imply that I ought to keep my promise and return the book to you in as good condition as I can, that is, that I ought to use service A? If so, the Prospective View would seem to reduce, not to the Subjective View (which, as noted in section 1.2, is something that Ross alleges), but to the Objective View. But in that case no progress has been made.

The solution to this problem requires drawing a distinction between *direct* and *indirect* obligation. This is a distinction that Ross himself makes.[31] Presupposing the Objective View, Ross says that my direct obligation is to keep my promise to you. If I pack and post the book on Tuesday and you consequently receive it on Wednesday, then I will have kept my promise to return it to you by Friday. But since my packing-and-posting will only have been a means of keeping my promise, it itself will have been, according to Ross, merely indirectly right. (Whether it will have been indirectly *obligatory* depends on whether there was any other means available to me to keep my promise.) This is not an entirely straightforward matter. Ross's position seems to presuppose that my packing-and-posting the book to you is one action and my keeping my promise is another, since the former is merely indirectly right but the latter is directly so. But some philosophers, who individuate actions coarsely, will claim that these actions are one and the same.[32] If this is correct, one could retain Ross's distinction, or at least the spirit of it, by talking of an action's being directly right or obligatory "under one description" but indirectly right or obligatory "under another description."[33] Those who individuate actions finely would presumably claim that my packing-and-posting is distinct from

---

[31] Ross 1930, pp. 44–6.   [32] See, e.g., Anscombe 1969; Davidson 1980.
[33] Cf. Anscombe 1969, p. 11 and elsewhere; Davidson 1980, pp. 5, 46, and elsewhere.

my keeping my promise and thus need not resort to such a move in order to retain Ross's distinction.[34] But they would still have to face the difficulty of determining whether my securing your reception of the book is identical with my keeping my promise. If it is, then, given the Objective View, my securing your reception of the book is directly obligatory. (This seems to be Ross's position.[35]) If it isn't, then my securing your reception of the book is on that view merely indirectly obligatory.

I think that the distinction between direct and indirect obligation is very important. It is one's direct obligations that dictate what one ought to do; indirect obligations are merely derivative. Given my adherence to the Prospective View, I of course do not agree with Ross that, in the present case, my direct obligation is to keep my promise. On the contrary, my direct obligation has to do with that which provides me with the best prospect of keeping my promise. Moreover, direct obligations are restricted to those *intentional* actions that one can perform; it is on *such* actions that one's obligations turn. Given my epistemic situation in Case 8, strictly keeping my promise is not something that I can intentionally do.[36] My doing so is therefore not directly obligatory. Using service B is, however, something that I can intentionally do, and my doing so provides me with the best prospect (among those actions that I can intentionally perform) of keeping my promise. Hence this is what, according to the Prospective View, my direct obligation concerns, and as a result I do not even have an indirect obligation strictly to keep my promise.

That what is directly obligatory is something that one can intentionally do is not a thesis that I take to be obviously true. I touched very briefly on the relation between obligation and intentional action in section 1.6. At that point, I postponed a full discussion of the issue to chapter 3. As before, at this juncture I will continue simply to beg your indulgence on the matter.

Let me now turn to the implications of the Prospective View regarding your having a right to receive the book by Friday. Some of these may be somewhat surprising.

---

[34] See, e.g., Goldman 1970, ch. 1.   [35] See Ross 1930, p. 46.

[36] In so saying, I am assuming that my promise is, strictly, to return the book to you by Friday in as good condition as I can (rather than to do that which provides me with the best prospect of achieving this).

Consider another version of the book-borrowing case:

Case 9:
I have a choice between two delivery services, A and B. All the evidence available to me is such that B provides me with a better prospect of keeping my promise to return the book to you (in as good condition as I can) by Friday.

According to the Prospective View, I have an obligation to use service B, not service A. The Correlativity Thesis would then appear to imply that you have a right that I use B and that you have no right that I use A. But now suppose that A is in fact the superior service and that B will not succeed in delivering the book to you at all. The result would seem to be that, according to the Prospective View, you do not have a right to delivery of the book at all, despite my promise to return it to you. Isn't this preposterous?

I think not. It is very often claimed that rights are grounded in interests. This is plausible. However, the nature of the grounding is not as straight-forward as one might think. Let us agree that you have an interest in receiving the book by Friday. This is what grounds the proposition that it would be *most suitable* for me to return the book to you by Friday. It does *not* ground the proposition that you have a *right* that I return the book to you by Friday, for two reasons: it may be that I *cannot* return the book by Friday; and it may be that that (intentional) act that provides me with the best *prospect* of returning it by Friday will not in fact achieve my doing so. Each of these points indicates that *your* right, though grounded (in part) in *your* interest, is nonetheless hostage to certain facts about *me* (my abilities, my evidence) in a way in which your interest itself is not. That to which you have a right is this: that I not perform any act such that some alternative that I could intentionally perform would provide me with a better prospect of keeping my promise and returning the book to you by Friday. As long as I act accordingly, your right has been satisfied, even if your interest has not.

There are of course objections to consider.

A

Suppose I had borrowed $100 from you rather than a book. Surely I would discharge my debt to you if and only if you received $100 in return from me. Hence, as the Objective View implies, it is to such repayment that you have a right – no more, and no less. So, too, in the matter of the book. You have a right to its being returned to you by Friday – no more, and no less. So much the worse for the Prospective View.[37] This is not persuasive. We must distinguish between what it would be most suitable to do and what it is obligatory to do. This is the *inescapable* lesson of Jackson's case. Perhaps we can regard "debt" as ambiguous between the two, in which case it can be admitted that, in *one* sense of the term, I would discharge my debt to you if and only if you received $100 in repayment from me. Even so, it is certainly not the case that I would fulfill my obligation to you if and only if you received $100 in repayment from me. On the contrary, my obligation is to do that which provides me with the best prospect of repaying $100 to you, and thus, given the Correlativity Thesis, it is to my so acting that you have a right.

One could of course resist this conclusion about what right you have, while cleaving to the Prospective View, by denying the Correlativity Thesis. But I see no plausibility in doing so. On the contrary, as I have already remarked, there is ample reason to declare rights as well as obligations to be partly a function of risk. Consider again that version of Case 3 in which Jill gambles successfully but recklessly with John's life by tossing a coin to decide which of drugs A and C to give him. Or consider again Thomson's case of one person playing Russian roulette on another without the latter's knowledge, and hence without his consent.

Another move that one might try making here is to say that people in general have two sets of rights, one set having to do with what actually occurs and one set having to do with what is likely to occur. We could then say both that you have a right to my repaying you $100 (or to my returning the book to you) and that you have a right to my doing that which provides me with the best prospect of doing so.[38] But this proliferation of senses of "right" is no more acceptable than the proliferation of senses of "ought" that was discussed and dismissed in the last chapter. Note again that the division of obligations into two (or more) categories only confounds the issue. It may at first be tempting to say that I have a special obligation to repay $100 to you (or to return the book to you) but also a general obligation to act responsibly or conscientiously in carrying out such a special obligation and thus to shun any option that does not provide me with the

---

[37] Cf. Montague 2004, p. 72: "A person violates no right of yours and acts contrary to no requirement simply by making it probable that she reveals the contents of your diary. Your right is violated only if the person actually reveals…the diary's contents."

[38] Something like this proposal is made in Broad 1985, pp. 127 ff.

best prospect of accomplishing it. But, for reasons given in the last chapter, that can't be right. To repeat just one of these reasons: such an account entails the possibility – indeed, the frequent inevitability – of moral dilemmas; for it can easily happen that fulfillment of the alleged general obligation conflicts with fulfillment of the alleged special obligation. This would be the case if my situation were such that the only method of succeeding in repaying you (or returning the book to you) were one that the available evidence indicated was less likely to succeed than some alternative. Surely, though, whatever we think of the possibility of moral dilemmas, they do not arise simply in virtue of our being so situated that what is actually most suitable is not prospectively most suitable. And, given the Correlativity Thesis, this implies that you do not have both a right to repayment (or receipt of the book) and a right to my doing that which is prospectively most suitable in this respect. It is only the latter right that you have.

B

Return to Case 9:

Case 9:
I have a choice between two delivery services, A and B. All the evidence available to me is such that B provides me with a better prospect of keeping my promise to return the book to you (in as good condition as I can) by Friday.

Suppose now that I use service B on Tuesday, as the Prospective View says I ought, expecting delivery of the book to you on Wednesday, but it then comes to light later on Wednesday that the book never reached you. If I have satisfied your right on Tuesday, then you have no right against me that I either retrieve and send the lost book or send you a replacement (if I can) by Friday. But surely you do have such a right. Therefore the Prospective View is to be rejected.

This objection neglects the fact that obligations can recur. Had I had no evidence that the book hadn't reached you, I would have had no obligation to send it again or send a replacement. Your interest in receiving the book would of course not have been satisfied but, as noted above, what rights you have in the matter are not simply a function of what is in your interest. However, given that I did come to learn that the book hadn't reached you, I did (once again) have an obligation to you in respect of it; your continuing interest in receiving the book, conjoined with my new evidence, rekindled my obligation and hence your right. Or more carefully: given such evidence, I re-incurred an obligation to do that which provided me with the best prospect of either sending the original to you or sending a replacement; and so you did indeed once again have a right that I do this.

C

But what if in Case 9 I use service A on Tuesday, contrary to the prescription of the Prospective View, and you nonetheless receive the book on Wednesday? Surely I have satisfied any right you have in the matter, even though the Prospective View implies otherwise. Therefore that view is once again to be rejected.

In this case your interest has indeed been satisfied, but your right has not. Despite having received the book, you have a grievance against me (just as John had a grievance against Jill when she tossed a coin to decide which drug to give him), a grievance that stems from my having infringed your right. It seems plausible to say that, in light of this, I owe you something, but just what it is that I owe you is a matter that I will not pursue here. (It is a complicated matter, as the remarks concerning compensation in the last section indicate.)

D

What if in Case 9 I choose the better prospect (service B) on Tuesday, the book gets delivered on Wednesday, but my subsequent evidence is that you have *not* received it? Surely your right against me has been satisfied, but the Prospective View implies that I am once again obligated to do that which provides me with the best prospect of sending you either the original or a replacement, and thus that your right against me has not been satisfied. Therefore the Prospective View is again to be rejected.

In reply: the Prospective View is perfectly correct to declare that, under the circumstances, *I* am once again *obligated* to do that which provides me with the best prospect of sending you (a copy of) the book; there is no need to retract this claim, since it is perfectly in keeping with the idea, which is the general lesson of Jackson's case, that one's obligations are tailored to one's evidential circumstances. That said, the claim that *you* continue to have a *right* that I act in this way, given that I used the prospectively best service and you did indeed receive the book, is admittedly more troubling. There are three possible positions one might hold on this issue while cleaving to the Prospective View.

First, one could reconcile oneself to accepting the claim that you continue to have the right, even though it is troubling. Given both that I satisfied my original obligation to you and that your interest in receiving the book has been satisfied, I do not recommend this position.

Second, one could reject the claim by virtue of rejecting the Correlativity Thesis. For reasons given above in subsection A of this section, I don't recommend this position, either.

Third, one could reject the claim while retaining the Correlativity Thesis by noting once again that this thesis stipulates that rights are correlative to *associative* obligations in particular rather than to all obligations (whether associative or otherwise) in general. It is perfectly consistent to say that I have an obligation to return the book to you without having an obligation *to you* to do this. I suggest that we say just this in the present case: given my evidential situation, I am once again obligated to do that which provides me with the best prospect of sending you (a copy of) the book, but, given the fact that you have already received the book, you no longer have a right against me that I act in this way and so I am not obligated *to you* to do so.[39]

It may help, in summary, to compare and contrast my position with that of Ross on the matter of returning the borrowed book. His position (in *The Right and the Good*) is captured in chart 2.1 above. The position that I endorse, in keeping with both the Prospective View and the Correlativity Thesis, is captured in chart 2.2, where: "Carefully dispatched" is now understood in particular to concern whether I initially did that which provided me with the best prospect of returning the book to you; "Evidence of book received" concerns my subsequent evidence regarding whether you received the book; "Obligation to resend" concerns whether I have a subsequent obligation (associative or non-associative) to do that which *provides me with the best prospect* of sending either the book or a replacement; and "Associative obligation to resend – Right to resending"

---

[39] A particularly dramatic sort of case in which obligations and rights can part company is one in which the person whom the obligation concerns does not exist. Suppose that, after lending me the book on Monday, you die before I have the opportunity to return it to you, but that I have every reason to believe that you are still alive. Then I will still be obligated to do that which provides me with the best prospect of returning the book to you by Friday, even though you, being dead, no longer have an interest in my doing so or a right against me that I do so. (In so saying, I am of course rejecting the possibility of posthumous interests and rights.) Once again, this is perfectly in keeping with the Correlativity Thesis, since the obligation in question is not an associative one; that is, it is not one that I owe *to you*.

Carefully dispatched	Book received	Evidence of book received	Obligation to resend	Associative obligation to resend – Right to resending
Yes	Yes	Yes	No	No
Yes	Yes	No	Yes	No
Yes	No	Yes	No	No
Yes	No	No	Yes	Yes
No	Yes	Yes	No	No
No	Yes	No	Yes	No
No	No	Yes	No	No
No	No	No	Yes	Yes

Chart 2.2

concerns whether I have a subsequent obligation *to you* so to act, that is, whether you have a right against me that I do so.

2.4 TEST CASE: SELF-DEFENSE

Consider now this case:

Case 10:
Alf is in love with Brenda. Alas, she does not return his affections. She is more interested in Charles. This upsets Alf. One day he reaches the breaking point. He storms over to Brenda's house, hammers on her front door, barges in when she cracks open the door to see what the fuss is about, waves a gun in her face, and tells her that he is going to "teach her a lesson she won't forget." (Alf seems not to appreciate the fact that, if he succeeds in doing what he threatens, then the lesson will be one that Brenda will not only not forget but also not remember.) Brenda has long anticipated such an emotional display by Alf. She has a gun of her own. As Alf steadies his hand and points his gun at Brenda, she shoots him in self-defense, killing him.

I wish to address two questions. First, did Alf do something that was overall morally wrong? Second, did Brenda do something that was overall morally wrong? The answers will of course depend on how we fill in certain details of the case. I will be concerned with the following details in particular: (1) whether Alf's behavior actually endangered Brenda (by which I mean: whether he would in fact have killed her, had she not killed him first); (2) whether, in light of the evidence available to Alf, his behavior imposed a grave risk of harm on Brenda; and (3) whether, in light of the evidence available to Brenda, Alf's behavior imposed a grave risk of harm on her. Given these three variables, eight broad types of case emerge, as shown in chart 2.3.

I will consider versions of Case 10 of each type (except Type D, which will not require separate treatment). My purpose in doing so is twofold.

97

Type	(1) Actual endangerment	(2) Grave risk relative to Alf's evidence	(3) Grave risk relative to Brenda's evidence
A	Yes	Yes	Yes
B	Yes	Yes	No
C	Yes	No	Yes
D	Yes	No	No
E	No	Yes	Yes
F	No	Yes	No
G	No	No	Yes
H	No	No	No

Chart 2.3

First, I will argue that, in certain versions of Case 10 in which the intuitively correct verdict is that Brenda was overall morally justified in killing Alf, this verdict cannot be reconciled with the Objective View but is endorsed by the Prospective View. This provides further confirmation of the Prospective View, independently of the considerations provided in the last chapter when discussing Case 3. Second, I will pursue the implications of the Prospective View in other versions of the case, in order once again to put this view to the test.

To facilitate the discussion, I will label the versions according to the type they exemplify. Thus, Case 10A will be a version of Case 10 that exemplifies Type A, Case 10B will be a version of Case 10 that exemplifies Type B, and so on. Also, for the sake of simplicity, I will suppose the following: for all versions of the case to be considered, the only relevant actual values at stake are personal benefit (a positive value) and personal harm (a negative value); for each of Alf and Brenda the available evidence concerning these actual values is accurate; Alf is not in a position to provide any benefit to anyone; Brenda is a singularly tough-minded individual who can be harmed only physically (she knows no fear, for example); and Alf is not in a position to prevent any harm other than the harm he threatens to do to Brenda (a supposition that is in one respect *too* simple – a point to which I will shortly return). Given these suppositions, the Objective View implies that Alf did nothing wrong; in acting as he did, he forwent no benefit to anyone, and Brenda's quick action ensured that he did her no harm. I will argue that this implication is unacceptable, since it deprives us of the best means of explaining why it is that, in some versions of the case, Brenda was overall justified in killing Alf.

It might be countered that the Objective View implies that Alf did nothing wrong only because of the simplifying supposition that the only actual values at stake are personal benefit and harm, and that many plausible substantive theories of obligation are inconsistent with this supposition. Whereas an act-consequentialist might be willing to entertain this supposition, a rule-consequentialist, for example, or a virtue-theorist would not be. A rule-consequentialist might say that Alf's attack on Brenda was not actually rule-best (that is, it actually violated a rule, general adherence to which is instrumentally better than general adherence to the rule to which his attack conformed), even though the attack was not successful. Similarly, a virtue-theorist might say that Alf's attack was actually vicious, even though it was not successful. Thus the Objective View is perfectly consistent with the claim that what Alf did was wrong.

I grant this point but want to put it aside. My particular concern here is with whether Alf violated any *right* of Brenda's. The most obvious right at issue concerns her being harmed. Since she was not actually harmed, any alleged right not actually to be harmed was clearly not violated. I suppose that a rule-consequentialist might contend that Brenda had a right that Alf not violate the pertinent rule, or a virtue-theorist might contend that she had a right that Alf not display the relevant vice, but such a contention is not often made and would need supporting argument. It seems to me far more plausible to say that, at least in some versions of Case 10, Alf infringed a right of Brenda's having to do with her being (at risk of being) harmed. It is this claim in particular that, on the simplifying approach, the Objectivist is not in a position to make.

An Objectivist might respond that he *is* in a position to say just this. Brenda has a right to privacy. Alf violated this right. In so doing, he did her actual harm (moral harm, even if not physical or psychological harm). Hence the Objective View is perfectly compatible with the claim that he did wrong, even on the simplifying supposition in question.

But this won't do, either. The simplifying supposition declares that the *only* actual values at stake in the case are personal benefit and harm (of a *non*-moral sort), and that Alf did not harm Brenda. Thus we are presuming that Brenda's privacy is *not* an issue, either because privacy is not an actual value, or because Case 10 is to be (re)construed in such a way that Brenda's privacy was not invaded. In either case, no right to privacy was violated, and hence the Objectivist has no pretext for smuggling into the case any harm that might consist in or arise from the violation of such a right.[40]

---

[40] In this connection, cf. n. 18 above.

A

Consider, first, this version of our case:

Case 10A:
(1) Alf's behavior actually endangered Brenda (since his gun was fully loaded and operational, he was fully intent on pulling the trigger, he was not physically incapacitated, she had no time to escape, she could not have saved herself except by killing him, etc.).
(2) In light of the evidence available to Alf, his behavior imposed a grave risk of harm on Brenda.
(3) In light of the evidence available to Brenda, Alf's behavior imposed a grave risk of harm on her.

Here almost everyone will agree that, all else being equal, Brenda's killing Alf was overall morally justified; that is, her doing so was overall morally justifiable; that is, she was overall morally justified in doing so; that is, her doing so was not overall morally wrong.[41] (I take all these expressions to be equivalent.) Let us for the moment suppose that the Objective View is true. There then arises an obvious puzzle: how can Brenda have been overall justified in killing Alf if, as the Objective View implies, Alf himself, since he failed actually to harm Brenda, did nothing wrong?

It is commonly assumed that all persons have a right to life (unless this right has been lost or renounced in some way), and that for one to have such a right involves at least having a claim against others that they not kill one.[42] Given the Correlativity Thesis, this implies that it is prima facie morally wrong for one person actually to kill another, since doing so constitutes an infringement of the latter's right to life. In other words, it implies that, under what I will call "normal" circumstances, one person's killing another is overall morally wrong. But it is also commonly assumed that circumstances may not be normal and that killing another person may then be overall morally justifiable. There are four main ways in which one might try accounting for the nature of such abnormal circumstances.

---

[41] The proviso "all else being equal" may not be necessary. I have in mind the sort of case, for example, in which, by virtue of killing Alf, Brenda somehow brought it about that someone else, who was morally innocent, also died. (E.g., Alf was carrying a child in his arms as he pointed his gun at Brenda, and Brenda was able to kill Alf only by shooting through the child's body, thereby killing it.) Some would deem Brenda's action in such a case overall morally wrong; others would say that it was still overall morally justifiable. The proviso brackets such issues.

[42] It may involve other kinds of right, too, such as the power to press or waive this claim.

First, it may be that the person killed has waived his or her right to life.[43] This is irrelevant to the present discussion, since neither Alf nor Brenda undertook such a waiver.

A second account goes as follows. Although there is a presumption against infringing a right, this presumption can be overridden by countervailing considerations. If it is overridden, then the infringement is justified, despite the moral cost incurred. If such is the case, then, as noted in section 2.2, the right, though infringed, is not violated. We could then try explaining Brenda's being overall justified in killing Alf by saying that, although in so doing she infringed Alf's right to life, she did not thereby violate this right, since the presumption against doing so was overridden by countervailing considerations.

Although it is presumably possible for rights on occasion to be justifiably infringed, the account just offered of why Brenda was overall morally justified in killing Alf strikes me as unpromising. The explanation is unstable, unreliable.[44] Let us agree that it would have been overall unjustifiable for Alf to kill Brenda, chiefly because Brenda had (and fortunately continues to have) a right to life. But then why was it overall justifiable for Brenda to kill Alf? If, given that they each had a right to life, Alf and Brenda both had their respective rights simply in virtue of being persons, then, since they were equally persons, there would seem to be no reason to declare Alf's right any less stringent than Brenda's. Thus, as far as these rights are concerned, if it would have been overall morally wrong for Alf to kill Brenda, then it was overall morally wrong for Brenda to kill Alf. Of course, there could have been extraneous considerations that might be thought to have tipped the balance in Brenda's favor: perhaps her continued existence will be a boon to mankind, whereas Alf's would not have been. But such thinking is pernicious. It could just as easily be that Alf's continued existence would have been a boon to mankind (despite being emotionally volatile, he was a brilliant scientist on the brink of discovering a cure for cancer), whereas Brenda's will not be (I'll forgo the sordid details). We would surely not then want to say that Brenda was after all not overall morally justified in defending herself.

A third attempt at explaining why Brenda was overall morally justified in killing Alf involves understanding the right to life that persons typically

---

[43] In some circumstances, it may be overall morally wrong to kill someone even though that person has waived his right to life. If so, that will not be because killing him violates this right.
[44] Cf. Thomson 1986, pp. 42 ff.

have not simply as an unconditional right not to be killed but as a conditional right not to be killed unless..., where the "..." involves a specification of some alleged exemption. Such a move is tantamount to conceiving of all rights as correlative to overall obligations and is, as I indicated in section 2.2, not at all plausible.[45] The exempting condition would have to be very long and complicated to accommodate all overall morally justifiable killings. Few, if any, people would know how to spell it out; thus few, if any, people would know just what a right to life is. Moreover, this problem would arise for rights generally, not just for rights to life. Thus few, if any, people would know just what rights we have. If so, invoking rights in an effort to justify moral judgments or to resolve moral problems would appear in general to be a foolhardy venture, and it is hard to see why it would help in the particular case of Alf and Brenda. Not only that, the effort, even if successful, would seem redundant. For how else are we to specify the exempting condition without having *already* determined that, in cases like that of Alf and Brenda, it is overall justifiable to respond lethally to a lethal threat? But, if that is the way the exempting condition is to be specified, then citing that condition cannot itself help explain why it was overall justifiable for Brenda to kill Alf, since that kind of case will already have been settled in the specification of the condition. The explanation would be circular, and hence empty.

A final and, I think, a much more plausible, intuitive, and promising attempt at explaining why Brenda was overall morally justified in killing Alf is to note that rights can, under certain circumstances, be forfeited, so that what was once overall unjustifiable (involving a violation of a right) becomes overall justifiable (since no right is any longer available for violation). It might then be said that, in threatening Brenda, Alf threatened to violate Brenda's right to life; in virtue of so doing, he forfeited his own right to life; thus the primary impediment (posed by his having a right to life) to Brenda's being overall justified in killing Alf is removed, and so she was overall justified in killing him.

Some have alleged that this very natural explanation is unacceptable because it, too, is circular.[46] The complaint is that, in light of the Correlativity Thesis, to say that one person, Q, has a right against another person, P, just is to say that P is obligated to Q; hence one cannot *explain* P's not being obligated to Q by noting that Q has no right against P. I find this

---

45 Cf. Thomson 1986, pp. 37 ff.
46 See Montague 1981, pp. 208–9. Cf. McMahan 1994, p. 278.

objection unpersuasive. First, it is not clear that Q's having a right against P is *identical* with P's having an obligation to Q; it seems natural, in many cases at least, to say that Q's right *grounds* P's obligation (even if, as the Correlativity Thesis declares, the two are strictly equivalent). Second, and more importantly, even if it were agreed that there is just one moral phenomenon here (viewed from two perspectives, P's and Q's), and not two, still, I think, the appeal to forfeiture could have explanatory power. Of course, there would be no explanation of P's not being obligated to Q to be found in the simple observation that Q has no right against P; but the former could still be explained by observing that, *in virtue of behaving in some way*, Q has *forfeited* his right against P. It is Q's behavior that would explain "both" the loss of Q's right and the cessation of P's obligation.

But is the rationale of forfeiture applicable to the particular case of Alf and Brenda? It is surely common to think that it is through overall moral wrongdoing that one forfeits a right. But remember that, on the Objective View (which is the view currently being presupposed), Alf did *no* wrong in threatening Brenda. How, then, could he have forfeited his right to life?

Well, one possibility is that there is an alternative route to forfeiture, by way of culpability rather than wrongdoing, and that Alf forfeited his right by virtue of being culpable. But culpable for what? Suppose that Alf was in the habit of behaving badly. Anyone who knew him would not be surprised that he threatened Brenda as he did. Why, just last week he beat his mother because she had the temerity to suggest that he stop pining over Brenda. Let us assume that Alf was culpable for having beaten his mother. Surely, it won't do to say that he forfeited his right to life *vis-à-vis* Brenda by virtue of being culpable for having beaten his mother. If culpability was the ground of forfeiture, it must be culpability for behavior (by Alf) that was suitably related to the behavior (by Brenda) that such forfeiture rendered justifiable.[47] Perhaps the most obvious candidate is this: culpability for having threatened Brenda. But note what this would entail, given the Objective View: Alf was culpable for having done something that it wasn't wrong for him to do. How could this be?

Many people apparently subscribe to the view that such a situation cannot arise. Whereas the possibility of overall moral wrongdoing without culpability is widely recognized – that is, after all, what excuses are traditionally taken to consist in – the possibility of culpability without overall moral wrongdoing is hardly ever discussed, let alone accepted. I think that

---

[47] Cf. McMahan 2005a, pp. 387 ff., and 2005b, section II C.

this is a mistake, and that what we may call "accuses" – the mirror-image of excuses – are indeed possible. (This is an issue that I'll take up in chapter 4.) But, having said this, I want to put the matter aside here. This is not because I think it must be a mistake to hold Alf culpable for his behavior, but simply that it may be, and thus that we cannot rely on his culpability as an explanation for his having forfeited his right to life. Let me explain.

Alf will be culpable for his behavior if he believed that he was doing something overall morally wrong or culpably failed to believe this;[48] otherwise he will not be culpable for his behavior. Did he believe that he was doing something overall morally wrong? Given part (2) of the present version of our case – Case 10A – it is quite possible that he did; but part (2) doesn't guarantee this, and so it is also possible that he did not. Did he perhaps culpably fail to believe that he was doing something overall morally wrong? Again, quite possibly; but, also, possibly not. Yet, even if Alf was not culpable for his behavior, it seems clear that almost everyone will agree that, under the circumstances of Case 10A, Brenda was overall morally justified in killing him in self-defense. As I see it, the most promising rationale for this verdict is that Alf forfeited his right to life, and the most promising rationale for this claim in turn is that what Alf did was overall morally wrong. Since the Objective View implies that, in virtue of not actually harming Brenda, Alf did nothing wrong, I submit once again that we must reject this view. Not only does Jackson's case – Case 3 – show it to be unacceptable; so too, for different reasons, does Case 10A. (Let me immediately add, though, that I take the present considerations against the Objective View to be less forceful than those raised in the last chapter. Everyone agrees – or would agree, if they were in Jill's shoes – that in Case 3 Jill ought to give John drug B. Certainly not everyone agrees that the rationale of forfeiture is the best explanation for the justification of a potential victim's killing her assailant in cases like Case 10A. Nonetheless, I submit, for the reasons given above, that this is indeed the best rationale available.)

There is a complication. I have claimed that the Objective View implies that Alf did no wrong in Case 10A (and hence that it cannot provide a satisfactory explanation, via the forfeiture of his right to life, of Brenda's being overall morally justified in killing him in self-defense). But does the Objective View really have this implication? At the outset of this section I

---

[48] In so saying, I am assuming that Alf satisfies whatever other conditions, having to do with freedom of action and any such related matters, are necessary for culpability.

made the simplifying supposition that Alf was not in a position to prevent any harm other than the harm he threatened to do to Brenda, and it was partly on the basis of this supposition that I claimed that the Objective View implies that he did no wrong. But I also remarked that this supposition is in one respect *too* simple. Let me now explain. The supposition is too simple because Alf clearly must have been in a position to prevent some harm other than that which he threatened to do to Brenda, namely, the harm that Brenda in fact did to him; for, had he not made the threat in the first place, Brenda would not have responded as she did. Thus the Objective View is consistent after all with the claim that Alf did something wrong, and so it might seem that it can after all account for his having forfeited his right to life. But in fact it still cannot account for this forfeiture, even if it is conceded that Alf did wrong in virtue of failing to prevent the harm that Brenda did to him. The reason for this is that the rationale of forfeiture requires that any wrong act performed by Alf that could justify Brenda's killing him in self-defense be an act that was wrong independently of the fact that she killed him. It cannot be that her killing him accounts for the wrongness of his act, which in turn accounts (via forfeiture) for the justification of her killing him. No act can be self-justifying in this way. Hence the Objective View remains incompatible with the rationale of forfeiture and is still to be rejected.

B

It is of course true, as I noted in the last chapter, that rejection of the Objective View does not entail acceptance of the Prospective View. Someone who leans toward the Objective View but acknowledges that Case 10A requires abandoning it might advocate making only a small amendment to it in order to accommodate the claim that Alf did wrong in this case. According to this amendment, one has done something overall morally wrong if *either* one has failed to do what is actually best *or* one would have failed to do what was actually best had one not been somehow prevented from doing so. Given this amendment, we are no longer constrained to conclude that Alf did no wrong in Case 10A, since part (1) of that case implies that he would have killed Brenda had she not prevented him from doing so by killing him first.

The amendment is not plausible. Just now I counseled rejection of the Objective View because it implies that Alf did no wrong in Case 10A. If, like me, you find that implication unacceptable, then what reason could you have for insisting that Alf's doing wrong requires under the circumstances that, if he didn't harm Brenda, then he at least endangered her? If, under the circumstances, actual harm was not necessary for wrongdoing, why then should actual endangerment have been? Suppose that Alf had had not a standard six-gun but a special thousand-gun, and that he knew that all but one of the chambers were loaded. And suppose that, as luck would have it, if Alf had pulled the trigger, he would have engaged the one chamber in a thousand that was empty and thus did not actually endanger Brenda (in the present sense of "endanger"). We now have this version of our case:

Case 10E:
(1) Alf's behavior did not actually endanger Brenda (since, even though he was fully intent on pulling the trigger, he would have engaged the one chamber in a thousand that was empty).
(2) In light of the evidence available to Alf, his behavior imposed a grave risk of harm on Brenda.
(3) In light of the evidence available to Brenda, Alf's behavior imposed a grave risk of harm on her.

Parts (2) and (3) of Case 10E are the same as those of Case 10A; it is only part (1) that has changed. In light of this change, the amended Objective View requires us once again to declare that Alf did no wrong (independently of the fact that he failed to prevent Brenda's killing him). I submit that this is unacceptable. Surely it would be much more plausible to say, as the Prospective View implies, that in Case 10E Alf did do wrong, even though he would have engaged an empty chamber, because of the enormous and unacceptable *risk* of harm that he imposed on Brenda in behaving as he did.[49] I suggest that imposing such a risk violated her rights, in light of which he forfeited his own right to life, in light of which Brenda's killing him was overall morally justified. And I take the plausibility of saying this to be further confirmation of the Prospective View.

---

[49] In Case 10E there was an objective probability of 0.999 that Alf's gun would fire, but that is not the sort of probability in terms of which the risk that he took is to be directly determined. After all, if causal determinism is true, there was also an objective probability of 0 that the gun would fire. (There can be several objective probabilities, each relative to some distinct reference class.) As noted in chapter 1, what directly determines the relevant risk that Alf took – relevant, that is, to the question whether his behavior was morally justifiable – is the epistemic probability that his gun would fire. Since Alf knew that all but one of the chambers were loaded, we may take the epistemic probability to be very high.

To repeat a point from section 2.2: it is possible to subscribe to the Prospective View and yet, by denying the Correlativity Thesis, maintain that the rights that people have regarding exposure to harm should be given a wholly objective account. That is, one might say that people in general have a right not to be (actually) harmed or, at least, a right not to be (actually) endangered (in the sense of "endanger" used previously). But this would not allow us to say that in Case 10E Alf violated any right of Brenda's. Yet it seems clear that we should say precisely this. For Alf did not simply do wrong in behaving as he did; he *wronged Brenda*. And it is in virtue of having been wronged in this way that Brenda both had special cause for complaint against Alf and was overall morally justified in killing Alf in self-defense. What right of Brenda's is it that Alf violated? The answer seems simple: the right that he not put her at risk of harm. (Remember that, given the distinction between the infringement and the violation of a right, the claim that people have a right not to be put at risk of harm does not imply that we are routinely violating the rights of others, even if it does imply that we are routinely infringing their rights.)

C

Let us now focus more tightly on the question of whether Brenda did wrong in killing Alf. The Prospective View is a general account of wrong-doing; if it applies to Alf, it applies equally to Brenda. This makes matters somewhat complicated, but what emerges is, I believe, a persuasive, coherent picture of who acts wrongly and why in the various versions of Case 10.

Consider again Cases 10A and 10E, in both of which, in light of his own evidence, Alf imposed a grave risk of harm on Brenda. I have suggested that, in these versions of our case, Alf forfeited his right to life. Above, I characterized this right as a right not to be killed. But, given the Prospective View, this cannot be quite right. If in general we don't have a right not to be harmed but rather have a right not to be put at *risk* of being harmed, then more particularly we don't have a right not to be killed but rather have a right not to be put at *risk* of being killed.[50] Let us now say that it is *this*

---

[50] Or rather, given the points raised in the last two sections: we have a right that others not perform an *intentional* action that risks their killing us, *given* that their evidence indicates that their doing so is not most suitable to (some aspect of) their situation. The reason for the first qualification is that killing always risks killing. It follows from this fact that, if we had an unqualified right not to be put at risk of being killed, then we would after all have a right not to be killed. The qualification blocks this inference, since unintentional killings do not

right that constitutes a right to life.[51] Then, I think, we can indeed once again say that, in the two versions of the case just mentioned, Alf forfeited his right to life, since in each version he violated Brenda's right to life.[52] (This is actually too simple, for a reason on which I will shortly elaborate.) Moreover, given that, in both versions, Brenda's evidence conformed to this fact, there would seem to be no reason to deny, on the Prospective View, that she was overall justified in responding as she did. Of course, in so responding, she risked causing Alf grave harm; however, there is no reason to think that, in running this risk, she was failing to do what was prospectively best. Thus the Prospective View provides a very natural account of how it is, in these two versions of Case 10, not only that Alf did wrong in attacking Brenda but also that Brenda did no wrong in defending herself against Alf's attack.

But consider now two more versions of our case:

Case 10B:
(1) Alf's behavior actually endangered Brenda (since his gun was fully loaded and operational, he was fully intent on pulling the trigger, he was not physically incapacitated, she had no time to escape, she could not have saved herself except by killing him, etc.).
(2) In light of the evidence available to Alf, his behavior imposed a grave risk of harm on Brenda.
(3) In light of the evidence available to Brenda, Alf's behavior did *not* impose a grave risk of harm on her (since she had very good reason to believe that his gun was *not* loaded).

infringe the qualified right. The reason for the second qualification is, once again, that the evidence available to the agent may be defective. (See section 3.4, subsection C, for further discussion and refinement.)
[51] Alongside, perhaps, some rights of a non-claim kind. See n. 42 above.
[52] The question arises: forfeited for how long? I am not sure of the answer. There would seem to be three main alternatives: the forfeiture lasts (a) only as long as Alf's threat does, (b) for as long as Alf is alive, (c) for some period of time in between. None of these alternatives is such that I find a compelling reason to embrace it in particular. With respect to (a): I readily grant that, if Alf's threat had ceased, and it had been evident to Brenda that it had ceased, prior to Brenda's taking any defensive action, then she would have been obligated not to shoot him. But, as was noted in the last section and will be discussed further below, she can be obligated not to shoot him without being obligated *to him* not to shoot him, and so such a turn of events need not be construed as reinstating Alf's right to life. With respect to (b): this position may seem unduly harsh. Suppose that Alf's threat had ceased prior to Brenda's taking any defensive action, that she had refrained from shooting him, and that both Alf and Brenda had then gone on to live for several decades, Alf never once threatening Brenda again. Should we really say that Alf's right to life remained forfeit for all those years? With respect to (c): we might say that Alf's right could be reinstated by his atoning for his behavior (or perhaps by some other means). I leave the matter open.

Case 10F:
(1) Alf's behavior did not actually endanger Brenda (since, even though he was fully intent on pulling the trigger, he would have engaged the one chamber in a thousand that was empty).
(2) In light of the evidence available to Alf, his behavior imposed a grave risk of harm on Brenda.
(3) In light of the evidence available to Brenda, Alf's behavior did *not* impose a grave risk of harm on her (since she had very good reason to believe that his gun was *not* loaded).

Cases 10B and 10F are just like Cases 10A and 10E, respectively, except for the change in part (3). Given this change, I think we may safely say that, in Cases 10B and 10F, Brenda's shooting Alf in "self-defense" did indeed constitute a failure to do what was prospectively best and thus that, on the Prospective View, the risk she thereby imposed on him constituted overall moral wrongdoing on her part.[53] But now we have another puzzle: how can it be that what Brenda did was overall wrong if, as I have just claimed, Alf had forfeited his right against her that she not impose a risk of harm on him?

The answer involves the distinction, introduced in section 2.2, between associative and non-associative obligations. Although, in light of Alf's wrongdoing, Brenda did not have an obligation *to him* not to risk killing him (that is, she didn't *owe it to him* not to do this), nonetheless, in light of her evidence, she did have an obligation not to do this, and so her shooting him in "self-defense" was *not* justified, *despite* his having forfeited his right to life.[54] Although she did not *wrong Alf* in shooting him, she nonetheless did *wrong*. (An alternative assessment of Brenda's behavior in Cases 10B and 10F is that, in light of the fact that Alf forfeited his right to life, she was overall justified in shooting him, but, in light of the fact that her evidence was such that she had no reason to think her life was in danger, she is to blame for having shot him. This would mean that Brenda has what I earlier called an accuse for shooting Alf. But again, although I accept the possibility of accuses in general, this seems to me the wrong diagnosis in the present instance. For if, as the Prospective View says, wrongdoing is in

---

[53] The scare-quotes are intended to reflect the fact that the term "self-defense" is quite misleading under the circumstances, given the evidence that was available to Brenda and the further assumption that her beliefs conformed to this evidence. (Perhaps she was simply being opportunistic, taking advantage of the situation in an effort to avoid being charged with murder.)
[54] Compare the discussion in subsection D of the last section.

general to be understood in terms of the risks one runs, then Brenda cannot escape the charge of wrongdoing in the cases in question.)

Consider now this version of our case:

Case 10C:
(1) Alf's behavior actually endangered Brenda (since his gun was fully loaded and operational, he was fully intent on pulling the trigger, etc.).
(2) In light of the evidence available to Alf, his behavior did *not* impose a grave risk of harm on Brenda (since he had very good reason to believe that the gun was *not* loaded; he was only trying to scare her).
(3) In light of the evidence available to Brenda, Alf's behavior *did* impose a grave risk of harm on her (since she had very good reason to believe that the gun *was* loaded, etc.).

Let us understand part (3) of this case to imply that Brenda's shooting Alf was prospectively best and thus that she was overall justified in killing him. This implies in turn that she was not overall obligated not to shoot him, despite the fact that, in light of the evidence available to Alf, he was not imposing a grave risk of harm on her. Initially, there may seem nothing unintuitive in this verdict; for it is reasonable to assume that Alf did overall wrong in trying to scare Brenda, even though he didn't thereby impose a grave risk of harm on her. Hence, it may seem, he forfeited his right to life. Hence Brenda was overall justified in killing him. But the first "hence" is unacceptable. It seems clear that, if Alf did do something overall morally wrong, still, given the evidence available to him, his behavior did not constitute wrongdoing so serious as to render his right to life forfeit. You may disagree, citing the fact that Alf's behavior actually endangered Brenda. Given my allegiance to the Prospective View, I find this fact irrelevant. But we can sidestep this issue here. Consider instead the following version of our case:

Case 10G:
(1) Alf's behavior did *not* actually endanger Brenda (since his gun was *not* loaded; he was only trying to scare her).
(2) In light of the evidence available to Alf, his behavior did *not* impose a grave risk of harm on Brenda (since he knew that the gun was not loaded).
(3) In light of the evidence available to Brenda, Alf's behavior *did* impose a grave risk of harm on her (since she had very good reason to believe that the gun *was* loaded, etc.).

Here I think it really is clear that any wrong that Alf did was not sufficiently serious to render his right to life forfeit.

(This point indicates the need to qualify the too simple claim made a short while ago that Alf's violating Brenda's right to life rendered his own right to life forfeit. We should distinguish between wrongly imposing a grave risk of harm and wrongly imposing a risk of grave harm. Degree of risk is a function both of the probability and of the degree of harm. A grave risk is one in which these two factors combine to make the risk a high one. But a risk of grave harm – such as death – need not itself be grave, since the relevant probability may be very low. The idea that one may forfeit one's right not to be put at risk of being killed through violating someone else's right not to be put at risk of being killed is I think plausible as long, but only as long, as the gravity of the risk one imposes, and not just the gravity of the harm one risks, is sufficiently great.[55])

It seems clear that, in Case 10G no less than in Case 10C, Brenda was overall justified in shooting Alf. But then we have yet another puzzle: how could Brenda be so justified, if Alf did not forfeit his right to life?

One answer is this. Since he did not forfeit his right to life, Alf retained this right, and so Brenda continued to have a prima facie obligation to him not to put him at risk of being killed; however, her evidence provided her with a reason to shoot him that overrode her obligation to him not to shoot him. I reject this answer. If in general, as the Prospective View implies, it is the evidence available to the agent that determines whether the agent does right or wrong, both prima facie and overall, and if Brenda's evidence in the versions presently under consideration (Cases 10C and 10G) is exactly like her evidence in the versions considered earlier (Cases 10A and 10E) in which her overall justification for shooting Alf turned crucially on the fact that she was *not* obligated to him not to shoot him, then we must say that in the present versions too she was not obligated to Alf not to shoot him.

A second answer is this. Since he did not forfeit his right to life, Alf retained this right; but since (as just argued) Brenda was not obligated to him not to shoot him, we must reject the Correlativity Thesis. As before, I reject this answer too. In severing the connection between rights and obligations, it makes a mystery of the moral significance of rights.

The answer I endorse is this. Since Brenda was not obligated to Alf not to shoot him, and since the Correlativity Thesis is true, it follows that Alf did not have a right that Brenda not shoot him – and, more generally, that he did not have a right that she not risk killing him. Thus he lost his right

---

[55] What counts as "sufficiently great"? I will offer no precise answer. The issue is discussed briefly in Alexander 1993, pp. 63–4, and 1999, p. 1,503, where it is said that whether the gravity of the risk is sufficiently great to warrant a preemptive response depends in part on the culpability of the attacker.

to life, even though he did not forfeit it. Alf certainly had an interest in not being killed, but, as noted in the last section, rights do *not* directly correlate with interests. Alf's interest in not being killed does not itself imply that he held a right not to be killed against all that might kill him – not even if it is stipulated that he neither waived nor forfeited such a right. He held no such right against the poisonous snake in his garden, because snakes are not the sort of creature that can have moral obligations. He would have held no such right against Brenda, if Brenda had been incapable of refraining from killing him; for, even though Brenda is the sort of creature that can have moral obligations, no one can have moral obligations that he or she cannot fulfill.[56] And, I contend, he held no such right against Brenda in Cases 10C and 10G because, although she could have refrained from killing him, her evidence was such that she had no obligation to do so. As in the last section, then, we see once again that one's right to life and, indeed, one's rights in general are hostage not only to the abilities but also to the evidence possessed by those against whom one's rights are held.

A certain asymmetry has emerged. In Cases 10B and 10F, Brenda's evidence was such that she had an overall obligation not to shoot Alf despite the fact that he had forfeited his right to life and thus had no right against her that she not shoot him. In Cases 10C and 10G, Alf had no right against her that she not shoot him precisely because she lacked any evidence in light of which she would have had an obligation not to do so, despite the fact that he had not forfeited his right to life. You might find this verdict about Cases 10C and 10G too difficult to swallow and urge that we say instead that, in these cases, Brenda had an *excuse* for shooting Alf but no overall *justification* for doing so. But I deny this. If in general, as the Prospective Views implies, it is the evidence available to an agent that determines whether the agent does right or wrong, we cannot shy away from this idea in those cases in which the evidence is misleading. That would return us to the Objective View, a view that has proven unacceptable.

You might not be satisfied with this response and seek to press the objection further.[57] Consider, you might say, a further variation on our case, one that is just like Case 10G except in its third part:

---

[56] Cf. section 3.5 below.   [57] Cf. McMahan 2005b, p. 391.

Case 10H:
(1) Alf's behavior did *not* actually endanger Brenda (since his gun was *not* loaded; he was only trying to scare her).
(2) In light of the evidence available to Alf, his behavior did *not* impose a grave risk of harm on Brenda (since he knew that the gun was not loaded).
(3) In light of the evidence available to Brenda, Alf's behavior did *not* impose a grave risk of harm on her (since she too knew that the gun was not loaded).

There is no doubt that, in this version of the case, Brenda's killing Alf in "self-defense" was *not* justified. But surely her ignorance in Case 10G cannot establish justification where otherwise there would have been none; hence in that case, just as in Case 10H, her killing Alf was not overall justified after all.

In response, I simply reject the claim that ignorance cannot justify behavior that would otherwise be unjustifiable. When rooted in misleading evidence rather than simply mistaken belief, ignorance can indeed affect the moral status of one's actions. That is precisely the import of the Prospective View. It is this that allows us to declare Alf's behavior overall morally wrong even if, as in Case 10E, he would not in fact have harmed Brenda had he pulled the trigger; and it is this that allows us to say that Brenda's behavior was overall morally justified even if, as in Case 10G, any wrong that Alf did was not sufficient for forfeiture.

D

The right to life is commonly taken to be one of the most basic "human" rights. Such rights are often said to be rights that we have simply in virtue of being humans (or persons). This claim is false, as the possibility of waiving or forfeiting the right to life shows. Several writers have noted this fact.[58] What I think has often not been adequately appreciated is just how precarious our possession of the right to life is, for such possession may be entirely beyond our control. Forfeiture of a right through wrongdoing is never beyond our control, since wrongdoing never is.[59] Nor is waiving a right ever beyond our control. But, as has just been seen in the discussion of Cases 10C and 10G, we can lose rights, even the right to life, which we have neither forfeited nor waived. This is a sobering thought. Still, one might try drawing some comfort from the fact that, in Cases 10C and 10G, it was nonetheless Alf's fault that he lost his right to life, since he acted

---

[58] Cf., e.g., Uniacke 1994, pp. 199 ff.; Rodin 2002, p. 76.   [59] Cf. section 3.5 below.

overall wrongly in trying to scare Brenda. (Although he knew, or had good reason to believe, that his gun was not loaded, he didn't know that Brenda was the sort of person who knows no fear. In light of the evidence available to him, his behavior therefore did impose an unreasonable risk, even if not a grave risk, of harm.) But such solace is premature. Suppose that, in another version of Type G, Alf was not even trying to scare Brenda; rather, he was just going through the motions of machismo, since this is what he had every reason to think that everyone (including Brenda) expected of him. Here it seems we should say that Alf did nothing wrong. Nonetheless, Brenda was overall justified in defending herself. Thus wrongdoing is not even necessary for the (involuntary) loss of a right to life, even when the person against whom the right was held remains capable of doing that which would previously have constituted the fulfillment of the correlative obligation. This is a very sobering thought.

The difference between forfeiture and mere loss is reflected in how third parties may respond to a situation. For simplicity, consider first cases in which both the second party (Brenda) and some third party (Charles, say) know all the relevant facts; their evidence is not misleading in any way. In those cases in which Alf endangers Brenda and the risk that he imposes on her is so serious that he forfeits his right to life, each of Brenda and Charles would be overall justified in killing Alf to save Brenda; indeed, it is arguable that Charles (and perhaps also Brenda) would be overall unjustified in not killing Alf to save Brenda. However, in those cases in which Alf endangers Brenda and the risk that he imposes on her, if any, is not such that it renders his right to life forfeit, then, although Brenda would be overall justified in killing Alf to save her life, Charles would not be overall justified in doing so (barring, perhaps, some extraneous considerations that might tip the balance in her favor; but, as before, this is problematic, since the considerations could favor Alf instead, and it is doubtful that we should then say that Charles would be overall justified in killing Brenda to save Alf). Another way of putting this point is to say that, if Alf forfeits his right to life, then he loses it *vis-à-vis* not only Brenda but also Charles, whereas, if he merely loses it without forfeiting it, he loses it *vis-à-vis* Brenda but not also Charles.[60]

Matters get complicated when Charles's epistemic situation is not perfect; for then, given the Prospective View, what he would be overall justified in doing (in light of the evidence available to him) might not

---

[60] Compare Davis 1984, pp. 192 ff. Contrast Thomson 1991, p. 306; Benbaji 2005, pp. 588, 595; Øverland 2005, pp. 138–9.

match the facts of the situation. It can therefore happen that Charles would be overall justified in killing Alf to save Brenda, even if Alf has not in fact forfeited his right to life, since Charles's evidence is such that Alf is acting in a way that does render his right to life forfeit. But this is nothing new. The sort of "disconnect" between truth and evidence that might affect the justifiability of Charles's intervening on Brenda's behalf has already been discussed with respect to Brenda's acting on her own behalf. (See the treatment above of Cases 10B, 10C, 10F, and 10G.)

The possibility that we might lose a "human" right that we have neither waived nor forfeited shows that moral luck is, in some ways at least, simply a fact of life.[61] Such luck may be either good or bad. Let me end by briefly giving some further illustrations of this fact.

Consider Alf. His moral luck was bad in Cases 10C and 10G, in that he lost his right to life even though he didn't forfeit it. (His personal luck was bad, too, since Brenda shot him.) Alf would have had the same bad moral luck in other variations of our case. Suppose, for example, that he had unwittingly and justifiably ingested some drug that rendered him unwittingly and uncontrollably homicidal; if he had threatened Brenda in such a way that she could not have defended herself except by killing him, then (as long as her evidence comported with the facts) she would have been overall justified in doing so. (This would be a version of Type C.) The only stable explanation of this is, I believe, that Alf would have lost his right to life in virtue of his behavior. And it need not even be *behavior* that grounds the loss of a right to life. Alf could simply have been in the wrong place at the wrong time. Suppose (as another version of Type C) that, trying to come to terms with Brenda's preference for Charles, Alf had gone for a long walk to think things through; that during this walk a sudden, strong gust of wind blew him off the top of a cliff; that he was bound to land on and thereby seriously injure Brenda, who happened to be standing at the bottom of the cliff and who would have cushioned his fall and saved him from serious injury, had she not had the opportunity and the remarkable skill to shoot him, thereby killing him but deflecting his body away

---

[61] Much resistance to the idea of moral luck is, I think, rooted in a failure to distinguish between luck regarding moral *obligation* and luck regarding moral *responsibility*, and, with respect to obligation in particular, to a failure to distinguish between luck regarding the *incurring* of obligation and luck regarding the *fulfillment* of obligation. (I discuss these matters more fully in Zimmerman 2006b.) The incurring of obligation is subject to all sorts of luck. In so far as rights are correlative to obligations, it follows that the possession of rights is also subject to all sorts of luck.

from her; and that she had duly shot him so that she might save herself (and, not incidentally, live happily ever after with Charles).[62] Tough luck for Alf, I think – not just personally, but morally; for Brenda was overall justified in her action.[63]

In other versions of our case, Alf's moral luck was good (though his personal luck remained bad – he was shot in every one). In Cases 10B and 10F, for example, Brenda was overall morally obligated not to shoot him (even though she was not obligated *to him* not to shoot him). It is Brenda's moral luck that, in these versions, was bad.

The discussion in this section has been complicated. It may help if I say something in summary about what I have tried and what I have not tried to accomplish.

I have tried to show that the Objective View cannot, while the Prospective View can, accommodate the intuitively correct verdict in Cases 10A and 10E that, in attacking Brenda, Alf did something overall morally wrong. In not harming Brenda but only putting her at risk of harm, Alf violated no right of

---

[62] Cf. Thomson 1991, p. 287, for a similar case.

[63] Contrast Rodin 2002, p. 89. Some writers seem to try to blunt the force of such cases by suggesting that Brenda's right to life is, or is about to be, infringed (indeed violated) by Alf. (Cf. Thomson 1991, pp. 300 ff.; Uniacke 1994, pp. 162 ff.) Surely not. To infringe a right is to fail to fulfill an obligation. One cannot have, and so cannot fail to fulfill, an obligation that one cannot fulfill. (Again, cf. section 3.5 below.) It is important to note, therefore, that the rationale of loss without forfeiture is one that not only the Prospectivist but also the Objectivist must take seriously. Perhaps in Case 10C, as originally described, the Objectivist would want to say that Brenda was justified in killing Alf because, in actually endangering Brenda as he did, Alf did wrong and thus forfeited his right to life (although, for reasons given earlier, I believe that the Objective View does *not* in fact endorse this claim), whereas the Prospectivist must say that, in light of the evidence available to him, Alf did no wrong and so did not forfeit his right to life, and thus that Brenda's being justified in killing him indicates that he lost this right without forfeiting it. However, in the current case of Type C in which Alf was blown off the cliff-top, even the Objectivist must acknowledge that Alf did no wrong and thus did not forfeit his right to life, so that, if Brenda was nonetheless justified in killing him, this indeed indicates that he lost his right without forfeiting it.

One might wonder, if the right to life is so precarious, whether there are any circumstances under which someone would *not* lose it, if his continued existence posed a threat to someone else's life. Certainly there are. One such set of circumstances would be a case (perhaps a case of euthanasia) in which the potential "victim" had waived the right not to be put at risk of being killed. In such a case, the killer has not lost his right not to be put at risk of being killed by the victim. Another case – or set of cases – concerns self-preservation rather than self-defense, where one person's continued existence threatens another's continued existence but not in virtue of the fact that the latter is at risk of being *killed* (whether voluntarily or otherwise) by the former. I leave open whether and how the former may lose his right to life under such circumstances.

Brenda's that the Objectivist can recognize. However, that he violated a right of hers is precisely what the Prospective View (conjoined with the Correlativity Thesis) claims to be the case. I have also tried to show that the Objective View cannot, while the Prospective View again can, accommodate (via the rationale of forfeiture) the intuitively correct verdict in Cases 10A and 10E that Brenda was overall morally justified in killing Alf. When we apply the Prospective View to other versions of Case 10, however, we arrive at verdicts which may at first be disquieting but are nonetheless, I contend, to be accepted – the verdict that in Cases 10B and 10F Brenda was not justified in killing Alf, even though he had forfeited his right to life, and the verdict in Cases 10C and 10G that Brenda was justified in killing Alf even though he hadn't forfeited (but had merely lost) his right to life.

I have not tried to defend all the judgments that I have made, although I do of course commend them to you. They are based not only on the Prospective View and the Correlativity Thesis but also on the rationale of forfeiture, and some of them go beyond that rationale and endorse the disturbing possibility of losing a right that one has neither waived nor forfeited. Certainly, these judgments can be, and have been, resisted.[64] I offer them to you for your examination. If in the end some of them are to be rejected, this will, I believe, be due to some problem with the rationales of forfeiture or of loss without forfeiture rather than with either the Prospective View or the Correlativity Thesis.

---

[64] For example, the idea that one can lose a right to life despite doing no wrong is rejected outright in Otsuka 1994, p. 82. Cf. also Rodin 2002, p. 89.

3

Prospective possibilism

In chapter 1, I argued against the Objective and Subjective Views of overall moral obligation and in favor of the Prospective View, but I formulated none of these views with any precision. In the last chapter, I pursued my defense of the Prospective View, extending my discussion to include an account of prima facie moral obligation and of moral rights, and in so doing provided a somewhat more precise formulation of the view. But in fact that formulation (the seventh) is still very rough, and it is now time to attend to the matter of developing the Prospective View in detail. In order to accomplish this, I will begin by discussing a debate that has recently taken place within the camp of those who subscribe, not to the Prospective View, but to the Objective View. This debate concerns the question of what exactly it means to say that one ought to choose that option that is actually best. Perhaps the most natural way of understanding what this means (it is certainly the way in which archetypical Objectivists such as G. E. Moore understand it) is that of the Actualist, but this understanding gives rise to a host of difficulties. An alternative construal, that of the Possibilist, avoids these difficulties but faces problems of its own. These are matters that I will discuss in section 3.1. My reason for doing so is that the same issues arise for the Prospectivist when trying to determine what exactly it means to say that one ought to choose that option that is prospectively best. The most natural way of understanding what this means constitutes a qualified form of Actualism and gives rise to the very same difficulties as Actualism does. I will argue, however, that a carefully qualified form of Possibilism once again avoids these difficulties and, moreover, avoids the problems faced by unqualified Possibilism. Developing and defending what I call Prospective Possibilism will be the task of sections 3.2–3.4. In section 3.2 I will explain how a holistic approach to overall moral obligation solves the problems that plague the piecemeal approach that characterizes Actualism; in section 3.3 I will argue that it is on intentional action in particular that we must focus if we are to avoid certain counterintuitive results, and I will give a precise account of unconditional overall moral obligation in such terms; and in section 3.4

118

I will extend this account so as to cover unconditional overall moral right and wrong, conditional overall obligation, subsidiary obligation, prima facie obligation, and the distinction between direct and indirect obligation. The resulting account endorses the principle that "ought" implies "can" and certain related principles. In section 3.5 I will explain more fully what these principles come to, and finally, in section 3.6, I will defend the principle that "ought" implies "can" against what I take to be the most serious objection to it. In so doing, I will show how my account of obligation provides an attractive and informative analysis of the ways in which obligations can shift over time.

3.1 ACTUALISM *VS.* POSSIBILISM

Recall the first formulation of the Objective View, which is exclusively concerned with overall moral obligation:

The Objective View (first formulation):
An agent ought to perform an act if and only if it is the best option that he (or she) has.

Recall, too, that by an "option" I mean something that the agent can do, where "can" expresses some form of personal control. In recent years, defenders of the Objective View have fallen into two main camps, those who adopt what has come to be called an Actualist interpretation of it and those who adopt a Possibilist interpretation of it. What Actualists propose is roughly this:

Actualism:
An agent ought to perform an act if and only if it is an option such that what *would* happen if the agent performed it is better than what *would* happen if he did not perform it.[1]

What Possibilists propose is roughly this:

Possibilism:
An agent ought to perform an act if and only if it is an option such that what *could* happen if the agent performed it is better than what *could* happen if he did not perform it,[2]

---

[1] Actualism is defended in Goldman 1976, Sobel 1976, Jackson and Pargetter 1986, and Goble 1993.

[2] One reason why this formulation is a bit rough is that, as the discussion below makes clear, Possibilism needn't be put in terms of a subjunctive conditional. Possibilism is defended in Goldman 1978, Greenspan 1978, Thomason 1981, Humberstone 1983, Feldman 1986, and Zimmerman 1996.

where "could" expresses the same sort of personal control as that involved in something's being an option. The difference between these two interpretations becomes apparent when we ponder the implication of future failings for present obligation.

Consider the following case (a milder version of the love-triangle featured in Case 10):

Case 11:
Alf has been invited to attend a wedding. The bride-to-be, Brenda, is a former girlfriend of his; it was she who did the dumping. Everyone, including Alf in his better moments, recognizes that Brenda was quite right to end the relationship; they were not well suited to one another, and the prospects were bleak. Her present situation is very different; she and her fiancé, Charles, sparkle in one another's company, spreading joy wherever they go. This irks Alf no end, and he tends to behave badly (though not murderously) whenever he sees them together. He ought not to misbehave, of course, and he knows this; he could quite easily resist the temptation to do so, but so far he hasn't. The wedding will be an opportunity for him to put this sort of boorishness behind him, and to grow up and move on. The best thing for him to do would be to accept the invitation, show up on the day in question, and behave himself. The worst thing would be to show up and misbehave; better would be to decline the invitation and not show up at all.

Ought Alf to accept or decline the invitation? (Here, as in chapter 1, "ought" expresses overall moral obligation and it is being presupposed that "all else is equal," that is, that nothing further hangs in the moral balance beyond what is implicit in the case.) The Possibilist answers with an unequivocal "Accept!" but the Actualist can only say "That depends." For, according to the latter, whether Alf ought to accept turns not just on what he *could* do, but on what he *would* do, were he to accept. Suppose that, if he accepted the invitation, he would show up and misbehave (whereas he wouldn't do this if he declined). He needn't misbehave (for, as noted, he could quite easily do otherwise[3]); nonetheless, this is what he would in fact do. Under these circumstances, the Actualist will say that Alf ought to decline the invitation.

In my experience, most people are inclined to accept the Actualist's verdict in Case 11. I think this is a mistake. But, whether the verdict is mistaken or not, what is clear, I believe, is that the basis for it provided by the Actualist is flawed. The best that Alf can do is to accept the invitation, show up at the wedding, and behave himself. The Possibilist says that this is

---

[3] I am assuming that, although some habits are hard to break, Alf's misbehaving does not constitute such a habit.

therefore what Alf ought to do, and in fact the Actualist *agrees* with this verdict. He (or she) agrees, that is, that Alf ought to do *all* of these things, since what would happen if he did act in this way is better than what would happen if he didn't. However, the Actualist denies that Alf ought to do *each* of the things just mentioned, since he denies that Alf ought to accept the invitation; indeed, he claims that Alf ought not to accept it. This is bizarre; it borders on incoherence.

Let me spell out the charge.[4] First, the Actualist must deny (where "*P*" ranges over persons and "*A*" and "*B*" range over acts)

(3.1) If *P* ought to do both *A* and *B*, then *P* ought to do *A*.[5]

(Let *A* = accept, *B* = behave.) He must also deny

(3.2) If *P* ought to do both *A* and *B*, then it is not the case that *P* ought not to do *A*.

(Let *A* = accept, *B* = behave.) He must also deny

(3.3) If *P* both ought to do *A* and ought to do *B*, then *P* ought to do both *A* and *B*.

(Let *A* = accept-and-behave, *B* = decline.) He must also deny

(3.4) If *P* both ought to do *A* and ought to do *B*, then *P* can do both *A* and *B*.

(Let *A* = accept-and-behave, *B* = decline.) And he must also deny

(3.5) If *P* ought to do *A* and cannot do *A* without doing *B*, then *P* ought to do *B*.

(Let *A* = accept-and-behave, *B* = accept.) The Possibilist, however, can affirm each of these five propositions.

Some Actualists explicitly recognize at least some of the commitments just noted and boldly embrace them.[6] I suspect that they are blustering; I cannot believe that they are really at ease with these commitments. Still, nor can I pretend that the Possibilist's victory is assured by these brief observations. For, although all five of the propositions surely strike a strong intuitive chord, each can be challenged independently of any commitment to Actualism. One challenge is that which the Good Samaritan Paradox

---

[4] What follows draws from Zimmerman 1996, sect. 6.2.
[5] Note that (3.1) does *not* say that, if *P* ought to do both *A* and *B*, then *P* ought to do *A* alone even if he doesn't do *B*.
[6] See, e.g., Jackson and Pargetter 1986; Goble 1993.

poses to (3.5).[7] Another challenge is that which proponents of the possibility of moral dilemmas pose to (3.4).[8] Their thesis is often put as follows: it is possible both that *P* ought to do *A* and that *P* ought to do *B*, even though *P* cannot do both *A* and *B*. This, of course, directly contradicts (3.4). But this superficial agreement between Actualists and proponents of dilemmas masks a deeper disagreement. Proponents of dilemmas often go beyond simply rejecting (3.4) to say that a genuine dilemma involves the inevitability of overall wrongdoing: no matter what the agent does, he cannot help but do overall wrong. This is something that the Actualist *denies*; for notice that, according to him, Alf would avoid doing any wrong at all if he were both to accept the invitation and to behave himself. On this point, I take it that the Actualist has the upper hand; the thesis that overall wrongdoing may be inevitable is false,[9] and it is therefore a mistake to reject (3.4) on this basis. But there is another thesis to which the Actualist is committed, one that underlies his rejection of (3.4) and which seems more objectionable still, namely: it can happen that one ought to do something, even though doing it will involve wrongdoing, and even though one can avoid doing any wrong at all. (According to the Actualist, Alf ought to decline the invitation, even though this involves wrongly failing to accept-and-behave, and even though he can accept-and-behave and thereby do no wrong at all.) This sanctioning of wrongdoing is deeply problematic.

I have to confess, however, that I too believe that not all of the propositions are acceptable as they stand. Although (3.2)-(3.4) seem to me beyond reproach, I think that (3.1) and (3.5) require modest modification, as follows:[10]

(3.1′) If *P* ought to do both *A* and *B*, and *P* can refrain from doing *A*, then *P* ought to do *A*;

(3.5′) If *P* ought to do *A* and cannot do *A* without doing *B*, and *P* can refrain from doing *B*, then *P* ought to do *B*.

---

[7] See Åqvist 1967 for an early discussion. This and related paradoxes are also discussed in Fred Feldman 1987, 1988, 1990, and Zimmerman 1996, pp. 72 ff. and 122 ff. See also n. 10 below.

[8] See, e.g., Lemmon 1962, Williams 1973, van Fraassen 1973, and Marcus 1980.

[9] This is put somewhat too boldly. For the needed qualifications, see Zimmerman 1996, ch. 7.

[10] The reason is that I take "ought" to imply not only "can" but "can refrain." I will discuss this issue further in section 3.5. For reasons given in Zimmerman 1996, pp. 72–4, I believe that (3.5′) is *not* vulnerable to the Good Samaritan Paradox.

Actualists must deny (3.1′) and (3.5′), too, but they can endorse their own qualified versions of the original propositions. For example, they can accept

(3.1″) If P ought to do both A and B and also does both A and B, then P ought to do A;[11]

(3.5″) If P ought to do A and cannot do A without doing B, then P ought to do both A and B.[12]

But such modifications are not as minor as the ones I endorse and so take us further away from the original intuitions.

You might think that the Actualist could evade these contentious commitments simply by insisting that we restrict "ought" to acts that are immediately performable. Whereas it makes sense to ask whether Alf now ought to accept or decline the invitation, it doesn't make sense (you may say) to ask whether he now ought to behave or misbehave at the wedding; that question can only arise when the opportunity for misbehavior is imminent. And if it doesn't make sense to say that he now ought to behave, it doesn't make sense to say that he now ought to accept-and-behave.

This would be a mistake, for two reasons. First, it just does make sense to say that someone now ought to do something later. Consider any compound act whose parts occur sequentially – Dave's opening a door, for instance, by first unlocking it and then turning the knob. It surely makes sense to ask whether Dave now ought to open the door. If the answer is "Yes," then it follows that he now ought to unlock the door and he now ought to turn the knob.[13] You may resist this. You may say that all that follows is that he now ought to unlock the door and that, once having done so, he *then* ought to turn the knob. Not so. If he fails to fulfill his obligation to unlock the door, it may well be that he will *not* have (any longer) an obligation to turn the knob; what would be the use? This will not alter the fact that he *did* have an obligation to open the door (and, hence, to turn the knob).

I will discuss such shifts in obligation in section 3.6 below. For the present, though, there's no need to pursue the matter because – and this is my second point – compound acts can have parts that occur simultaneously,

---

[11] See Jackson and Pargetter 1986, p. 248.
[12] See Goble 1993, p. 144.
[13] This follows, at least, if he cannot open the door without doing these things (and he can refrain from doing them). See (3.1′) and (3.5′).

Living with Uncertainty

and certain such acts give rise to the same sort of challenge to Actualism as Case 11 poses. Consider this case:

Case 12:
Jill is operating on John. She has a choice between two procedures. Procedure A would be the better of the two, as long as she performed it with care; if she were to perform it carelessly, failing to pay attention to what she was doing, John's condition would deteriorate. Procedure B, however, is something she can do with her eyes closed; if she were to perform it, John's condition would improve somewhat. Jill has an unfortunate penchant for letting her mind wander during surgery, and the fact is that, were she to perform procedure A, she would not pay sufficient attention to what she was doing, although this is something that she could manage quite easily.

Ought Jill to perform procedure A? The Possibilist says "Yes," the Actualist "No," even though the latter agrees with the former that she ought to perform A carefully. This leads the Actualist once again to the denial of (3.1)–(3.5).

The idea that our moral obligations should be tailored to our easily avoidable moral failings is repugnant. That is why I deem the Possibilist's verdicts in Cases 11 and 12 – that Alf ought to accept the invitation, and that Jill ought to perform procedure A – to be correct. (More cautiously: I take them to be correct, given that the agents' evidence is accurate, so that there is no mismatch between actual and prospective values. Notice that these verdicts are perfectly consistent with the claims that Alf ought to decline the invitation *if* he is going to misbehave, and that Jill ought to perform procedure B *if* she is going to operate carelessly. I think these claims are also correct, but they concern matters of *conditional* obligation, which is not the issue here. It is an issue to which I will return in section 3.4.) But although Possibilism yields the correct verdicts in these cases, it appears to founder in other cases. Here is one of a type that is often discussed:[14]

Case 13:
To be cured, John requires two doses of some drug. One dose of drug A today and another dose of A tomorrow will completely cure him; one dose of drug B today and another dose of B tomorrow will partially cure him; any other form of treatment will kill him. Jill knows this. Her (and John's) problem is that, whereas the first dose of each of A and B is readily available, as is the second dose of B, the second dose of A is locked inside a safe whose combination nobody knows. There are a million possible combinations. Jill can easily turn the dial in any of the million

---

[14] Cf. Feldman 1986, pp. 52 ff.; Goble 1993, pp. 140 ff.; Goble 1996, pp. 325 f.; Zimmerman 1996, pp. 124 f.

relevant ways, but it would of course be a miracle if she were to hit upon the correct combination, and miracles do not happen. The fact is, were she to try to open the safe, she would fail.

What ought Jill to do today: give John a dose of A, a dose of B, or neither? The answer seems plain: she ought to give him a dose of B. But this is the Actualist's answer, not (apparently) the Possibilist's. Strictly, Jill can open the safe, precisely because she can turn the dial in any way she wants, including the way that corresponds to the combination. The best that she could do thus appears to involve her giving John a double dose of A. For this reason, the Possibilist seems committed to saying that she ought to give him the first dose of A.

Although the Actualist appears to give the right answer in this case to the question about what Jill ought to do today, the basis for his answer of course remains flawed. Notice that he is committed to saying, not only that Jill ought to give John a dose of B today, but also that she ought to give him a dose of A today and another dose of A tomorrow. This is surely unacceptable, and we see once again that the Actualist is committed to denying each of (3.1)–(3.5). Moreover, as before, these commitments cannot be evaded by insisting that we restrict "ought" to acts that are immediately performable, since a case can be given that has the same implications for Actualism as those of Case 13 but in which the relevant features are simultaneous. Consider the following:

Case 14:
To be cured completely, John requires a single dose of A injected in *exactly* the right spot; if injected elsewhere, such a dose will prove fatal. The trouble is that, although Jill knows this, she doesn't know just where the relevant spot is. She's pretty sure that it lies somewhere in the general region of the *gluteus maximus*, but beyond that she hasn't a clue. An alternative treatment would be to inject a single dose of B anywhere within that same region. This will provide only a partial cure, however. Although Jill can, strictly, inject A in the right spot, it would be a miracle if she succeeded in doing so, and miracles do not happen. The fact is, were she to inject A, she would not inject it in the right spot.

Actualism implies that Jill ought to inject B, not A, which is fine. But it also implies that she ought to inject A in the right spot, which is not so fine.

It seems, therefore, that neither Actualism nor Possibilism is acceptable. What are we to do?[15]

---

[15] Some philosophers would answer this question by urging that we steer a middle course between Actualism and Possibilism. See, for example, Carlson 1995, ch. 7, Vorobej 2000, and Bykvist 2002. In what follows, I will not heed this advice, since doing so requires giving up many of the attractions of Possibilism noted above and discussed further below.

3.2 A HOLISTIC APPROACH

Part of my answer to the question just raised is of course that we must pay attention to the matter of risk, a matter not explicitly mentioned in any of the cases given in the last section but one that clearly lurks in the background. After all, it would seem more plausible to say, not that Alf definitely *would* misbehave if he accepted the invitation, or that Jill definitely *would* operate carelessly if she performed procedure A, or that she definitely *would* fail to open the safe if she tried, or that she definitely *would* hit the wrong spot if she injected drug A, but rather that, given their ignorance, these agents would run an unacceptable *risk* of doing these things. It was precisely in order to accommodate the moral significance of ignorance that I urged rejection of the Objective View in favor of the Prospective View, whose final formulation in chapter 1 was this:

The Prospective View (sixth formulation):
An agent ought to perform an act if and only if it is the prospectively best option that he has.

(Remember that, in this formulation, "prospectively best" is to be understood in terms of the maximization of expectable value for the agent, at his definitive level of evidence, adjusted in whatever way is necessary for the various considerations raised in section 1.6 to be adequately accommodated.) But simply switching from the Objective View to this formulation of the Prospective View does *not* by itself do anything to resolve the issues raised in the last section, because *this formulation simply constitutes a "probabilized" version of Actualism*, inheriting all the defects of the original, unqualified version given in the last section. (This point also applies to the more elaborate seventh formulation of the Prospective View provided in the last chapter.) Suppose, as seems plausible, that in Case 13 it is only highly probable, and not certain, that Jill would fail to open the safe if she tried; the prospective value of her giving John a dose of drug A today is therefore very low (given that, aside from her ignorance of the correct combination of the safe, her evidence is otherwise adequate), whereas the prospective value of her giving him both a dose of A today and another dose of A tomorrow of course remains very high. Or suppose that in Case 14 it is only highly probable that Jill would inject A in the wrong spot, if she injected it at all; the prospective value of her injecting it is therefore very low, whereas the prospective value of her injecting it in the right spot remains very high. The present formulation of the Prospective View thus denies each of (3.1)–(3.5) and constitutes no improvement over unqualified Actualism.[16]

The problem that besets Actualism is structural. It is its piecemeal approach to the moral evaluation of acts that accounts for its incompatibility with (3.1)–(3.5). Consider again

(3.1) If P ought to do both A and B, then P ought to do A.

Clearly, what would (actually or probably) happen if P did both A and B could be marvelous even though what would (actually or probably) happen if P did A was awful, which is precisely why Actualism (whether unqualified or "probabilized") is inconsistent with (3.1). Similar remarks apply to (3.2)-(3.5). The remedy is to eschew *independent* evaluations of both A and B on the one hand and of A on the other; the proper approach to overall moral obligation, that is, is to understand it *holistically*. (This lesson holds in general, whether you are an Objectivist, a Subjectivist, or a Prospectivist. Of course, my purpose in this chapter is to apply the lesson in my development of the Prospective View.) Whenever an agent has a choice between options, that choice concerns not only actions that are immediately performable but also actions that lie some distance in the future. (At the time that he responds to the invitation, Alf's options of behaving and misbehaving at the wedding are not immediately performable. At the time that Jill gives John the first dose of whatever drug she gives him, the option of giving him the second dose – at the proper time – is not immediately performable. And so on.) Agents' choices thus always concern whole *courses* of action that include, as parts, some actions that are immediately performable (in the sense that they can be immediately initiated, at least, even if not immediately completed) but also many that are not immediately performable. In saying that the latter are not immediately performable, I mean that the agent cannot *now* initiate them *now*; in so far as they are options that the agent has, the agent *can* now initiate – and complete – them *later*. There are thus two time indices implicitly at work, and we would do well to note them explicitly. We should, that is, distinguish

---

[16] See Goble 1996 for a discussion and endorsement of a similar proposal, including once again a bold embracing of the commitments that I am rejecting.

between claims of the form "*P* can at *T* do *A* at *T*," which concern actions that are immediately performable, and claims of the form "*P* can at *T* do *A* at *T**," which (given that *T** is distinct from, and thus later than, *T*) concern actions that are not immediately but only remotely performable. (So, for example, we can say that Alf can now accept the invitation now and that, although he cannot now behave himself at the wedding now, he can now behave himself there later, in that there is a course of action upon which he can now embark and which includes his behaving himself at the wedding later.) Moreover, just as the sort of personal control expressed by "can" may be either immediate or remote, so too may moral obligation be either immediate or remote. Thus we should distinguish between claims of the form "*P* ought at *T* to do *A* at *T*," which express immediate obligation, and claims of the form "*P* ought at *T* to do *A* at *T**," which (given that *T** is distinct from, and thus later than, *T*) express remote obligation.

Let us say that a course of action, *C*, that is performable by an agent is a *maximal* course of action just in case no other course of action that is performable by the agent includes *C*.[17] The idea underlying the holistic approach that I wish to propose is this: an agent ought to perform an act if and only if every maximal course of action performable by the agent that does *not* include the act is inferior (in respect of what is relevant to the determination of overall moral obligation) to some maximal course of action performable by the agent that *does* include the act.[18] Applied to the Prospective View, this approach yields the following formulation (initially – there are further refinements still to come):

The Prospective View (eighth formulation):
An agent, *P*, ought at some time, *T*, to do some act, *A*, at some time, *T** (which may or may not be later than *T*), if and only if
(1) *P* can at *T* do *A* at *T**,
(2) *P* can at *T* refrain from doing *A* at *T**, and
(3) for every maximal course of action, *C*, that *P* can at *T* perform and which excludes *P*'s doing *A* at *T**, there is some maximal course of action, *C**, such that

---

[17] Cf. Goldman 1978, p. 201, on "maximal sequences of acts."
[18] See Goldman 1978, Feldman 1986, ch. 2, and Zimmerman 1996, ch. 2, for examples of this approach.

(a) *P* can at *T* perform *C**,
(b) *C** includes *P*'s doing *A* at *T**, and
(c) *C** is prospectively better, for *P* at *T*, than *C*.[19]

When understood in such terms, the Prospective View constitutes a "probabilized" version of Possibilism, not Actualism, and so avoids the

---

[19] Several points should be noted.

(a) To say that *P* can at *T* perform a course of action, *C*, is of course not to say that *P* can at *T* complete *C* at *T* but only that *P* can at *T* embark on *C* at *T*. It is to say, more precisely, that any act that *C* includes is such that, for some time *T**, *P* can at *T* perform that act at *T**.

(b) I am presupposing that acts are to be individuated finely, so that (for example) Jill's injecting a dose of drug A into John's backside is distinct from her curing John, and similarly her attempt to inject the drug is distinct from her attempt to cure him. If this presupposition is false, then the account of obligation that I give in this chapter would have to be qualified in order to allow for the possibility that acts be obligatory (or right, or wrong) under one description but not under another. Cf. section 2.3 above.

(c) This account of unconditional overall obligation says (roughly) the following: (i) every (not-*A*)-course is prospectively worse than some *A*-course. It doesn't say: (ii) some *A*-course is prospectively better than every (not-*A*)-course. Claim (ii) presupposes the comparability, in terms of prospective value, of all performable maximal courses of action; claim (i) does not. (Cf. Zimmerman 1996, pp. 58–9.) This is an issue that need not concern us further here.

(d) On pp. 26–7 of Zimmerman 1996, the account of obligation that I offered was put in terms of accessible possible worlds rather than performable maximal courses of action. Thus, instead of "*P* can at *T* do *A* at *T**" I wrote in terms of "there is a world accessible to *P* at *T* in which *P* does *A* at *T**." I take these two expressions to be equivalent. In this work I use "can" rather than "accessible," since the former is simpler and more common. In the earlier work I used "accessible" rather than "can," because I wanted to accommodate the fact that, strictly, it is not only actions that can be obligatory. (Cf. Zimmerman 1996, pp. 40–1.) This, too, is an issue that need not concern us further here.

(e) The present formulation of the Prospective View also overlooks another issue that need not concern us here: the possibility that *P* be confronted with an infinite number of performable maximal courses of action. (Cf. Zimmerman 1996, pp. 60–1.)

(f) The account of obligation that I gave in my earlier book was couched in terms of "deontic value" rather than "prospective value." The former term was simply a place-holder for whatever should in the end be said to be that in terms of which the obligatory and the non-obligatory are to be distinguished. The account was thus intended to be compatible with any substantive theory of obligation, whether that of the act-consequentialist, the rule-consequentialist, the virtue-theorist, and so on; and it was intended to accommodate any version of any such theory, whether that of actual-value maximization, that of expected-value maximization, and so on. (On pp. 27 ff. of Zimmerman 1996, I explained how it is that any version of any theory of obligation can in principle be cast in maximizing terms.) "Prospective value" is of course more restrictive. As I have repeatedly said, it is intended to be compatible with any substantive theory of obligation, but of course it is not intended to accommodate every version of such a theory; on the contrary, it selects a unique version – unique, that is, once whatever adjustments, of the sort discussed in section 1.6, that need to be made have been made.

problematic commitments of the latter. (But what, then, of the problems with Possibilism noted in the last section? Unlike Actualism, Possibilism's problems are not structural in nature and do not therefore transfer to all qualified versions of it. I will argue that the version I eventually develop avoids the problems noted earlier.)

The stipulation that moral obligation turns on the relative prospective values of *maximal* courses of action, and not also on any parts of such courses, avoids the kind of vacillation in values that stems from the piecemeal approach of the Actualist and forces him to deny each of the five propositions discussed in the last section. (Another way to put this point: on the present holistic approach, it is only maximal courses of action that count as the agent's "alternatives." Individual acts, or less-than-maximal courses of action, do not also count as alternatives that compete with maximal courses when it comes to determining what an agent ought to do.) To see this, consider again

(3.1′) If P ought to do both A and B, and P can refrain from doing A, then P ought to do A.

(For present purposes, there's no need to render the time indices explicitly.) Given its current formulation, the Prospective View implies that (3.1′) is true. If P ought to do both A and B, then any maximal course of action, C, that excludes P's doing both A and B will be prospectively worse than some maximal course of action, $C*$, that includes his doing both A and B. Since any course of action that excludes P's doing A excludes his doing both A and B and any course of action that includes his doing both A and B includes his doing A, it follows that any maximal course of action that excludes his doing A is prospectively worse than some maximal course of action that includes his doing A. Given that there is a maximal course of action that excludes his doing A, it therefore follows, on the Prospective View, that P ought to do A.

Consider now

(3.2) If P ought to do both A and B, then it is not the case that P ought not to do A.

As just noted, if P ought to do both A and B then, on the present view, any maximal course of action that excludes his doing A is prospectively worse than some maximal course of action that includes his doing A. It is therefore not the case that any maximal course of action that includes his doing A (and thus excludes his not doing A) is prospectively worse than some maximal course of action that excludes his doing A (and thus includes his not doing A). Hence it is not the case that P ought not to do A.

Consider next

(3.3) If P both ought to do A and ought to do B, then P ought to do both A and B.

Suppose that any maximal course of action, C, that excludes P's doing A is prospectively worse than some maximal course of action, $C*$, that includes his doing A. $C*$ must either include or exclude P's doing both A and B. If the latter, then $C*$ excludes P's doing B. In such a case, given that any maximal course of action that excludes P's doing B is prospectively worse than some maximal course of action, $C**$, that includes his doing B, it follows that $C*$ is prospectively worse than $C**$, which must include his doing both A and B. The prospectively best maximal courses of action will thus include P's doing both A and B.

Consider next

(3.4) If P both ought to do A and ought to do B, then P can do both A and B.

Given (3.3), if P both ought to do A and ought to do B, then P ought to do both A and B. Since, according to clause (1) of the present formulation of the Prospective View, whatever an agent ought to do he can do, it follows that P can do both A and B.

Consider finally

(3.5′) If P ought to do A and cannot do A without doing B, and P can refrain from doing B, then P ought to do B.

If P ought to do A, then, on the present view, the prospectively best maximal courses of action include his doing A. If P cannot do A without doing B, then these courses of action must include his doing B as well. Given that some maximal course of action excludes P's doing B, it follows that P ought to do B. (Recall from section 1.6 the following two principles:

The First Inheritance Principle (IP1):
If P ought not to do A, then if it is the case that if P does B, he will thereby do A, then P ought not to do B.

The Second Inheritance Principle (IP2):
If P ought not to do A, then if P cannot avoid its being the case that if he does B, he will thereby do A, then P ought not to do B.

I said there that IP1 was false but that IP2 was a rough version of something true. I can now explain. As for IP2: it is equivalent to (3.5), which is itself a rough version of (3.5′). As for IP1: what matters is not simply whether *P will* do *A*, if he does *B*, but whether he *must*. Consider Alf: the fact that he ought not to misbehave but *will* do so, if he accepts the invitation to Brenda's wedding, does not imply that he ought not to accept the invitation, precisely because he could both accept the invitation and behave himself.)

The present formulation of the Prospective View is, therefore, markedly superior to its previous formulations, confirming as it does the five propositions just discussed. Unfortunately, it still faces problems. Consider Case 13 again. In this case, the Actualist is committed to saying both that Jill ought to give John a dose of B today and that she ought to give him a dose of A today and another dose of A tomorrow. This is surely unacceptable, and on its present formulation the Prospective View implies no such conflict in prescriptions. The trouble is that it resolves the conflict by declaring that Jill ought not to give John a dose of B today because she ought instead to give him a dose of A today (and another dose of A tomorrow). This gets things precisely the wrong way around. Surely, given the very high risk of death associated with giving John a dose of A today, what Jill ought to do is give him a dose of B today; hence it is not the case that she ought to give him a dose of A today, and hence not the case that she ought both to give him a dose of A today and to give him another dose of A tomorrow.

3.3 INTENTIONAL ACTION

Let's take a closer look at Case 13. I have said that, in this case, Jill can open the safe and then completely cure John, even though she would fail to do this if she tried. (A similar point was made regarding Case 14.) Some would declare this statement incoherent, claiming that a necessary condition of its being the case that one can (in the relevant sense) do something is that one would do it if one tried.[20] This charge is too strong, for there surely is a pertinent, personal sense of "can" in which Jill can open the safe (and then completely cure John); all she has to do is turn the dial in the requisite way, and clearly she can do that. However, it seems equally clear that there is a pertinent sense in which she cannot open the safe: she doesn't *know how* precisely to open it. I think what this indicates is that, although she *can* (in some "simple" sense) open the safe, her circumstances are such that she

---

[20] Something like this is suggested in Moore 1912, ch. 5, and in Nowell Smith 1960.

cannot *intentionally* do so.[21] And this is important. It is plausible to say that what one ought to do turns crucially not simply on what one can do but on what one can intentionally do. How could Jill be morally obligated to open a safe whose combination she doesn't know and cannot discover (except by accident)?

One way to accommodate the observation just made would be to say that it is only ever intentional actions that can be morally obligatory (or right, or wrong).[22] If this were correct, we could confine our attention to courses of action whose only parts are intentional actions and give an account of obligation in terms of the relative prospective values of such courses of action. But I don't think this would be quite the right move. In general, doing something intentionally typically requires doing many things unintentionally, and it seems perfectly appropriate to evaluate such unintentional side-effects of intentional actions in moral terms. Suppose, for example, that Dave's unlocking the door consists in his causing certain

---

[21] Cf. the works cited in n. 47 to chapter 1. I confess that the precise relation between what one can intentionally do and what one knows how to do is unclear to me, for several reasons.

First, it is not in general the case that, if one knows how to do something, then one can intentionally do it. I may know how to ride a bike, for example, even though there is no bike available for me to ride. (Cf. Stanley and Williamson 2001, p. 416; Snowdon 2003, pp. 8–9.) Perhaps it is true, though, that if one knows how to do something *and* can (simply) do it, then one can intentionally do it. I suspect, though, that, if this is true, it is true only for some kinds of "know-how." A teacher, for example, may know "in principle" how to do something and yet lack the necessary skill to do it intentionally. (Here the distinction between "savoir faire" and "savoir comment faire," noted in Rumfitt 2003, seems pertinent.)

Second, the converse thesis – viz., that if one can intentionally do something, then one can (simply) do it and knows how to do it – is problematic. Certainly, "can intentionally" implies "can (simply)," but whether "know-how" is also required is debatable. One reason to doubt the implication is that (i) basic actions (understood as actions that one can intentionally perform, without doing so by way of performing other actions) perhaps should not be said to be actions that one knows how to perform. Perhaps it is incorrect to say that I "know how" to raise my arm, for example, if there is no means by which I raise it. (Cf. Snowdon 2003, p. 12.)

Another reason to doubt the implication in question is that (ii) it may be the case that one can intentionally do something without *knowing* how to do it, as long as one satisfies some sufficiently robust epistemic condition with respect to it. Should we say, for example, that an amateur golfer *knows* how to sink a long and difficult putt? That may be an exaggeration. Yet, if he sinks it, it seems that he may well have done so intentionally.

I therefore leave open the precise connection between "can intentionally" and "know-how." I also leave open the question whether "know-how" is reducible to knowledge-that. (On this last matter, see the articles by Stanley and Williamson, Snowdon, and Rumfitt mentioned above.)

[22] Cf. Lemos 1980 and Howard-Snyder 1997 and 2005 for related proposals.

mechanisms internal to the lock – mechanisms about which he is wholly oblivious – to change position. It seems plausible to say that, if he ought to (or may, or ought not to) open the door, then he ought to (or may, or ought not to) cause these mechanisms to change position, and if he ought to (or may, or ought not to) refrain from opening the door, then he ought to (or may, or ought not to) refrain from causing them to change position. Yet his causing them to change position would be an unintentional action, as would his refraining from doing so.[23] I think, therefore, that we must try to accommodate the observation in a different way.

One suggestion is this. We could say that the "core" of a course of action consists of all and only those parts of it that constitute intentional actions and then claim that it is such cores, and only such cores, whose prospective values are relevant to determining an agent's obligations; any unintentional actions included in a course of action can be morally obligatory (or right, or wrong), but they will not be relevant to determining what it is that an agent ought to do. This proposal would give us the answer we're looking for in Case 13; for although Jill can intentionally give John a dose of A today, she cannot intentionally open the safe and hence cannot intentionally give him a dose of A tomorrow.

But I'm afraid that this still won't quite do. Consider a variation on Case 13 in which, it seems, Jill *can* intentionally open the safe and give John a dose of A tomorrow, but where the probability of her succeeding in doing so if she tried is still prohibitively low. Suppose, for example, that the safe that contains the second dose of A is not protected by a combination lock. Instead, to open it, Jill need "only" sink a long and difficult putt; once the ball drops in the hole, the safe will open. Even if Jill has the skill of Tiger Woods, it would seem unacceptably risky for her to attempt the putt; yet she can (simply) sink it and, if she were to do so, it seems that she would have done so intentionally.[24]

The solution is straightforward. We should, as the illustration suggests, focus on *attempts* in particular, rather than intentional actions in general; it is

---

[23] Some writers use the term "action" to refer only to "positive doings" and not also to "negative doings" such as refrainings. (See, e.g., Davis 1979, p. 82.) Throughout this work I am using the term to refer to both kinds of behavior. Some writers use "refrain" to refer to intentional omissions only and not also to unintentional ones. (See, e.g., Brand 1971, p. 49; Moore 1979, p. 420.) Throughout this work I am using the term more broadly to refer to omissions generally.

[24] On this point, see n. 21 above.

on the attempts that one can make that one's obligations directly turn.[25] I assume that, whenever one acts, one makes an attempt to do something, and that, whenever one makes an attempt, one makes it intentionally. Attempts are thus themselves to be understood as intentional actions, in a minimal sense of "action." They consist of decisions or choices to perform actions in a fuller sense.[26] And I propose that we revise our definition of the "core" of a course of action so that a core is said to consist in all and only those parts of it that constitute attempts that the agent can (intentionally) make. On this basis, I propose that we reformulate the Prospective View one last time (the change from the last formulation is contained entirely in the final subclause):

The Prospective View (final formulation: unconditional overall obligation):
P ought at *T* to do *A* at *T** if and only if
(1) *P* can at *T* do *A* at *T**,
(2) *P* can at *T* refrain from doing *A* at *T**, and
(3) for every maximal course of action, *C*, that *P* can at *T* perform and which excludes *P*'s doing *A* at *T**, there is some maximal course of action, *C**, such that
  (a) *P* can at *T* perform *C**,
  (b) *C** includes *P*'s doing *A* at *T**, and
  (c) *C**'s core is prospectively better, for *P* at *T*, than *C*'s.

This proposal gives us the answer we're looking for, not just in the original version of Case 13, but also in its modified version. It is precisely because her attempt to open the safe (whether by way of hitting upon the correct combination or by way of sinking the putt) is so unlikely to afford Jill the opportunity to give John a second dose of A that she ought not to

---

[25] So saying is reminiscent of Ross's Attempt Thesis, discussed in section 1.2 above, according to which one is never obligated to bring something about but is only ever obligated to set or exert oneself – that is, to attempt – to bring something about. (See Ross 1939, p. 154.) However, there are two major differences between Ross and me on this matter. First, unlike Ross, I am concerned not with what the agent believes concerning the suitability of making an attempt but with the prospective value of the attempt. Second, I do not deny that things other than attempts can be obligatory, even if what one is obligated to do turns directly on the attempts that one can make.

[26] Thus I assume that all action involves intentional action; no one can act unintentionally without acting intentionally. (This is a version of the common claim that all action is intentional under some description. Cf., e.g., Davidson 1980, pp. 46, 50.) Note that I am not claiming that, whatever one does, one makes an attempt to do, precisely because some actions are unintentional. Nor am I saying that, whenever one acts, one makes an effort; for, although some attempts require effort, others do not. On the nature of attempts, see O'Shaughnessy 1973; McCann 1975; Hornsby 1980, ch. 3; Corrado 1983; Ludwig 1992.

make the attempt. Rather, what she ought today to do is to attempt to give him a dose of B today and then attempt to give him another dose of B tomorrow; no maximal course of action upon which Jill can today embark and which excludes her making these attempts is one whose core is prospectively as good as all those whose core includes her making them. Hence the current formulation of the Prospective View implies that she ought indeed to make the attempts. Furthermore, on the plausible supposition that, under the circumstances, Jill would succeed in giving John both doses of B if and only if she made the relevant attempts, the current formulation of the Prospective View implies that she ought indeed to give him both doses.

Not only does the present formulation of the Prospective View give the right answer in Case 13, it gives the right answer in the other cases that have just been presented. Case 14 is like Case 13: although Jill can inject a dose of A in exactly the right spot, any attempt to do so would be far too risky. As for Case 11: the expected value of Alf's making a sincere attempt to behave himself at the wedding is higher than that of his not doing so. Given that all else is being held equal (remember that this is implicit in the presentation of all such cases;[27] in the present context, this proviso implies, among other things, that prospective value coincides with expected value), it follows that there is a maximal course of action whose core includes his making the attempt, the prospective value of which is greater than that of the core of any maximal course of action whose core excludes the attempt. Hence the present formulation of the Prospective View implies that he ought to make the attempt; furthermore, given that his circumstances are such that he would succeed in behaving himself if and only if he made the attempt to do so, the Prospective View implies that he ought indeed to behave himself.

Of course, Alf's situation could have been different. We can imagine, on another version of the case, that he finds it very difficult to control himself whenever he sees Brenda and Charles together. It's not that he simply yields to a temptation that he could easily resist, but rather that he feels a deep and urgent need to make a scene, resistance to which calls for monumental self-control. In such a case, it is very likely that any attempt to behave himself, however sincere, will fail, so that the expected value of such an attempt will be relatively low. Under these circumstances, the Prospective View on its current formulation does not imply that Alf ought

---

[27] See n. 8 to chapter 1.

to accept the invitation and behave himself. On the contrary, it implies that he ought to decline the invitation, for the good of all concerned.

Case 12 is to be treated in similar fashion: under the circumstances, a sincere attempt on Jill's part to perform procedure A with care is likely to succeed, and so this is what the Prospective View on its current formulation says she ought to do. Were it the case that Jill found it extremely difficult to concentrate with the intensity needed to perform procedure A successfully, the verdict would of course be different.

The current formulation of the Prospective View also yields the correct answer in other cases that we have discussed. Recall this case from chapter 1, in which it is presupposed that drug A would in fact completely cure John, drug B would relieve his condition but not cure him completely, drug C would kill him, and giving John no drug at all would leave him permanently incurable:

Case 2:
All the evidence at Jill's disposal indicates (in keeping with the facts) that giving John drug B would cure him partially and giving him no drug would render him permanently incurable, but it also indicates (in contrast to the facts) that giving him drug C would cure him completely and giving him drug A would kill him.

I said in section 1.4 that the Prospective View implies that Jill ought to give John drug C. I noted in section 1.6 that, given IP2, this implies that Jill ought to kill John, but that it doesn't imply that she ought to kill him intentionally. We can now see how and why this is so. Jill's giving John drug C would be an intentional action, the attempt to perform which has a higher expected value than that of any alternative attempt. With all else being held equal, it follows that there is a maximal course of action, $C*$, whose core includes Jill's attempting to give John drug C, the prospective value of which is greater than that of the core of any maximal course of action that does not include her making this attempt. Hence the Prospective View implies that she ought to (attempt to) give him the drug. She cannot do this without killing him, and so her killing him is also part of $C*$, and thus the Prospective View also implies that she ought to kill him. But it doesn't imply that she ought to kill him intentionally. In attempting to give John drug C, Jill would not be attempting to kill him. Presumably she could attempt this, and so her doing so is part of the core of some maximal course of action performable by her. But this core does not include either her attempting to give John drug C or her giving him the drug, and so it is prospectively worse than the core of $C*$; thus the

137

Prospective View, far from implying that Jill ought to kill John intentionally, implies that she ought *not* to do so.[28]

Or consider this case from chapter 2:

Case 8:
I have a choice between three delivery services, A, B, and C. I know that B will deliver the book in pretty good condition. I also know that either A or C will deliver it in somewhat better condition, and that either A or C will deliver it mangled, but I have no idea which will provide the good service and which the bad (although it is in fact A that would provide the superior service).

When I first presented this case, I said that the Prospective View implies that I ought to use service B, since doing so provides me with the best prospect of keeping my promise to return the book to you in as good condition as possible. But I also noted that it might be objected that keeping my promise provides me with an even better prospect of keeping my promise, and that the Prospective View therefore implies that I ought to use service A, not B, since it is A that would actually afford me the means of returning the book to you in as good condition as possible. My response was to note that one's obligations turn on the intentional actions that one can perform and thus that, since I cannot intentionally keep my promise, I am not obligated, directly or indirectly, to do so.[29] At that point, I didn't elaborate on this response, but I am now in a position to do so. Given that my obligations turn on that subset of intentional actions that I can perform that consists in the attempts that I can make, and given that any attempt strictly to keep my promise must involve my attempting either to use service A or to use service C, whose expected value is low relative to that of an attempt to use service B, it is clear that (holding all else equal) the Prospective View on its current formulation preserves the verdict that I ought to (attempt to) use service B.

3.4 EXTENSION OF THE ACCOUNT

The most recent formulation of the Prospective View is limited, in that it concerns only unconditional overall moral obligation. It can be straightforwardly extended in a number of ways.

---

[28] Cf. Howard-Snyder 2005, pp. 271–2, for a different but related treatment of such issues.
[29] See n. 36 to chapter 2.

A

First, there are the matters of unconditional overall moral rightness and wrongness. These may be understood as follows:

The Prospective View (final formulation: unconditional overall rightness):
P may at T do A at T^* if and only if
(1) P can at T do A at T^*,
(2) P can at T refrain from doing A at T^*, and
(3) for every maximal course of action, C, that P can at T perform and which excludes P's doing A at T^*, there is some maximal course of action, C^*, such that
  (a) P can at T perform C^*,
  (b) C^* includes P's doing A at T^*, and
  (c) C's core is prospectively no better, for P at T, than C^*'s.[30]

The Prospective View (final formulation: unconditional overall wrongness):
P ought at T not to do A at T^* if and only if
(1) P can at T do A at T^*,
(2) P can at T refrain from doing A at T^*, and
(3) for every maximal course of action, C, that P can at T perform and which includes P's doing A at T^*, there is some maximal course of action, C^*, such that
  (a) P can at T perform C^*,
  (b) C^* excludes P's doing A at T^*, and
  (c) C^*'s core is prospectively better, for P at T, than C's.[31]

In other, rougher words: whereas A is overall obligatory just in case every (not-A)-course's core is prospectively worse than some A-course's core, it is overall right just in case every (not-A)-course's core is prospectively no better than some A-course's core, and it is overall wrong just in case every A-course's core is prospectively worse than some (not-A)-course's core.

B

Next, there is the matter of conditional overall moral obligation. Before I give a formal account of such obligation, let me present an informal characterization of the contrast between it and unconditional obligation.

---

[30] Cf. Zimmerman 1996, p. 32. Cf. also n. 19 above.
[31] Cf. Zimmerman 1996, p. 33. Cf. also n. 19 above.

To say that P ought unconditionally to do A is to say (roughly) that every (not-A)-course's core is prospectively worse than some A-course's core. Similarly, to say that P ought to do A on the condition that p is true is to say (roughly) that every (p & not-A)-course's core is prospectively worse than some (p & A)-course's core. The underlying idea is that, when it comes to conditional obligation, comparison of performable courses of action is to be restricted to cases in which the condition in question obtains.

As an illustration, consider an example given in section 1.7. Suppose that Matt ought (that is, has an unconditional overall moral obligation) to attend a meeting on the first floor of his building; that he ought to attend a meeting on the second floor, if he fails to attend the meeting on the first floor; that he ought to attend a meeting on the third floor, if he fails to attend either of the first two meetings; etc. On the rough account of unconditional and conditional obligation just given, what this amounts to is the following (where "M1" refers to Matt's attending the meeting on the first floor, "M2" to his attending the meeting on the second floor, and "M3" to his attending the meeting on the third floor): every (not-M1)-course's core is prospectively worse than some M1-course's core; every (not-M1 & not-M2)-course's core is prospectively worse than some (not-M1 & M2)-course's core; every (not-M1 & not-M2 & not-M3)-course's core is prospectively worse than some (not-M1 & not-M2 & M3)-course's core; and so on. Or consider an example given earlier in this chapter: Dave ought to open the door by first unlocking it and then turning the knob, but it is not the case that he ought to turn the knob if he doesn't unlock the door. On the current account, what this amounts to is the following (where "U" refers to Dave's unlocking the door and "T" to his turning the knob): every not-(U & T)-course's core is prospectively worse than some (U & T)-course's core, but it is not the case than every (not-U & not-T)-course's core is prospectively worse than some (not-U & T)-course's core. Or consider, finally, Case 11, in which it seems correct to say, not only that Alf ought to attend the wedding, but also that he ought not to attend it if he's not going to behave himself. On the current account, what this amounts to is the following (where "A" refers to Alf's attending and "B" to his behaving himself): every (not-A)-course's core is prospectively worse than some A-course's core, but every (not-B & A)-course's core is prospectively worse than some (not-B & not-A)-course's core.[32]

---

[32] Remember that Alf's not behaving himself does not require his misbehaving himself. If he doesn't attend the wedding, then he will neither behave nor misbehave himself at the wedding.

The more exact, formal account of conditional obligation is this:

The Prospective View (final formulation: conditional overall obligation):
P ought at T to do A at $T*$, on the condition that p is true, if and only if
(1) P can at T do A at $T*$ while p is true,[33]
(2) P can at T refrain from doing A at $T*$ while p is true, and
(3) for every maximal course of action, C, that P can at T perform and which includes P's refraining from doing A at $T*$ while p is true, there is some maximal course of action, $C*$, such that
   (a) P can at T perform $C*$,
   (b) $C*$ includes P's doing A at $T*$ while p is true, and
   (c) $C*$'s core is prospectively better, for P at T, than C's.[34]

(Corresponding accounts of conditional overall moral rightness and wrongness can of course be given.)

Such an approach to conditional obligation is extremely fruitful; it makes intuitive sense of many statements of the form "P ought to do A, if…" and helps resolve many so-called deontic paradoxes. This is a matter that I have discussed in detail elsewhere, however,[35] and so I won't repeat myself here, except briefly to pursue an issue raised in section 1.7: that of subsidiary obligation. In connection with the example of the meetings, I said there that Matt has a primary unconditional obligation to attend the meeting on the first floor; that he has a secondary conditional obligation to attend the meeting on the second floor, if he fails to attend the meeting on the first floor; and so on. I added that, if he does indeed fail to attend the meeting on the first floor, this will trigger a secondary unconditional obligation to attend the meeting on the second floor. Such judgments presuppose that all maximal courses of action performable by Matt are comparable in terms of prospective value,[36] and also that at least one of these courses is such that no alternative course has a greater prospective value – that is, that at least one of these courses has a prospective value of "rank 1." Given this presupposition, we can say:[37]

The Prospective View (final formulation: unconditional primary overall obligation):
P ought[1] at T to do A at $T*$ if and only if

---

[33] Equivalently (cf. n. 19 above): there is a world accessible to P at T in which (i) P does A at $T*$ and (ii) p is true.
[34] Cf. Zimmerman 1996, p. 119.   [35] See Zimmerman 1996, ch. 4.
[36] This is not a presupposition of the account given so far. See n. 19 above.
[37] Cf. Zimmerman 1996, pp. 132–3.

(1) P can at T do A at $T*$,
(2) P can at T refrain from doing A at $T*$, and
(3) for every maximal course of action, C, that P can at T perform and which excludes P's doing A at $T*$, there is some maximal course of action, $C*$, such that
    (a) P can at T perform $C*$,
    (b) $C*$ includes P's doing A at $T*$,
    (c) $C*$'s core is prospectively better, for P at T, than C's, and
    (d) $C*$ has a prospective value of rank 1.

The Prospective View (final formulation: conditional subsidiary overall obligation):
P ought^n at T to do A at $T*$, on the condition that p is true, if and only if
(1) P can at T do A at $T*$ while p is true,
(2) P can at T refrain from doing A at $T*$ while p is true, and
(3) for every maximal course of action, C, that P can at T perform and which includes P's refraining from doing A at $T*$ while p is true, there is some maximal course of action, $C*$, such that
    (a) P can at T perform $C*$,
    (b) $C*$ includes P's doing A at $T*$ while p is true,
    (c) $C*$'s core is prospectively better, for P at T, than C's, and
    (d) $C*$ has a prospective value of rank n.

And, where n is greater than 1:

The Prospective View (final formulation: unconditional subsidiary overall obligation):
P ought^n at T to do A at $T*$ if and only if, for some proposition p,
(1) P ought^n at T to do A at $T*$, on the condition that p is true, and
(2) p is true.[38]

Corresponding accounts of subsidiary moral rightness and wrongness can of course be given. In this way, we can account for the compounding of wrong done by Matt if, for example, in addition to failing to attend the meeting on the first floor, he also fails to attend the meeting on the second floor.

C

Let me turn, next, to the matter of prima facie moral obligation.[39] In section 2.1, when I gave the seventh formulation of the Prospective View, I characterized an act as being overall obligatory just in case it provides the agent with a prospect of doing what suits his situation *as a whole* better than

---

[38] Cf. n. 98 to chapter 1.
[39] An account of such obligation was given in Zimmerman 1996, ch. 5. The following account is quite different and much simpler.

that provided by any other option that he has, and I characterized an act as being prima facie obligatory just in case it provides the agent with a prospect of doing what suits *some particular aspect* of his situation better than that provided by any other option that he has. As noted in section 3.2, though, as it stands, this characterization suffers from the fact that it constitutes a "probabilized" form of Actualism and thus has several unacceptable implications. The characterization must therefore be amended, so that it may be reconciled with the holistic approach to obligation that I have advocated in this chapter.

Such reconciliation is straightforward. I have proposed, roughly, that A is overall obligatory just in case every (not-A)-course's core is prospectively worse than some A-course's core. I take this to be equivalent to saying that A is overall obligatory just in case every (not-A)-course's core is prospectively less suited to the agent's situation as a whole than some A-course's core. The corresponding account of prima facie obligation is obvious: A is prima facie obligatory just in case every (not-A)-course's core is prospectively less suited to some particular aspect of the agent's situation than some A-course's core. Or more exactly:

The Prospective View (final formulation: unconditional prima facie obligation):
P prima facie ought at T to do A at $T*$ if and only if
(1) P can at T do A at $T*$,
(2) P can at T refrain from doing A at $T*$, and
(3) there is some aspect, S, of P's situation at T such that, for every maximal course of action, C, that P can at T perform and which excludes P's doing A at $T*$, there is some maximal course of action, $C*$, such that
  (a) P can at T perform $C*$,
  (b) $C*$ includes P's doing A at $T*$, and
  (c) $C*$'s core is prospectively more suited to S, for P at T, than C's.

(Corresponding accounts of conditional prima facie obligation, subsidiary prima facie obligation, and of both unconditional and conditional prima facie rightness and wrongness can also be given.) As it stands, this is an account of prima facie obligation in general, whether associative or otherwise. As I noted in section 2.2, an associative obligation is one that is owed to someone in particular. It's not clear to me precisely what condition an obligation must satisfy in order to be associative; that is, it's not clear to me precisely what makes it the case that P not only has an obligation to do A but also[40] has an obligation to Q to do A. However, given the Correlativity

---

[40] Cf. n. 11 to chapter 2.

Thesis concerning rights and obligations (regarding which see section 2.2), we can at least say this: Q has a right at T against P that P do A at $T*$ only if each of clauses (1)-(3) of the account of unconditional prima facie obligation just given is satisfied. This point echoes one of the major themes of chapter 2, namely, that one's rights are hostage not only to the abilities but also to the evidence possessed by the person(s) against whom the rights are held.

Consider, by way of example, such (alleged) rights as the rights to fidelity and non-maleficence. An Objectivist like the early Ross will say that these rights are correlative to direct prima facie obligations on the part of others, these being simply the obligations, respectively, to keep one's commitments and to refrain from harm.[41] A Prospectivist like me will give a different, more complicated account. On the assumption that keeping a commitment is suited to the prior making of a commitment, the Prospective View implies that Q has a right against P that P keep his commitment to Q only if, for every maximal course of action, C, performable by P that excludes P's keeping his commitment to Q, there is some maximal course of action, $C*$, performable by P that includes P's keeping his commitment to Q whose core is prospectively more suited to P's having made his commitment than C's core is. Or, to put the point another way: the Prospective View implies that Q's "right to fidelity" is, more precisely (but still somewhat roughly), a right against P that P perform some maximal course of action whose core is prospectively most suited to his having made his commitment to Q. If this course of action includes P's actually keeping his commitment to Q, then Q has a right against P that P keep his commitment; but *not otherwise*. Similarly, on the assumption that refraining from causing harm is suited to the opportunity either to cause harm or not, Q's "right to non-maleficence" against P is a right that P perform some maximal course of action whose core is prospectively most suited to P's having the opportunity either to cause Q harm or not. If this course of action in fact includes P's causing Q no harm, then Q has a right against P that P cause him no harm; but, again, *not otherwise*. (And so, in the particular matter of the right to life: Q has a right against P that P perform some maximal course of action whose core is prospectively most suited to P's having the opportunity either to kill Q or not. Such a course of action may, but may not, include P's not killing Q.)

---

[41] Cf. Ross 1930, pp. 21, 46, 48.

D

Finally, there is the matter of accounting for the distinction between direct and indirect obligation. When discussing Case 8 in chapter 2, I said that, on the Prospective View, my direct obligation is to perform some intentional action that, among the intentional actions that I can perform, provides me with the best prospect of keeping my promise, and that this implies that I ought to use service B. This way of putting things is only roughly right, though. On the holistic approach to obligation proposed in this chapter, it is only entire courses of action that can be directly obligatory; their parts – the individual actions that they include – will be merely indirectly obligatory. Moreover, for reasons given in the last section, it is only entire courses of *attempts* that can be directly obligatory.

As noted earlier, when an agent has a choice between options, that choice is in effect a choice between maximal performable courses of action. On the Prospective View, it is the core of a maximal course of action that determines whether the agent ought to perform that course of action. However, not every part of that core need be relevant to determining this. It can happen that an agent has a choice between two (or more) maximal courses that are equally prospectively best. For example, in a variation on Case 8, I might be able to do that which provides me with the best prospect of keeping my promise by attempting to use, and using, either service A or service B, in which case neither service will be such that I am obligated to use it, even though each service will be such that my using it is part of the core of some prospectively best maximal course of action performable by me. In order to isolate what it is that an agent is directly *obligated* to do, then, we must focus on those maximal *parts* of cores that are common to *all* the prospectively best maximal performable courses.

To say that P *can* at T perform a course of action, C, is to say that every act, A, that C includes is such that, for some time, $T*$, P can at T do A at $T*$. Let us now also say that P *ought* at T to perform a course of action, C, just in case every act, A, that C includes is such that, for some time, $T*$, P ought at T to do A at $T*$. And let us finally say that a course of action is a course of attempts just in case every action that it includes is the minimal sort of action that consists in making an attempt. I then propose:

The Prospective View (final formulation: direct unconditional obligation):
C is directly unconditionally obligatory for P at T if and only if C is a course of attempts such that

(1) P can at T perform C,
(2) P ought at T to perform C, and
(3) there is no course of attempts, $C*$, distinct from C such that
    (a) P can at T perform $C*$,
    (b) P ought at T to perform $C*$, and
    (c) $C*$ includes C.

(This applies to all unconditional obligation, whether overall or prima facie, primary or subsidiary. A corresponding account can be given for conditional obligation.) An obligation will be indirect, of course, just in case it is not direct.

3.5 OBLIGATION AND CONTROL

We may say that an act has a *deontic status* just in case it is morally either obligatory, right, or wrong (whether overall or prima facie, unconditionally or conditionally, primarily or subsidiarily, directly or indirectly), and that an act is *optional* just in case the agent both can perform it and can refrain from performing it, in the relevant personal sense of "can."[42] Then the Prospective View implies (on its final formulation) that an act has a deontic status only if it is optional. I will call this the Principle of Optionality.

The Principle of Optionality includes, but goes well beyond, the principle that "ought" implies "can" – that is, the principle that an act is morally obligatory only if the agent can perform it (in the relevant personal sense of "can"). The latter principle enjoys strong, though not unanimous, support among philosophers. Some take it to be a conceptual truth. I think they are probably right to do so, although the matter is difficult.[43] We should note two points. First, even if the principle is a conceptual truth, doubting it is not necessarily unreasonable. Second, even if it is not a conceptual truth, it is intuitively very plausible, so that, to be reasonable, any doubts one has about it must be supported by argument.

Many arguments for rejecting the principle that "ought" implies "can" have been offered. Here I will address only one of these: the Argument from Self-imposed Impossibility. This strikes me as the strongest argument against the principle. I have addressed other arguments elsewhere, and

---

[42] This is a *personal* sense of "optional." An act may be said to be *morally* optional just in case the agent morally both may perform it and may refrain from performing it.
[43] Cf. Zimmerman 1996, pp. 77–8.

there is no need to repeat myself here.[44] In fact, I have also addressed the Argument from Self-imposed Impossibility elsewhere, but my thinking on the matter has changed, and so I will discuss it anew. This is something I will undertake in the next section. In this section, I want to say something more about the Principle of Optionality.

According to the Principle of Optionality, "ought" implies not only "can" but also "can refrain," and "may" has both these implications too. The underlying idea is of course that, if an act is not a genuine option, then, no matter what kind of evaluation (whether moral or non-moral) may be made of it, it is not a candidate for deontic evaluation in particular.[45] As noted, the claim that "ought" implies "can" is intuitively very plausible; the idea that one can be obligated to do something that one cannot do suggests, paradoxically, that morality's demands can be unfair. The claim that "ought" implies "can refrain" is also very plausible; the idea that one can be obligated to do something that one cannot avoid doing suggests, paradoxically, that morality's demands can be empty or trivial. Finally, the claim that "may" has these same implications is also intuitively plausible; the idea that something that one cannot do or cannot avoid doing can be permissible suggests, paradoxically, that morality's permissions can be pointless. These suggestions can of course be challenged. Again, though, I have addressed such challenges elsewhere. My concern at this point is to elaborate on the relevant sense of "can." I'm afraid that this elaboration will be strictly limited and therefore disappointing. Although the sense of "can" at issue is one with which we are all familiar, it is unfortunately also one that is notoriously difficult to specify precisely.

At the outset of each chapter so far, I have said that by an "option" I mean something that the agent can do, where "can" expresses some form of personal control. (Prior to this chapter, I also used "alternative" as an alternative to "option." In this chapter, however, I have said that "alternative" is to be used more restrictively, to refer only to a *maximal* performable course of action. I will continue to use "option" broadly, though, to refer to any performable act or course of action.) In section 1.2, I characterized the form of personal control in question as that which many

---

[44] Cf. Zimmerman 1996, ch. 3.
[45] Among non-deontic moral evaluations are those that concern: what is ideal (as opposed to obligatory); responsibility, i.e., laudability and culpability (as opposed to obligation); and character (as opposed to action).

believe to be threatened by causal determinism. This is both meager and misleading. What follows is a modest attempt to do better.

I have said that A is optional for P just in case P both can do A and can refrain from doing A. This presupposes that its being the case that P can do A is one thing, and its being the case that P can refrain from doing A is another. This presupposition is surely correct. If P cannot refrain from doing A, then P will do A; and if P will do A, then P can do A. (Likewise, if P cannot do A, then P won't do A; and if P won't do A, then P can refrain from doing A.[46]) But it certainly sounds odd to say that, if P can do A but cannot refrain from doing A, then P is in control of doing A. Moreover, if its being the case that P will do A implies that P can do A, then surely no one should think that there is any incompatibility between its being the case that P is causally determined to do A and its being the case that P can do A. So I must qualify my claim that "can" expresses some form of personal control.

Perhaps the most obvious qualification is this: for P to be in control of doing A, it must be the case not only that P can do A but also that P can refrain from doing A. I am inclined to think that this obvious qualification is false. Or more precisely: although there *is* a form of control that consists in an act's being optional (the by-now-standard label for this form of control is "regulative" control), it is plausible to contend that there is also a form of control that P may have over doing A that does not require it to be the case that P can refrain from doing A. This is (or appears to be) the lesson of so-called Frankfurt-style cases, thought-experiments that have been concocted to challenge the claim that moral responsibility requires regulative control. Harry Frankfurt has argued that, even though P's being morally responsible for having done A requires that P have done A freely, it doesn't require that P could have refrained from doing A.[47] Many have accepted Frankfurt's argument, and many have rejected it.[48] I am inclined to accept it, although the issue is difficult. Let us suppose that the argument succeeds. Then there is a form of control (for which the by-now-standard label is "guidance control"[49]), constituted by the sort of freedom that suffices (*ceteris paribus*) for moral responsibility, which itself does not require

---

[46] Again (see n. 23 above), by "refrain from doing A" I mean simply "not do A."
[47] Frankfurt 1969.
[48] Among those who accept it are: Fischer 1994, Fischer and Ravizza 1998, Haji 1998, Hunt 2000, Pereboom 2000, and Zagzebski 2000. Among those who reject it are: Blumenfeld 1971, van Inwagen 1983, Widerker 1995, Kane 1996, and Otsuka 1998.
[49] The labels "regulative control" and "guidance control" were introduced in Fischer 1994.

that the agent have been able to refrain from doing that for which he is responsible. And this makes matters really quite tricky, because it's natural to use "can" to express this form of control. Yet *this* sense of "can" – call it "can*" – cannot be the same as that discussed in the last paragraph, because it is clearly *not* correct to say that, if *P* will do *A*, then *P* can* do *A*; for it can certainly happen that *P* does *A* but does *not* do it freely (in whatever sense of "freely" is required for *P* to have guidance control over doing *A* and thus for *P* to be morally responsible for having done *A*).

Fortunately for present purposes, this tricky issue can be side-stepped. That is because, even though its being the case that *P* can do *A* does not suffice for its being the case that *P* can* do *A*, its being the case both that *P* can do *A* and that *P* can refrain from doing *A* does suffice for its being the case that *P* can* do *A* (and also, of course, for its being the case that *P* can* refrain from doing *A*). In brief, even though being in guidance control of doing *A* doesn't imply being in regulative control of doing *A*, the converse implication does hold – or so I contend. And since we're working under the assumption that "ought" and "may" require optionality, that is, regulative control, we can stick with the original, broader sense of "can" (and "can refrain") and need not concern ourselves with just how this sense is to be distinguished from the narrower sense of "can*."[50]

The question still remains, of course, what the broader sense of "can" amounts to. Some say that its being the case that *P* can, in the relevant sense, do *A* consists in its being the case that *P* has both the ability and the opportunity to do *A*.[51] Well, perhaps so, but this advances our understanding only a little, if at all, since "ability" itself admits of broader and narrower construals. For example, there is doubtless a sense in which *P* has the ability to do *A* only if *P* can* do *A* – that is, only if *P* has guidance control over doing *A*. Moreover, there is also doubtless a sense in which, in Case 13, Jill lacks the ability to open the safe, since she cannot intentionally open it. Yet she *can* open it (and thus *does* have the ability to open it) in the broad sense in question. And, again, it is this broad sense that is at issue in the principle that "ought" implies "can" and in the Principle of Optionality. For, as noted in section 3.3, it may be that *P* ought to do *A* even if *P* cannot intentionally do *A*; for example, perhaps Dave ought to

---

[50] The question arises: if Frankfurt-style cases can be used to show that moral responsibility doesn't require regulative control, why can't they also be used to show that an act's having a deontic status also doesn't require that the agent have regulative control over the act? I address this question in Zimmerman 1996, pp. 85–9.

[51] An early example is Nowell Smith 1960.

cause certain mechanisms in the door's lock to change position, even though he cannot intentionally do this because he is unaware of their existence.

In this section, I have so far identified two distinctions concerning control. The first is that between *regulative* and *guidance* control. The second is that between what I will call *intentional* and *coincidental* control. P has regulative, intentional control over A just in case P both can intentionally do A and can intentionally refrain from doing A; P has guidance, intentional control over A just in case P can* intentionally do A. P's control (whether regulative or guidance) over A is coincidental rather than intentional in those cases in which P can or can* do A or refrain from doing A but cannot intentionally do so. There are also other distinctions concerning control that are worth noting. One distinction (mentioned in section 1.2) is that between *complete* and *partial* control. P has complete control over A just in case A's occurrence is not contingent on anything that lies beyond P's control; otherwise, P's control (if any) over A is merely partial. As noted before, no one ever has complete control over anything. Thus the Principle of Optionality is to be understood to imply that an act has a deontic status only if the agent has regulative, partial control over it.

Another distinction mentioned in section 1.2 is that between *direct* and *indirect* control. P has indirect control over A just in case he has control over it by way of having control over something else; P has direct control over A just in case he has control over it that is not indirect. On my view, we have direct control only over our attempts – minimal actions that, as I said in section 3.3, consist in decisions or choices to perform actions in a fuller sense. For example, suppose (from Case 14) that Jill injects a dose of drug B into John's backside. This action consists (I assume) of her attempting to inject the drug together with her attempt's causing the drug to enter John's body. She has direct control over the attempt and thereby indirect control over the drug's passage (and also of the causal consequences of this passage). The action itself, consisting of both the attempt and the passage, is something over which she has a sort of hybrid control, in so far as her control over one of its elements is direct while her control over another of its elements is indirect.

Other distinctions concerning control may be drawn. Here let me mention explicitly just one more (introduced in section 3.2): the distinction between *immediate* and *remote* control. P has immediate control over A just in case P has control at T over doing A at T; P has remote control over A just in case P has control at T over doing A at some later time $T*$. This distinction is closely allied, but is not identical, to that between direct and indirect control. It is typically but not necessarily the case that P's control over A is direct just in case it is immediate. (It is at least conceptually possible that P can at T do A at T only by way of doing B at T. In such a case, P's control over A would be immediate but indirect. Perhaps, too, we should say that a person who is asleep has direct but remote control over the first decision that he will make upon awakening.) At the beginning of this section, I put the Principle of Optionality in this way: an act has a deontic status only if it is optional. This is pretty rough. Let me now put it more carefully:

The Principle of Optionality:
P ought or may (whether overall or prima facie, unconditionally or conditionally, etc.) at T do A at $T*$ only if

(1) P can at T do A at $T*$, and
(2) P can at T refrain from doing A at $T*$.

(Here T may or may not be identical with $T*$. If it is not, then it is earlier than $T*$.) I noted in section 3.2 that, just as we may distinguish between immediate and remote control, so too we may distinguish between immediate and remote obligation (and permission). The Principle of Optionality implies that, whereas immediate obligation (or permission) requires immediate control, remote obligation (or permission) only requires remote control. As will be seen in the next section, this turns out to be very important.

Finally, it should be appreciated that all the distinctions just mentioned cut across one another. Thus immediate control may (in principle, at least) be direct or indirect; direct control may be complete or partial; partial control may be intentional or coincidental; and so on. In any particular case, then, whether someone has control over something is a matter of some complexity.

3.6 SHIFTS IN OBLIGATION

Consider, now, this objection to the principle that "ought" implies "can" (and so, too, to the Principle of Optionality). Return to the example, given in chapter 2, in which you lend me a book on Monday that I promise to return to you by Friday.

"It's a date," I say. "High noon at the *Pig and Whistle*! We'll have a couple of beers."

151

On Tuesday, I start reading your book. It's fabulous. It's fascinating. I love it. I can't put it down. Friday comes, and I don't want to give the book back. So I leave it on my shelf at home and turn up at the bar without it.

"Hi," you say, "like the book?"

"Loved it."

"I'll be glad to get it back."

"I can imagine."

Awkward silence. "Well," you say, "where is it?"

"Back at my place."

"What do you mean? You promised to return it to me today."

"That I did."

You seem annoyed. "Then why haven't you brought it with you? A promise is a promise."

"There's no denying that," I say breezily.

"What I mean," you say, gritting your teeth, "is that you ought to keep your promise."

"Oh, well, I do deny that."

"Why on earth would you deny that?" You sound irritated.

"Simple," I say. "I know I promised to return your book. But I didn't realize how great it was. It's wonderful! Terrific! I want to keep it. So naturally I haven't brought it with me. Of course, that means I can't return it to you now, and since 'ought' implies 'can,' *that* means that I don't have an obligation to return it to you now. So just calm down, why don't you, and buy me a drink."

To my surprise, my suggestion serves only to upset you further. Evidently, you are not impressed by my argument. But why not? Isn't it perfectly cogent?

Of course, it is not perfectly cogent. On the contrary, it is sheer sophistry. Although it may be easy to shirk one's duties, it is not so easy to divest oneself of them – certainly not as easy as the argument that I have given you suggests. By leaving the book on my shelf, I rendered myself unable to return it to you as promised; but such self-imposed impossibility clearly doesn't annul my obligation. In light of this fact, a counterargument may seem obvious: I can't return the book; I ought to return it; and so "ought" does not imply "can" after all. This is the Argument from Self-imposed Impossibility. It is one that several philosophers have given in one form or another,[52] and it is, I think, the strongest argument against the

---

[52] Cf. Henderson 1966, p. 106; Robinson 1971, p. 197; Stocker 1971, p. 314; White 1975, p. 149; Richman 1983, p. 85; Sinnott-Armstrong 1988, pp. 116–17.

principle that "ought" implies "can." I believe it fails. Contrary to what I said to you at the bar, I agree that I did indeed have an obligation to return the book to you as promised, but I also believe that "ought" implies "can." I believe, that is, that, in this sort of case at least, one can have one's cake and eat it too. In what follows, I'll explain how this is so and pursue the implications, chief among which is the fact that wrong-doing and the failure to fulfill an obligation are not as closely related as is usually assumed.

A

I borrowed the book from you on Monday. It was, we may assume, certainly possible for me *then* to return it to you on Friday, and so it is certainly plausible to say that I was obligated *then* to return it on Friday. So saying is perfectly in keeping with the Principle of Optionality, which, as noted in the last section, implies that remote obligation only requires remote control. By the time I got to the *Pig and Whistle* on Friday, I could no longer keep my promise to you. That is, I could not at noon on Friday return the book to you then. It follows from the Principle of Optionality that I was not obligated at noon on Friday to return the book to you then. Quite so. What I was then obligated to do was something else (something that I could then do then): apologize to you, perhaps (instead of telling you to calm down); make arrangements to return the book to you as soon as possible (instead of suggesting that you buy me a drink); make some sort of amends (by buying *you* a drink, for instance); and so on. Let us assume, for simplicity, that my evidence regarding my options and their relative values was accurate, so that what was prospectively best coincided with what was actually best; and let us assume that, as of Monday, the cores of all the best maximal courses of action performable by me included my returning the book to you at noon on Friday. Then, in failing to return the book to you, I failed to fulfill an obligation. (The obligation is an overall obligation, if "best" is construed in terms of suitability to my situation as a whole; it is a merely prima facie obligation, if "best" is construed merely in terms of suitability to some particular aspect of my situation.) The fact that on Friday I no longer had an obligation to return the book to you at noon does not alter the fact that I once did have an obligation to do so. A remote obligation is a genuine obligation, after all, and the failure to fulfill such an obligation can constitute genuine wrongdoing (whether the wrongdoing is

153

overall or merely prima facie). In this case it seems that I did indeed commit a genuine wrong, and that you thus had a genuine grievance – even though I was not obligated at the time to return the book to you then. (Your grievance would be negated, if my obligation to return the book were merely prima facie, overridden by some contrary, stronger prima facie obligation. It is not negated merely by the fact that I rendered myself unable to fulfill it.)

Let us suppose that it was my choice to leave home at 11:30 without your book that rendered me unable to return the book to you at noon. Then a partial picture of the case is provided by figure 3.1, in which the nodes represent possible choices – items over which an agent can exercise direct control – and the branches represent courses of action:

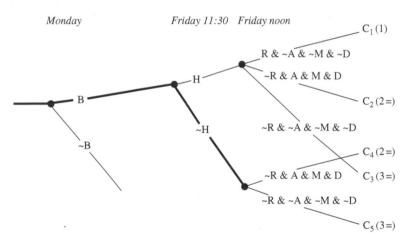

Figure 3.1

Here B = Borrow (the book), H = (have the book in) Hand, R = Return (the book), A = Apologize (to you), M = Make (arrangements to return the book later), and D = (buy you a) Drink. The numbers represent the deontic rankings of the maximal courses of action, C_1-C_5, performable by me on Monday. (Clearly the picture is greatly over-simplified. Many performable maximal courses of action are not depicted at all, and those that are depicted are only partially described.) The thick line represents the path I actually took up to noon on Friday. Notice that, following my choice at 11:30, when I took a turn for the worse, the best course of action performable by me as of then was one in which I

154

did *not* return the book at noon (because I couldn't return it) but did apologize, make arrangements to return it later, and buy you a drink. That, therefore, is what the Prospective View implies I was then obligated to do. But, again, this does not alter the fact that, in not returning the book at noon, I did wrong in failing to fulfill my remote obligation (the obligation that I had from Monday until Friday at 11:30) to return it then.

B

The question naturally arises: when a remote wrong is done, *when* is it done? We should distinguish between the time at which an agent *goes* wrong and the time at which the wrong *occurs*. "Do wrong" is ambiguous between the two. In an earlier work, I proposed the following general account of going wrong:

The First Principle of Wrongdoing (PW1):
P goes wrong at T with respect to doing A at $T*$ if and only if
(1) P ought at T to do A at $T*$,
(2) P refrains from doing A at $T*$, and
(3) it is not the case that P ought, just after T, to do A at $T*$.[53]

This account implies that I went wrong at 11:30 with respect to returning the book to you at noon, which seems to me exactly what should be said; for that, after all, is when I took a turn for the worse, as figure 3.1 illustrates. We can, and I think should, nonetheless say that the wrong that I did occurred at noon; for that is when I was due to return the book. (I will return to the question of when, in general, a wrong occurs in subsection F below.)

PW1 applies to all wrongdoing, whether remote (in which case T is distinct from and earlier than $T*$) or immediate (in which case T is identical with $T*$). It implies that all wrongdoing involves a failure to fulfill an obligation – a claim that may well be thought to be analytic. It also implies that all failures to fulfill an obligation constitute wrongdoing – that is, as I will put it, that all failures to fulfill an obligation constitute an *infringement* of

---

[53] Zimmerman 1996, p. 104. (For reasons that will emerge in subsections D and E below, I have switched from talk of "going wrong in not doing A" to talk of "going wrong with respect to doing A.") By clause (3) I mean that, for any time T' after T such that P ought at T' to do A at $T*$, there is an earlier time T'' after T such that it is not the case that P ought at T'' to do A at $T*$. The "just" in "just after" is intended to accommodate the possibility of the restoration of obligation (another matter to be addressed in subsection E).

that obligation. (If the obligation in question is an overall obligation, the infringement may be said to constitute a violation. This matches the terminology used in section 2.2 regarding the failure to fulfill a right.) This claim, too, may initially be thought to be analytic. It is, I think, clearly true of all cases of immediate obligation, but, once cases of remote obligation have been brought into the picture, one may wonder whether it should be said to hold for *all* such cases. We should surely agree that I went wrong with respect to returning the book to you, but perhaps that is only because of the *way* in which I failed to fulfill the obligation that I had. What if it hadn't been my decision to leave my home without your book that had incapacitated me (with respect to my returning it to you on time) but some other, wholly fortuitous event that had done so (I was mugged, say, and the book was stolen; or I was struck by lightning, and the book was incinerated)? Or what if I hadn't been incapacitated but you had simply released me from my obligation (you told me that I could hold on to the book; or you urged me to donate it to the local library instead of returning it to you)? Or what if I had been neither incapacitated nor released from my obligation but had come to learn on Wednesday that you were planning to bludgeon your neighbor with the book (it's a heavy book), once I had returned it to you on Friday, and make it look as if I had committed the crime? Surely, one may say, any such event would have transformed my situation by causing a shift in obligation, in that I would no longer have been obligated to return the book to you at noon on Friday; but, equally surely, had I not returned it, I would not then have gone wrong with respect to returning it to you then.[54]

Here is how I proposed handling such cases in my earlier work.[55] Regarding cases involving incapacitation, I suggested that we ask whether I could have avoided the allegedly transforming event in question. For example, if I could have avoided being mugged or struck by lightning (which seems likely, for I could presumably have left home at a different time or taken a different route to the *Pig and Whistle*), then, I said, if it was

---

[54] There may be a difference between the three kinds of cases just given, in that it is plausible to maintain that my being incapacitated or released from my obligation causes the obligation to cease, whether the obligation is overall or merely prima facie, whereas my coming to learn of your plan to bludgeon your neighbor doesn't put an end to my prima facie obligation to return your book but only makes it be the case that I am no longer overall obligated to return it. Perhaps so. If so, let us suppose in such a case that it is with overall obligation in particular that we are concerned.

[55] Zimmerman 1996, pp. 107 ff.

indeed the case that *all* the best courses of action performable by me included my returning the book, then those courses also included my avoiding the event; hence the occurrence of the transforming event *did* involve wrongdoing on my part, just as in the case in which I left home without your book, and in virtue of this my failure to return the book *did* constitute an infringement of my obligation to return it. Of course, I might well not have known that I was obligated to avoid the transforming event, but that is no surprise; for the truth about one's obligations and the evidence that one has concerning them can easily fail to correspond. If I didn't know that I was obligated to avoid the transforming event, then I would have an excuse for not doing so (unless my ignorance was culpable); but that wouldn't mean that I didn't do wrong in not doing so. Alternatively, if some of the best courses of action performable by me did not include my avoiding the event (and note: if I couldn't have avoided the event, then *all* of the performable, and hence *all* of the *best* performable, courses of action did not include my avoiding it), then those courses did not include my returning the book to you either, and so I never was obligated to return it to you after all; hence the occurrence of the event did not involve any wrongdoing on my part, but also it did not involve any genuine transformation of my obligation. Again, I might not have known that I was not obligated to return the book, but, as before, it is no surprise that truth and evidence should fail to correspond in this way. Thus in neither case would a faultless shift in obligation (that is, a shift not itself involving wrongdoing) have occurred.

Regarding cases not involving incapacitation, I suggested that we say something similar. On the one hand, if the allegedly transforming event genuinely resulted in a shift in obligation – that is (in the present set of cases), if it did indeed make it the case that I was no longer obligated to return the book – then I was obligated to avoid the event. On the other hand, if I was not obligated to avoid the event, then (in the present set of cases) *either* I never was obligated in the first place to return the book to you *or* I remained obligated to return it despite the occurrence of the event. Once again, in neither case would a faultless shift in obligation have occurred.

Although the theory of obligation that I defended in my earlier work was intended to accommodate all general approaches to obligation, whether that of the Objective View, the Subjective View, or the Prospective View, I confess that I secretly subscribed to the Objective View, and it is now clear to me that the account of going wrong that

I proposed was biased toward that view. My proposal was predicated on two assumptions, one that I had made only implicitly, the other explicitly. The first, implicit assumption was that the relevant value-rankings of possible courses of action never change; if $C*$ is ever better than C, it is always better than C. The second, explicit assumption was that what is presently performable by someone always was performable by that person (once he or she had come into existence), each new choice serving only to cut the agent off from courses of action that had been open to him (or her) up until that point.[56] For example, figure 3.1 depicts the fact that, when I made my choice on Monday to borrow your book, I thereby cut myself off from all the "non-borrow" courses of action that had been performable up until then. (Of course, had I made the choice not to borrow the book, I would thereby have cut myself off from all the "borrow" courses of action that had been performable up until then.) Likewise, when I made my choice to leave home at 11:30 on Friday without your book in hand, I cut myself off from all those courses of action, including C_1-C_3, that included my taking it with me. Given these two assumptions, it follows that shifts in remote obligation (such that P ought at T to do A at $T*$ – where T is earlier than $T*$ – but it is not the case that P ought just after T to do A at $T*$) can occur only when an agent makes a choice that cuts him off from courses of action that, up to that point, had been the best performable by him (and which had included his doing A at $T*$). This is precisely what is depicted in figure 3.1 when at 11:30 on Friday my obligation shifted, such that I then became obligated, for example, to apologize to you at noon, whereas up to that point I had not been obligated to do so. Every such shift constitutes a turn for the worse, a turn that constitutes the infringement of an immediate obligation and in virtue of which the failure to fulfill any attendant remote obligations constitutes an infringement of those obligations. Thus no shift is faultless.

The first assumption, I now believe, is false. As a result, so too is PW1.

C

On the Prospective View, moral obligation is to be determined by reference, not directly to the actual outcomes and values of an agent's options, but to his evidence concerning these outcomes and values. Such evidence may shift over time and, as a result, the relevant value-rankings of the

---

[56] Zimmerman 1996, p. 26. Cf. Feldman 1986, p. 21.

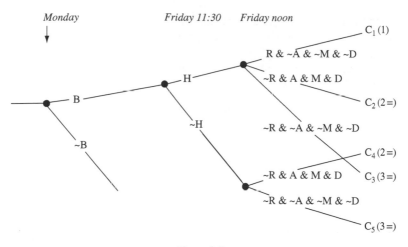

Figure 3.2

alternative courses of action open to an agent may also shift over time. Consider the case in which I came to learn on Wednesday of your plan to bludgeon your neighbor. Given that my evidence concerning the relevant actual values was accurate, the prospective value of the core of any performable maximal course of action that included my keeping my promise will have plummeted, and it is surely plausible to say that I was therefore no longer obligated to return the book to you.[57] But we should not infer that I never was obligated to return the book; for, prior to my discovery, there was presumably some performable maximal course of action whose core included my returning the book and whose prospective value was relatively high.

The case may be depicted as follows. As of Monday, the relative prospective values of (the cores of) my alternative courses of action may well have been exactly as depicted in figure 3.1. These are replicated in figure 3.2 above. The only changes from figure 3.1 to figure 3.2 are the following: the bold line (indicating which path I in fact took) has been deleted, and a vertical arrow has been inserted that indicates the time (on Monday) relative to which the prospective values hold.

[57] See n. 54 above.

Now consider the situation that obtained on Wednesday, once I came to learn of your plan. The picture, given in figure 3.3, is dramatically different:

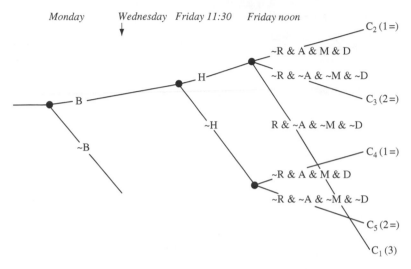

Figure 3.3

Figure 3.2 depicts the fact that, as of Monday, the prospectively best course of action open to me was C_1 (a course that of course included my returning the book to you on Friday), and hence that I was obligated on Monday to return the book on Friday. Figure 3.3 depicts the fact that, as of Wednesday, C_1 was far from being the prospectively best course of action open to me, and that, as a result, I was no longer obligated to return the book on Friday. My obligation shifted, but not through any wrongdoing on my part. PW1 implies that I did go wrong (as long as I refrained from returning the book). Given the Prospective View, PW1 is thus unacceptable.

If PW1 is to be rejected, what alternative account of going wrong should take its place? The answer to this question is, fortunately, quite straightforward. I propose (initially) the following, which supplements clauses (1)–(3) of PW1 with one further clause:

The Second Principle of Wrongdoing (PW2):
P goes wrong at T with respect to doing A at T^* if and only if
(1) P ought at T to do A at T^*,
(2) P refrains from doing A at T^*,

160

(3) it is not the case that P ought, just after T, to do A at $T*$, and
(4) if T is distinct from $T*$, then there is some act, B, such that
 (a) P ought at T to do B at T,
 (b) P refrains from doing B at T, and
 (c) clause (3) is true in virtue of subclause (b).

Let me explain. The retention of the three original clauses, (1)-(3), preserves the implication that all wrongdoing involves a failure to fulfill an obligation, but the addition of the new clause, (4), allows us to say that not all failures to fulfill an obligation need constitute wrongdoing – that is, that not all such failures need constitute an infringement of the obligation in question. This new clause implies that one goes wrong in failing to fulfill a remote obligation to do A only if one fails to fulfill an immediate obligation to do some act B and it is this failure that accounts for the failure to fulfill the obligation to do A.

Let us apply this account to the various cases already considered that have to do with my returning your book. Regarding the original case in which I simply decided to keep the book for myself, PW2 implies that I went wrong with respect to returning the book to you; this is because I committed the immediate wrongdoing of leaving home at 11:30 without the book, and it was in virtue of this wrongdoing that I no longer could, and so was no longer obligated, to return the book at noon. Regarding the cases in which I was no longer obligated to return the book because of some other kind of transforming event – the book was stolen or incinerated, or you waived your claim to it, or I learned of your plan to bludgeon your neighbor with it – PW2 implies that, if I did not return it, I did *not* go wrong with respect to returning it, *as long as* it is agreed that no immediate wrongdoing of mine accounts for the occurrence of the shift in obligation. Notice that PW2 can go "either way" on this issue, for it implies that I *did* go wrong with respect to returning the book at noon if some immediate wrongdoing of mine *did* account for the shift in obligation. Thus PW2 is compatible with my earlier view that all failures to fulfill an obligation, whether remote or immediate, constitute wrongdoing. But it is also compatible with my present view that, although all failures to fulfill an immediate obligation constitute wrongdoing, not all failures to fulfill a remote obligation constitute wrongdoing. Moreover, it provides an explanation of why those remote failures that constitute wrongdoing do so, and why those that don't, don't: it all depends on whether the remote failure is grounded in an immediate failure.

D

Let me now turn to two objections to PW2.

First, it might be objected that PW2 is circular. Consider the original case, in which, I have claimed, I went wrong at 11:30 with respect to returning the book to you at noon on Friday. PW2 implies that this claim is true, *given* that I had an immediate obligation to leave home at 11:30 with book in hand and that my failure to do so accounts for its being the case that I was no longer obligated to return the book at noon; for, as just noted, PW2 requires that any remote wrongdoing be grounded in some immediate wrongdoing. Surely, though, it was wrong of me to leave home at 11:30 without your book only because I had an obligation to return it to you at noon; for otherwise it would have been perfectly justifiable for me not to bring the book with me. But, in that case, my immediate wrongdoing was grounded in my remote wrongdoing, and this is inconsistent with the claim that my remote wrongdoing was grounded in my immediate wrongdoing.

In response: there is no inconsistency. Let us agree, as is surely plausible, that I had an obligation not to leave home without your book only because I had an obligation to return the book to you. This is a matter of an indirect obligation arising in virtue of a direct obligation. In light of this, we might, I suppose, say that my immediate wrongdoing was grounded in my remote wrongdoing, but only in the following sense: the *wrongness* of my leaving home bookless is to be explained by reference to the *wrongness* of (some course of action that included) my failing to return the book. This is perfectly consistent with the claim that the remote wrong would not, indeed could not, have been *committed* without some such immediate wrong being *committed*, and hence that in *this* sense my remote wrongdoing was grounded in my immediate wrongdoing.

A second objection is this: PW2 implies that people go wrong in ways in which in fact they don't. Consider this variation on the original case. I wrongly left home at 11:30 without your book, thereby incapacitating myself with respect to returning it to you at noon, thereby making it the case that I was no longer obligated to return it to you at noon. PW2's verdict: I went wrong at 11:30 with respect to returning the book at noon. But suppose now that you called me on my cell phone at 11:45, telling me that I could keep the book. When I turned up at the bar without your book, you were not at all surprised (perhaps you thought I had left it in my car). You of course didn't ask me for it back. Instead, the two of us had a good, friendly chat about the book over a couple of good, friendly drinks and then parted company. Surely I did no wrong in not returning the book to you, contrary to PW2's verdict.

In response: the claim that "I did no wrong in not returning the book" does not contradict PW2's verdict. What that principle implies is that "I went wrong with respect to returning the book." The two phrases, though similar, are subtly different. Return to the original case in which I left home bookless and you did *not* then call me to tell me that I could keep it. I take it that we can by now all agree that "I went wrong (at 11:30) with respect to returning the book." Perhaps, too, it doesn't sound too odd to say that "I did wrong in not returning the book," despite the fact that, by the time I was due to return the book, I no longer had an obligation to return it. In the present variation, in which you did call me and release me from my obligation (or, rather, you *attempted* to release me from it; your attempt misfired, though, because I had already sloughed it off when I left home without the book), it strikes me as somewhat odd (for reasons that are unclear to me) to say that "I did wrong in not returning the book." But, even so, that is strictly irrelevant. The question remains whether I went wrong (at 11:30) with respect to returning the book, and I can see no reason to deny that I did. It was wrong (at 11:30) for me to leave home (at 11:30) without the book. The wrongness of my doing so is, as just noted, to be explained by reference to the wrongness (then) of my failing to return the book (at noon). Hence I did go wrong (at 11:30) with respect to returning the book.

E

In this subsection, I want briefly to elaborate on the ways in which shifts in obligation can occur and to end by qualifying – actually, simplifying – the account of going wrong contained in PW2.

We can distinguish two broad categories of shifts in obligation, which I will call *extinction* and *supersession*.[58] When an obligation is extinguished, it ceases to exist. Such extinction may be immediate or remote. Immediate extinction is familiar. Consider the obligation to do some act A at some time T, an obligation that survives up until T. As soon as T is past, that obligation will cease to exist – it will be extinguished – whether or not it has been fulfilled.

---

[58] At p. 113 of Zimmerman 1996 I used "supersession" more broadly, to cover all kinds of shifts in obligation.

We may call such extinction *termination*, although it also falls under the more general heading of *incapacitation*, in as much as no one has control over, and hence no one can have obligations regarding, the past. Incapacitation may also be remote, as figure 3.1 illustrates. When I left home at 11:30 without your book, my obligation to return it to you at noon was extinguished.

Another form of remote extinction is *cancellation*, of the sort that occurred in the case in which you released me on Wednesday from my obligation to return your book on Friday. In such a case, cancellation is triggered by the waiving of a right. (Cancellation can also be triggered by the forfeiture of a right.) As far as I can tell, it is only associative obligations – those obligations that are correlative to rights – that can be cancelled. When you waived your right to your book, I was no longer obligated *to you* to return it to you (given that my evidence comported with the fact that you had indeed released me from my promise). It could still have been the case, though, that I was obligated (whether to someone else or to no one) to return it to you. Notice also that the cancellation of an obligation is compatible with its later being replaced by a "duplicate." It is possible that, although my obligation to you on Wednesday to return the book on Friday was cancelled, I incurred a new obligation to you on Thursday to return it to you on Friday. (See the discussion of the recurrence of obligation in subsections B and D of section 2.3.)

Extinction can be either faultless or not. In the original case, my incapacitating myself with respect to returning your book was wrong, and as a result I went wrong with respect to returning it. But in other cases (for example, incapacitation due to the book's being stolen or incinerated), the incapacitation was faultless. So too with cancellation. Your releasing me on Wednesday from my obligation occurred (as I have intended the case to be understood) by virtue of no wrongdoing on my part, but it could have been otherwise. I might, for example, have wrongly led you to believe that I would donate the book to the local library (whereas I intended all along to keep it), and it might have been this that prompted your waiving your right to it.

When an obligation at some level is superseded, it is overridden.[59] It ceases to retain its status as an obligation at that level, but it continues to

---

[59] The kind of overriding at issue here is *dynamic*. In this sense, even overall obligations can be overridden. Such overriding is to be distinguished from the sort of *static* overriding that occurs when a prima facie obligation is prevented from being an overall obligation by virtue of conflicting with another, stronger prima facie obligation.

exist (as a conditional obligation) at some lower level. Consider the following variation on our original case. Suppose that I came to learn on Wednesday, not that you were planning on bludgeoning your neighbor with the book that I had borrowed, but that the book's author was in town and was due to appear the next day at the local library, where he would sign any copies of the book that were presented to him. Let us suppose that I knew that you would love to have your copy signed by the author and recognized that having this done would be a uniquely suitable way of thanking you for having loaned me the book. Prior to Wednesday, the prospectively best performable maximal course of action included my returning the book to you unsigned on Saturday, and so that was what it was then my primary obligation to do. On Wednesday, though, this obligation was overridden by the obligation to return the book to you signed. My situation may be pictured, in part, as in figure 3.4, where RS = Return the book Signed, and RU = Return the book Unsigned.

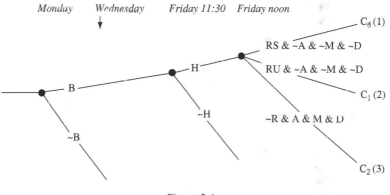

Figure 3.4

As the figure shows, that course of action, C_1, which previously was best and included my returning the book unsigned, was on Wednesday relegated to being second best. As is not true in the case of cancellation, in this case my obligation to return the book unsigned still survived, though, in the sense that it became a *secondary, conditional* obligation: I was still obligated to return the book to you unsigned *if* I didn't return it to you signed. No such conditional obligation pertains in the case of extinction.

Supersession differs from extinction in another, related respect. Because an obligation survives supersession, it is available for restoration; that is, it can regain its previous status as an unconditional obligation. (It is for this reason that the "just" in "just after" appears in the formulation of PW2.) When I learned on Wednesday of the author's impending visit, my obligation to return the book unsigned was overridden by the obligation to return it signed. However, if I had subsequently discovered that you would have preferred to present the book in person to the author for signing at a later date, my obligation to return it to you unsigned would have been restored. Neither of these shifts in obligation, as I intend them to be understood, would have involved wrongdoing on my part, but such shifts certainly can involve wrongdoing, as I will now explain.

Consider, as one final variation on our original case, the following. Despite having borrowed your book on Monday, with the promise that I would return it to you at noon on Friday, on Wednesday I told my ailing mother that I would visit her in hospital at noon on Friday. Let us assume that, having thus raised my mother's expectations in this way, my commitment to her took precedence over my commitment to you, and that my overall, unconditional obligation as of Wednesday (with respect to what I ought to do at noon on Friday) was therefore to visit my mother and not return the book to you. But now let us suppose that, despite this fact, I met with you and returned the book to you on Friday after all. This case seems to me to demonstrate two points.

First, supersession is not necessarily faultless. It is surely reasonable to suppose that it was wrong of me to tell my mother that I would visit her at noon on Friday (for I could easily have arranged to visit her at some time that would not conflict with my meeting with you). But it is also reasonable to suppose that it would not have been wrong of me to do this had I not already arranged to meet with you; the wrongness of my doing so was thus entirely parasitic on the wrongness of my not meeting with you. And yet I met with you! This brings me to my second point, which is that not only can it happen that an obligation is both not fulfilled and not infringed (which, on the face of it, is fairly surprising), but it can also happen that an obligation is both fulfilled and infringed (which strikes me as really quite surprising). A further modification is therefore called for in the account of what it is for one to go wrong, and that is simply to delete the requirement that one refrain from doing that which one is obligated to do. I therefore now propose that we accept the following:

The Third Principle of Wrongdoing (PW3):
P goes wrong at *T* with respect to doing *A* at *T** if and only if

(1) P ought at T to do A at $T*$,
(2) it is not the case that P ought, just after T, to do A at $T*$, and
(3) if T is distinct from $T*$, then there is some act, B, such that
  (a) P ought at T to do B at T,
  (b) P refrains from doing B at T, and
  (c) clause (2) is true in virtue of subclause (b).

F

Finally, when should we say that a wrong *occurs*? In my earlier work, I proposed roughly the following account:

The Fourth Principle of Wrongdoing (PW4):
A wrong occurs at $T*$ if and only if, for some person P, act A, and time T,
(1) P ought at T to do A at $T*$, and
(2) P refrains from doing A at $T*$.[60]

This account implies, appropriately I think, that in the original case a wrong *occurred* at noon on Friday – the time at which I was due to return your book – even though I had *gone* wrong half an hour earlier with respect to returning it. But if, as I now believe, not all failures to fulfill an overall obligation constitute an infringement of that obligation, then PW4 must be revised; for where there is no infringement, no wrong occurs. I therefore propose that we accept the following account instead:

The Fifth Principle of Wrongdoing (PW5):
A wrong occurs at $T*$ if and only if, for some person P, act A, and time T,
(1) P goes wrong at T with respect to doing A at $T*$, and
(2) P refrains from doing A at $T*$.

Like PW4, this account is compatible with the position, which I used to hold, that wrongdoing occurs if and only if there is a failure to fulfill an obligation, but it is also compatible with the position, which I have just defended, that not all failures to fulfill an obligation involve wrongdoing and, hence, not all such failures involve the occurrence of some wrong. However, given its clause (2), PW5 may appear, unlike PW3, to be incompatible with the position, which I have also just defended, that one can infringe an obligation and yet fulfill it. There is no such incompatibility, however, as I will now explain.

---

[60] Zimmerman 1996, pp. 100–1.

Consider the case, presented in the last subsection, in which I went wrong on Wednesday (by virtue of my promise to my mother) with respect to returning your book to you at noon on Friday, even though I ended up returning it to you then. I take this case to show that one can infringe an obligation to perform some action and yet perform that action. I also take it to show that one can go wrong with respect to performing some action, even though no wrong *that is constituted by one's not performing that action* occurs. However, I do *not* take this case to give us any reason to say either that not all wrongdoing involves a failure to fulfill an obligation or that one can go wrong with respect to performing some action without some wrong occurring at the time at which the obligatory action is due to be performed. As I have stressed, all remote wrongdoing involves immediate wrongdoing. Since, as I see it, all immediate wrongdoing consists in the failure to fulfill an immediate obligation, it follows that all remote wrongdoing involves the failure to fulfill some obligation. Thus, when I went wrong on Wednesday with respect to returning your book on Friday, I did so by infringing the immediate obligation not to tell my mother that I would visit her in hospital on Friday; and I infringed this obligation by failing to do what I was then obligated to do. PW5 thus implies that a wrong occurred on Wednesday. Moreover, PW5 also implies that a wrong occurred on Friday. Although I returned your book to you, thereby fulfilling my obligation to do so (even though I had already gone wrong with respect to doing so), I of course also failed to visit my mother at that time, thereby failing to fulfill my obligation to do that. This wrong – the wrong constituted by my not visiting my mother – occurred at noon on Friday.

4

Ignorance and responsibility

The previous three chapters have been devoted to setting out in some detail the way in which ignorance affects moral obligation. Three views were distinguished. According to the Objective View, ignorance does not affect obligation at all; on this view, it is the facts that determine what one ought morally to do, irrespective of one's knowledge of those facts. (The relevant facts are those that concern the actual values of one's alternatives.) According to the Subjective View, on the contrary, ignorance does affect obligation; on this view, it is one's beliefs that determine what one ought morally to do, and if one's beliefs part company with the relevant facts, then so much the worse for those facts. Ignorance affects obligation according to the Prospective View, too; on this view, however, it is not one's beliefs but one's evidence that determines what one ought morally to do, and if one's evidence parts company either with the relevant facts or with one's beliefs about the facts, then, once again, so much the worse for those facts and those beliefs. It is the Prospective View that I have sought to defend and develop.

I want now to address a different issue: the way in which ignorance affects moral responsibility. I am concerned here with "responsibility" in its backward-looking sense: responsibility for things that have happened in the past. ("Responsibility" also has a forward-looking sense: responsibility for things that may happen in the future. In this sense, it is, I think, synonymous with "obligation.") There are two main modes of such responsibility: praiseworthiness or laudability, on the one hand, and blameworthiness or culpability, on the other.[1] Many proponents of the Objective View say that, whereas one's evidence is irrelevant to what

---

[1] There is also a neutral and, because neutral, rather uninteresting mode of responsibility, for which there is no standard name. (In Zimmerman 1988, pp. 61 ff., I call it "indifference-worthiness.") One difficulty, to which I will return below, is that it is plausible to claim that laudability is just one of perhaps several kinds of praiseworthiness, and culpability just one of perhaps several kinds of blameworthiness.

one's obligations are, it is directly relevant to one's moral responsibility. Recall Case 2 from chapter 1, in which it is presupposed that drug A would in fact completely cure John, drug B would relieve his condition but not cure him completely, drug C would kill him, and giving John no drug at all would leave him permanently incurable:

Case 2:
All the evidence at Jill's disposal indicates (in keeping with the facts) that giving John drug B would cure him partially and giving him no drug would render him permanently incurable, but it also indicates (in contrast to the facts) that giving him drug C would cure him completely and giving him drug A would kill him.

As noted in section 1.4, G. E. Moore, one of the chief proponents of the Objective View, would say in this case (given that all else is equal) that, although Jill would do overall wrong – that is, would fail to do what she is overall obligated to do – if she gave John drug C, she would not be to blame if she did so; indeed, she would be to blame if she did not do so.[2] This position has been endorsed by other writers.[3] I of course reject it. I have argued that in Case 2 Jill ought overall to give John drug C, precisely because of the nature of the evidence available to her. I nonetheless recognize the distinction between ascriptions of obligation and ascriptions of responsibility, and so the question remains whether Jill would be to blame for giving John drug C. Contrary to what Moore and others would say, on my view Jill could indeed be to blame for giving John this drug, even though that is what she ought overall to do. In this chapter I will try to explain how this is so. In so doing, I will argue that it is one's beliefs, rather than one's evidence, that determine what it is for which one is to blame. (The sort of uncertainty at issue, then, will be doxastic rather than epistemic.) The relevant beliefs in this case, however, are those that concern not the *values* of one's alternatives but their overall moral *rightness* or *wrongness*.

---

[2] See n. 39 to chapter 1. It is not absolutely clear whether, in saying this, Moore intends by "to blame" or "blameworthy" to refer to that mode of moral responsibility that I have called culpability. (See the last note.) Indeed, there is some indication that he doesn't intend this, since he explicitly equates "*P* is to blame" and "*P* ought to be blamed," which in turn, in keeping with his advocacy of the Objective View, he understands in terms of *P*'s being blamed actually having better consequences than *P*'s not being blamed. It is absurd to claim that *P* is culpable if and only if blaming *P* would actually have better consequences than not blaming *P*, although that is perhaps what Moore thinks and appears also to be what others think. Cf. Schlick 1966, p. 61; Smart 1973, p. 54; Dennett 1984, p. 162.
[3] See, e.g., Parfit 1984, p. 25; Jackson 1986, pp. 352–3; Timmons 2002, p. 126.

4.1 MORAL OBLIGATION *VS.* MORAL RESPONSIBILITY

The ambiguity of the term "responsible" between its backward- and forward-looking senses may be responsible (in a third, purely causal sense) for the fact that many writers appear implicitly to embrace the following thesis:

The Equivalence Thesis:
One is morally responsible (in the backward-looking sense) for having done some-thing if and only if one had a moral responsibility (in the forward-looking sense) – that is, a moral obligation – not to do that thing but did it nonetheless.

(Because of the dangers posed by the ambiguity of "responsible," I will henceforth use it only in the backward-looking sense.) One problem with the Equivalence Thesis is that it confuses responsibility in general with culpability in particular; it overlooks laudability. Whereas it may seem plausible to say that one is culpable for having done something if and only if one had an obligation not to do it that one did not fulfill, there is no plausibility at all in tying laudability to unfulfilled obligations in this way. A second problem with the Equivalence Thesis is that it overlooks the distinction between overall and merely prima facie obligation. It is surely not the case that one incurs culpability simply in virtue of having failed to fulfill a prima facie obligation, if that obligation was overridden by some other obligation that one had. A final problem with the Equivalence Thesis is that, even when restricted to culpability and to overall obligation, it is still false, and false in both directions. It is false to say that one is culpable for having done something *if* one had an overall obligation not to do it that one did not fulfill, because it is possible to have an excuse for having done something overall wrong. And it is false to say that one is culpable for having done something *only if* one had an overall obligation not to do it that one did not fulfill, because it is possible to have what I will call an "accuse" despite having done nothing overall wrong.

The possibility of excuses for wrongdoing is commonly, though not universally, acknowledged. It is sometimes said that a genuine or successful excuse serves to show that an agent has not really done anything wrong.[4] This claim, however, collapses the traditional distinction between justifica-tions and excuses and ignores the fact that ascriptions of obligation, with

---

[4] Cf. Wallace 1994, pp. 127 and 135; Rivera López 2006. See Zimmerman 2004 for a rebuttal.

which justifications have to do, are essentially a matter of how acts are to be evaluated, whereas ascriptions of responsibility, with which excuses have to do, are essentially a matter of how agents are to be evaluated. This is a common observation. Stated in this way, the observation is in fact slightly misleading, for two reasons. First, both kinds of ascriptions concern both agents and acts; after all, it is *agents* that are obligated to act in certain ways, and it is for their *acts* that agents may be held responsible. Second, both kinds of ascription concern not just acting in particular but behavior (including omission) in general and also the consequences of behavior. Nonetheless, the point is that ascriptions of obligation are what may be called "act-based" or "act-focused," in that they concern the assessment of agents' behavior, and the consequences of their behavior, relative to behavior in which they could otherwise engage or have engaged. Ascriptions of responsibility, by contrast, concern the assessment of agents in light of the behavior in which they have engaged.

The possibility of accuses is rarely acknowledged, although a few philosophers have accepted it. This is somewhat puzzling, given the common observation just mentioned. It is a possibility that I will develop and defend in section 4.3 below.

Since the time of Aristotle, it has been customary to distinguish two conditions of moral responsibility, one metaphysical, having to do with the agent's *freedom* of will, the other mental, having to do with the agent's freedom of *will*.[5] The distinction can get blurred. Aristotle himself used the term "voluntary" in reference to both conditions and, as noted in section 3.5, the term "control" is often used to refer to that kind of freedom that is constituted by what one can intentionally do in particular (rather than simply by what one can do, intentionally or otherwise, in general), and such control obviously has a mental component. It is nonetheless clear that the metaphysical strand of responsibility is indeed to be distinguished from the mental strand, in as much as the former has to do with one's independence from and mastery of one's environment, whereas the latter has to do with one's internal constitution. In recent years, the metaphysical aspect of responsibility has received far more attention from philosophers than the mental aspect, due not only to the perennial fascination with the threat that causal determinism poses to freedom of action or will, but also to the particular puzzles that have recently been brought to light by Harry Frankfurt's challenge to what he calls the principle of alternate possibilities

---

[5] Cf. Aristotle 1941, pp. 964 ff. (Book III of *Nicomachean Ethics*).

and by Bernard Williams' and Thomas Nagel's discussion of the possibility
and nature of moral luck.[6] In this chapter, however, it is on the mental
aspect of responsibility that I will concentrate.

Although the Prospective View ties one's obligations to one's evidence,
I noted in section 1.7 that this view does not imply that it is easy to know
what one's obligations are. That it may sometimes, indeed often, be
difficult to discover what one ought overall morally to do is an unfortunate
fact of life. Even on those occasions when one's obligations are knowable,
it may still of course happen that one doesn't know what one ought to do;
for one's beliefs may fail to comport with one's evidence. Thus it is possible
for someone to do something that is morally wrong without believing that
it is morally wrong. This seemingly plain fact has sometimes been denied.
Some have claimed that it is a necessary, analytic truth that, if one does
moral wrong, then one acts in the belief that one is doing moral wrong.
There are two ways to construe this claim: as a claim about analysis, or as a
claim about synonymy. Either way, it cannot be accepted.

A strong endorsement of the claim, understood as a claim about analysis,
is to be found in the work of Galen Strawson, who says:

[W]hile it may perhaps be too simple, it is not in any way illegitimate...simply to
define morally wrong action as action that is (i) of a certain kind..., and (ii) believed
by its performer to be morally wrong.[7]

Although Strawson doesn't unequivocally embrace such an analysis (for
fear it may be "too simple"), he clearly accepts that it would not involve
any logical or conceptual incoherence (it would not be "illegitimate"), and
it is clear from other things he says that he thinks that a belief about moral
wrongdoing is, as he puts it, a "necessary constitutive condition" of moral
wrongdoing. But this claim is unacceptable; it involves conceptual circularity. There is a constraint that any proposed analysis must meet, and it is
this: if a concept *F* is constituted by, or analyzable in terms of, a concept *G*,
then *G* is conceptually prior to *F* (that is, a grasp of *F* presupposes a grasp
of *G*). Strawson's claim about wrongdoing violates this constraint and is
therefore to be rejected. It might be objected that it must be possible to
grasp *F* (the analysandum) without grasping *G* (the analysans), for

[6] See Frankfurt 1969, Williams 1981, and Nagel 1976.   [7] Strawson 1986, p. 220.

173

otherwise proposed analyses could never be assessed for accuracy. But this is beside the point. Although it surely is true that an analysandum can be grasped in some way and to some extent without its respective analysans being grasped, a successful analysis is one that shows that the analysandum is *best* and *most fully* grasped by means of grasping the analysans, and this cannot be the case if grasping the analysans presupposed grasping the analysandum; for that would be viciously circular.

It might be said that the alleged analytic truth in question involves synonymy rather than analysis, but this too is unacceptable. If two expressions are synonymous, then what one expresses is identical with what the other expresses, and so what one expresses cannot be entertained without that which is expressed by the other being entertained. But it is clear that one can entertain the notion of one's doing moral wrong without entertaining the notion of one's believing that one is doing moral wrong.

You might agree with what I have just said and yet maintain that it is a necessary, synthetic truth that, if one does moral wrong, then one acts in the belief that one is doing moral wrong. Although this claim cannot be rejected for either of the purely formal reasons just given, it is surely highly suspect nonetheless for a reason similar to one that I gave in section 1.3 when discussing the Subjective View. Surely we don't want to say that Hitler, for example, did no wrong just because he did not believe that he was doing wrong. It seems clear, then, that it is perfectly possible for one to do moral wrong without believing that one is doing so.

Consider, for example, Case 10, introduced in section 2.4. In that case Alf, upset by Brenda's favoring Charles over him, pointed a gun at her and threatened to teach her a lesson she wouldn't forget. I discussed various versions of this case. Consider any version in which, in light of the evidence available to him, Alf's behavior imposed a grave risk of harm on Brenda. Given the Prospective View (and the simplifying assumption that Alf's evidence concerning the actual values at stake was accurate), it follows that Alf's behavior was overall morally wrong. But it could well be that he did not believe this. Indeed, there are many ways in which such ignorance might arise. Perhaps Alf, in his passion and fury, simply did not consider the question whether it was wrong to threaten Brenda. Or perhaps he did consider this but didn't reach a conclusion on the matter. Or perhaps he believed that it was not wrong to threaten her because he had misconstrued some pertinent empirical evidence. Or perhaps he had misconstrued some pertinent evaluative evidence. Or perhaps he had misconstrued none of the pertinent evidence, and believed that threatening her was not prospectively best, but still believed that it was not wrong to do so because he rejected the Prospective View's verdict that one ought to do what is prospectively best. And there are doubtless still other ways in which Alf might have failed to recognize that it was wrong for him to threaten Brenda.

Question: is Alf to blame for having threatened Brenda, or does he have an excuse in virtue of his ignorance that his behavior was wrong? (That is: overall morally wrong. This qualification will be implicit throughout this section.) Surely such ignorance does not always excuse one's behavior, since one may be culpable for one's ignorance. This is commonly acknowledged. What is not commonly acknowledged, though, is that culpability for such ignorance is rare. On the contrary, our common practice indicates that we think that such culpability is frequently incurred; for we often blame people for performing actions that were wrong (or that we take to have been wrong) on the grounds that, even if they *didn't* know that what they were doing was wrong, they *should have* known this. Many would say just this in Alf's case. I believe that this practice is misguided, however, and is itself likely to result in wrongdoing.

Here is my argument. Call the item of behavior in question A, and grant that (1) Alf did A, A was wrong, but Alf was ignorant of this fact since, at the time he did A, he did not believe that it was wrong. Now (2) one is culpable for ignorant behavior only if one is culpable for the ignorance in or from which it was performed. Hence (3) Alf is culpable for having done A only if he is culpable for the ignorance in or from which he did A. However, (4) one is culpable for something only if one was in control of that thing. Hence (5) Alf is culpable for having done A only if he was in control of the ignorance – in particular, the failure to believe that what he was doing was wrong – in or from which he did A. But (6) one is never directly in control of whether one believes or does not believe something; that is, any control that one has over one's beliefs and disbeliefs is only ever indirect. Moreover, (7) if one is culpable for something over which one had merely indirect control, then one's culpability for it is itself merely indirect. Furthermore, (8) one is indirectly culpable for something only if that thing was a consequence of something else for which one is directly culpable. Hence (9) Alf is culpable for having done A only if there was something else, B, for which he is directly culpable and of which the ignorance – the disbelief – in or from which he did A was a consequence. But (10) whatever B was, it cannot itself have been an instance of ignorant behavior, because then the argument would apply all over again to it; B must, then, have been some item of behavior, some act or omission of Alf's, that Alf believed at the time to be wrong. Hence (11) Alf is culpable for having done *A* only if there was some other act or omission, *B*, for which he is directly culpable and of which his failure to believe that *A* was wrong was a consequence, and *B* was such that Alf believed it at the time to be wrong.

The picture that emerges is thus one of a chain of events or occurrences, each a consequence of its predecessors, at whose origin lies some item of behavior that Alf believed at the time to be overall wrong and for which he is directly culpable. Not at the origin, but lying somewhere further down the chain, are, first, the ignorance in or from which Alf did *A* and, second, Alf's performance of *A*. For these and other such items on the chain Alf is only indirectly culpable. We may call such a chain a chain of culpability. Now, Alf has, of course, been picked at random. What is true of him is also true of Brenda, Charles, Doris, Edward, and so on. We thus arrive at the following general thesis:

The Origination Thesis:
Every chain of culpability is such that at its origin lies an item of behavior for which the agent is directly culpable and which the agent believed, at the time at which the behavior occurred, to be overall morally wrong.[8]

As far as I can tell, ignorant behavior is rarely to be traced to a non-ignorant origin. It would be surprising, for example, to find any such episode of witting wrongdoing in Alf's history to which his wrongful threatening of Brenda can be traced. In the absence of any such episode, the Origination Thesis implies that Alf is not culpable for his ignorant behavior. And there is no reason to think that Alf is atypical in this respect. Thus the Origination Thesis implies that in general culpability for ignorant behavior is rare. This may be appropriately described as a deflationary conclusion, since it implies that our common practice of frequently blaming people such as Alf for their ignorant behavior is too expansive.

My argument is of course open to challenge. Each of premises (2), (4), (6), and (7) might be questioned. (I suppose that (8) might be questioned, too, but I won't try to defend it. I regard it as analytic.)

---

[8] This thesis is overlooked even by Holly Smith, who is perhaps closer to accepting it than anyone other than myself who has written on the topic. Although she gives an account of culpable ignorance according to which all responsibility for such ignorance is rooted in something else (which she calls a "benighting act") for which one is culpable, she fails to acknowledge that culpability requires, at bottom, a belief concerning wrongdoing. Cf. Smith 1983, pp. 547–8 and 556, and 1991, pp. 279–80.

A

Consider premise (2), according to which one is culpable for ignorant behavior only if one is culpable for the ignorance in or from which it was performed. Even those who seem most strongly opposed to the Origination Thesis appear to accept this premise,[9] but that of course doesn't mean that we should accept it. Should we?

It is clear that we should *not* accept premise (2) on the basis of the more general claim (of which (2) is an instance) that one is culpable for behaving in or from some mental state, *M*, only if one is culpable for *M* itself. There are many counterexamples to this general claim. One might be culpable for acting in anger, for example, without being culpable for one's anger. After all, perhaps one cannot help being angry. This would serve to relieve one of responsibility for one's anger (I believe – this is an implication of premise (4), which I will discuss shortly); but it wouldn't serve to relieve one of responsibility for acting in anger, since such behavior might be avoidable even if one's anger itself is not. So, too, one might be culpable for acting cruelly even if one cannot help, and thus is not culpable for, one's cruel impulses. Similarly for jealousy and indefinitely many other mental states. Why, then, should ignorance – that is, the failure to believe that one is doing wrong – be an exception?

The answer, I think, is that what distinguishes acting angrily (or cruelly, or jealously, and so on) from acting ignorantly does not have to do with any question of avoidability. It has to do with the fact that, typically, one can act angrily while being aware that one ought not to perform the act in question, whereas one of course cannot act in or from ignorance of the fact that one ought not to do something while being aware that one ought not to do it. Thus one can be culpable for acting angrily in a way in which one cannot be culpable for acting ignorantly. This stems, I believe, from the fact that lack of ignorance is a root requirement for responsibility. Given that it is such a requirement, (2) is true. But while I think that this does help explain why (2) is true, clearly I cannot appeal to it when using (2) in an attempt to show that lack of ignorance is a root requirement for responsibility; for that would be to beg the question.

How else might one try to argue for premise (2)? I'm not sure; nonetheless, I take it to be very plausible. It is worth remarking that this premise is also deeply embedded in our everyday practice of blaming people for

---

[9] See, e.g., Sverdlik 1993, p. 141; Montmarquet 1993, p. 3, and 1995, pp. 44–5.

their ignorant behavior – even if that practice is, as I have claimed, in some ways misguided. As I have noted, we often blame people for performing actions that they *didn't* know were wrong on the grounds that they *should have* known they were wrong. (Contrast this practice with, for example, the fact that we do *not* typically restrict our blaming people for acting in anger to those cases in which they should not have been angry in the first place. We may find the anger perfectly justifiable and yet condemn them for yielding to it.) Accordingly, if we judge that it is not the case that the people in question should have been aware that what they were doing was wrong, we excuse them for their ignorant behavior. What seems usually to be overlooked, however, and may help explain our tendency to over-estimate the number of cases in which people are to be blamed for their ignorant behavior, is that, even if it is true on some occasion that someone *should have* known something that he (or she) didn't know, it does *not* follow that that person is *culpable* for not knowing what he didn't know. To say that he should have known what he didn't know is, presumably, to attribute his ignorance to some *wrongdoing* on his part. But wrongdoing doesn't suffice for culpability! It is ironic that someone who recognizes the possibility that one have an excuse for wrongful behavior performed in or from ignorance should be blind to the possibility that one have an excuse for wrongful behavior that results in ignorance; yet that seems precisely to be the mistake committed by those who claim that its being the case that one should have known what one didn't know suffices (*ceteris paribus*) for one's being culpable for one's ignorance.[10]

B

Consider, now, premise (4), according to which one is culpable for some-thing only if one was in control of that thing. This premise expresses what in the last section I called the metaphysical condition of culpability. In section 3.5 I noted various ways in which one may have control over something. I distinguished between regulative control and guidance con-trol, between intentional control and coincidental control, between com-plete control and partial control, between direct control and indirect control, and between immediate control and remote control. There are doubtless still other distinctions that can be drawn. Premise (4) does not

---

[10] See, e.g., Guerrero 2007. Guerrero also makes what I take to be the mistake of subscribing to the Objective View rather than the Prospective View.

address these distinctions and is, to that extent, unclear. We needn't worry about these distinctions here, though. We can sidestep them by understanding premise (4) to say simply that culpability for something requires *some* form of control over that thing, control that is *either* immediate *or* remote, *either* direct *or* indirect, and so on. So understood, premise (4) is both extremely plausible and very widely accepted. Nonetheless, it has been challenged.

One philosopher who has recently argued at length for the rejection of premise (4) is Eugene Schlossberger. He has claimed that moral responsibility, properly understood, is simply a matter of moral evaluability, which is not essentially a function of one's being free or acting freely, that is, of one's being in control of one's actions. One may be properly morally evaluated, he says, either positively or negatively, in light not just of one's actions but also of one's beliefs, emotions, and other "items," regardless of whether one enjoys freedom with respect to these items.[11] In saying this, Schlossberger echoes such writers as Robert Adams, who says that the graduate of the Hitler *Jugend* is to be blamed for his vile beliefs, no matter how he came by them.[12] Others have made similar claims.[13] And there is surely something right about this. We find the Nazi's beliefs and actions reprehensible, and we condemn him for them, regardless of whether he was in control either of the acquisition of these beliefs or of his acting on them.

The lesson to be learned from this, though, is not that premise (4) is to be rejected. It is, rather, that there are a *variety* of ways in which a person is open to moral evaluation; attributions of moral responsibility constitute only *one* such way. Thus we may indeed say that the beliefs and actions of the youthful Nazi are morally reprehensible, and even that he is morally reprehensible in light of them, without saying that he is morally responsible for them. We might condemn him, blame him, but such condemnation or blame is not, or at least should not be, tantamount to holding him morally responsible (culpable) for his beliefs and actions – not, that is, unless he exercised freedom with respect to them.[14] Similarly, someone who cannot resist the impulse to help someone else and as a result does so unfreely, is surely morally admirable, in some way, both for having the impulse and for

---

[11] Schlossberger 1992, pp. 4–7, 79, 101, 112, 117–18.   [12] Adams 1985, p. 19.
[13] See, e.g., Brandt 1959, pp. 470–3; Milo 1984, pp. 41 ff.
[14] Hence my remark in n. 1 above that not all blameworthiness need take the particular form of culpability.

acting on it; but we need not infer that this person is morally responsible (laudable) for these things. Someone who has such an impulse but who can resist it and yet acts on it anyhow (or, at least, acts on it freely despite its irresistibility[15]) – such a person is to be assessed quite differently.[16] For he is acting "on his own," independently, and this makes a world of difference; it makes him (*ceteris paribus*) morally responsible for his action.

I am not distinguishing between types of moral evaluation solely in order to save premise (4). That would be to beg the question. The fact is that, regardless of what position we take on moral responsibility, it must be admitted that morality is complex, involving a multiplicity of items to be evaluated and ways to evaluate them. Agents, their traits, characters, beliefs, actions, and so on are all items that are candidates for some type of moral evaluation; and such terms as "good" and "bad," "right" and "wrong," "praiseworthy" and "blameworthy," "admirable" and "reprehensible," and so on can be variously applied, sometimes some more aptly than others, to such items. This of course does not prove that the sort of reprehensibility displayed by the youthful Nazi is not culpability; but it does point to the need to support such homogenization of moral evalua-tion with argument, especially since there would appear to be something quite different, qualitatively, about our moral evaluation, for example, of someone who acts on Nazi beliefs that he has had no opportunity or reason to question compared with our moral evaluation of someone who acts on such beliefs having had such opportunity and reason.[17]

Schlossberger acknowledges the need to support his rejection of premise (4) with argument. In particular, he attempts to show that his account of responsibility is just as successful as the traditional account (according to which premise (4) is true) in grounding the various "reactive attitudes" having to do with gratitude, resentment, reward, punishment, and so on, with which moral responsibility is often directly associated.[18] Let me briefly examine this claim, with specific reference to reward and punishment.

---

[15] I include this parenthetical remark in case responsibility requires only guidance and not regulative control. Cf. Fischer 1994, ch. 8.

[16] Cf. Mark Twain, as reported in van Inwagen 1983, pp. 63–4: "I am morally superior to George Washington. He couldn't tell a lie. I can and I don't."

[17] I don't mean to be advocating extreme heterogenization of moral evaluation. Sometimes the moral differences between two things will be quantitative rather than qualitative. What I am suggesting is that homogenizers bear the burden of proof.

[18] Schlossberger 1992, pp. 6–7. On the relation between responsibility and the reactive attitudes, cf. Strawson 1962; Zimmerman 1988; Wallace 1994; Fischer and Ravizza 1998.

It is often claimed, somewhat controversially, that the culpable deserve to be punished, and also, less controversially, that the inculpable deserve not to be punished. Schlossberger maintains that this claim is true even on his account of responsibility. In particular, he says that retribution is to be understood in terms of what he calls "abstract justice" and that such justice need invoke only moral evaluability and need not concern freedom.[19] It is abstractly just, he says, that those who are negatively morally evaluable fare less well than those who are positively morally evaluable; for one's "life situation" should match or fit one's "moral situation."[20] This is plausible, but I don't think it affords a satisfactory account of the (in)justice of punishment. For consider someone who is morally reprehensible (he is a cruel sadist, say, and often acts on his sadistic impulses) but uncontrollably so. I submit that the uncontrollability of his impulses and (I am now assuming) of his acting on them makes him *not* culpable for acting on them, and such inculpability means that he deserves *not* to be punished. Perhaps there is something to be said for the view that an uncontrollable sadist deserves to fare less well than an uncontrollable altruist. But whether or not this is so, surely an uncontrollable sadist is innocent in a way in which a sadist in control of his sadistic actions is not, and such innocence means that he deserves *not* to be punished. He is a moral monster, perhaps, and he, his character, and his actions are to be deplored (though perhaps he is not to be deplored to his face; that might be cruel, and controllably so). Perhaps his liberty of action should be curtailed despite his inculpability, in order to prevent his harming others. But this doesn't mean that he deserves to be punished.[21]

(It could still be argued, I suppose, that even if homogenization with regard to culpability and other types of reprehensibility is to be avoided, still homogenization with regard to laudability and admirability is not.[22] For, while there is force to the observation that those who are inculpable – even if reprehensible – deserve not to be punished, is there analogous force to the claim that those who are "unlaudable" – even if admirable – deserve not to be rewarded? Surely such reward doesn't constitute an injustice in the way that punishment of the inculpable does, for it involves no unwelcome imposition. But even if this is so, such reward doesn't constitute

---

[19] Schlossberger 1992, p. 166.   [20] Schlossberger 1992, pp. 168 ff.
[21] Cf. Frankfurt 1988, pp. 40–1, on the distinction between blame and contempt. Cf. also Frankfurt 1988, p. 185; Wolf 1987, pp. 53–5.
[22] This would constitute an asymmetry related to the one advocated in Wolf 1980.

justice either. Just as punishment involves a particular kind of condemnation, so too the sort of reward that is analogous to punishment involves a particular kind of recognition. Moreover, just as, arguably, those who are culpable deserve to be punished, so too those who are laudable deserve to be rewarded in the manner analogous to punishment. Someone who is admirable but not laudable would be lacking in such desert.)

C

Premise (7), according to which culpability that is merely indirect requires control that is merely indirect, doesn't follow from premises (4) and (8), but it is a natural assumption to make alongside those two assumptions. Given that culpability may be either direct or indirect and that control may also be either direct or indirect, it is surely plausible to say that the former distinction tracks the latter – once it has been accepted that culpability in general requires control. To see this, consider a variation on an example from chapter 3. Suppose that Jill injects a dose of some drug into John's backside. I said in section 3.5 that I take this action to consist in her attempting to inject the drug together with her attempt causing the drug to enter John's body. Let me now be a little more precise. Suppose that a is Jill's decision or attempt, b is the depression of the syringe, c is the drug's entering John's body, d is his health's deteriorating, and e is his being angry. Let us suppose that a causes b, which causes c, and so on. (There will of course be consequences of a other than those just mentioned; but those mentioned will serve as a representative sample.) In light of the occurrence of a–e Jill will have performed various actions. The case may be depicted as in figure 4.1.

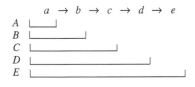

Figure 4.1

The arrows represent causation. A (which consists simply of a) is the minimal action (if it can be called an action at all) constituted by Jill's decision. B (which consists of a's causing b) is the action of Jill's pushing the syringe. (In von Wright's terminology, b is the "result" of B.[23]) C (which consists of a's causing c) is the action of Jill's injecting the drug. D is the action of her impairing John's health. E is the action of her angering John. (Note that, in light of the causal connections between a and e, Jill may be said to do E by doing D, D by doing C, and so on.) Suppose now that Jill is culpable for what happened. Given premise (4), it follows that she was in control of what happened. She had direct control over a, we may assume, and thereby indirect control over each of b–e. Consequently, she had direct control over A and a sort of hybrid control over B–E. So, too, for her responsibility in the matter. Jill is directly culpable for a (that is, A), indirectly culpable for b–e, and bears a sort of hybrid culpability for B–E.

D

Consider, finally, premise (6), according to which one is never in direct control of whether one believes or does not believe something. This premise has been challenged by James Montmarquet, who argues that one can be culpable for one's ignorance regarding whether it is overall morally wrong to do something by way of being careless regarding what to believe, that such carelessness is typically in one's direct control, and that, when this is so, one's state of (dis)belief is also in one's direct control.[24]

Montmarquet's argument is by way of an analogy. Suppose that one has direct control over the degree of care with which one whistles a tune. This does not imply that one's whistling is only in one's indirect control. On the contrary, direct control over the former is typically accompanied by direct control over the latter; if one whistles carelessly, for instance, then both the carelessness with which one whistles and the whistling itself are typically in one's direct control. Analogously, suppose that one has direct control over the care one takes regarding what to believe about what one ought to do. It would be a mistake to infer that any beliefs that one forms can only be in one's indirect control. On the contrary, direct control over the degree of care one takes in forming a belief is typically accompanied by direct control over the belief itself.

How, exactly, is it that one might take care regarding what one believes? According to Montmarquet, this involves "the familiar twin goals of [the pursuit of] truth and the avoidance of error," which themselves presuppose a certain quality of "openness" on one's part.[25] To take care in this regard

---

[23] See von Wright 1971, p. 66.   [24] Montmarquet 1999.
[25] See Montmarquet 1993, p. 21, and 1999, p. 845.

is just to have an open mind – a mind that is sensitive to what is true and false and to (dis)believe accordingly – and this is something that is typically in one's direct control.

I believe that Montmarquet's analogy is flawed and that it fails to establish that we can ever be in direct control of whether we (dis)believe something. I will argue that one cannot have direct control either over the care one takes regarding what to believe about something or over the belief itself. I will argue further that, even if one could have direct control over the former, one could not have such control over the latter, in precisely the sort of case that concerns Montmarquet.

My argument for the claim that one cannot have direct control either over the care one takes regarding what to believe about something or over the belief itself is grounded in a rather conventional theory of action, one that I adumbrated in the last subsection when discussing Jill's injecting a drug into John.[26] On this theory, all actions, whether physical or mental, are complex events that involve one event, a volition (a decision, an attempt), causing a certain other event or state. This other event or state (which, again following von Wright, I will call the "result" of the action) is of course an "external" effect of the volition, but it is "internal" to the action. Further effects are "external" to the action and thus mere consequences of the action, although these further effects may themselves be the results of other actions. Thus, and for example, if I flip a switch by raising my hand, then the following will have occurred: a volition (typically, a decision to raise my hand in order to flip the switch) causing my hand to rise, thereby causing the switch to go up. The action of my raising my hand comprises the volition's causing my hand's rising; the action of my flipping the switch comprises this same volition's causing the switch's going up. My hand's rising is an effect of my decision to raise it but the result of my raising it; the switch's going up is an effect of my decision to raise my hand, of my hand's rising, and of my raising my hand, but it is the result of my flipping the switch. And so on. (A graphic representation of this case could be given in the manner of figure 4.1 above.) For the sake of this illustration, we may assume that the action of my raising my hand is "basic," in that it is not itself performed by way of performing any other action (unless we count the volition internal to it as a minimal kind of

---

[26] This theory is elaborated in Zimmerman 1984. Cf. the account attributed to Ross in section 1.2 above.

action in its own right); the action of my flipping the switch is of course non-basic.

On this view, all actions (other than mere volitions) consist in the bringing about of a result. This is most easily seen in the sort of case that I have just described, where English provides a ready term not only for the action ("raising," "flipping") but also for the result ("rising," "going up"). But it holds also in those cases where no obvious term for the result is available. (Consider the action of walking. This involves the bringing about of a certain motion of one's feet, but there is no English term I know of that precisely expresses this motion.) It holds also in cases of mental action (such as multiplying 6 by 7 "in one's head," or offering up an unspoken prayer).

On such a theory of action, freedom of action can be seen to rest in freedom of the will. To return to the original case: under the circumstances, I control my flipping the switch just in case I control my raising my hand, and I control my raising my hand just in case I control my decision to raise it. It is the decision over which I have direct control; its effects, which include not just the consequences of my basic action but also its result, are something over which I have only indirect control. On this view, then, no action (other than a mere volition) – not even a basic action – is in an agent's direct control. Rather, as noted in the last section, control over an action is "hybrid": direct with respect to the volition but indirect with respect to the result.

It is plausible to think that all basic actions are intentional. But, even if so, one can be in control of actions that are (non-basic and) unintentional. Suppose that, in raising my hand, I not only flip the switch, but I also turn on the light, illuminate the room, and alert a prowler to the fact that I am home.[27] It may well be that I am in control of all that is involved here, including the prowler's being alerted, even if I am wholly oblivious to the presence of the prowler. In the terminology introduced in section 3.5, my control over the prowler's being alerted will be merely "coincidental" rather than "intentional," but it is a form of control nonetheless.

One can be in control of omissions as well as actions. It can happen, for instance, that my hand rises not because I raise it, but because I let it rise – I omit to prevent its rising. (It is being raised by someone or something else; I could do something about this, but I do not.) According to the present theory, it is once again the case that my control over my hand's rising must be indirect, by way of direct control over a decision to let it rise. (If there is

---

[27] The case is taken from Davidson 1980, p. 4.

no such decision, its rising will occur wholly independently of me.) In this case, my hand's rising is arguably not a *causal* consequence of my decision to let it rise, but it is a consequence nonetheless, in that my hand would not have risen, under the circumstances, if I had not decided to let it rise.

As with basic actions, it is plausible to think that all basic omissions are intentional. But still one can be in control of omissions that are (non-basic and) unintentional. For example, it may be that, in letting my hand rise, I unintentionally let the prowler be alerted.

Consider now Montmarquet's case of whistling. He claims that one can exercise direct control both over the care with which one whistles and over one's whistling itself. It is an interesting question whether there are two actions here or one. Is whistling carefully a single action, as whistling loudly is? Or does whistling carefully consist in doing one thing (taking care, focusing one's attention) while doing another (whistling)? I incline toward the latter view. In either case, though, it is clear that the present approach implies that neither the care with which one whistles nor the whistling itself is in one's direct control. For whether there is one action here or two, control over actions (other than mere volitions) is not direct but hybrid.

Turn now to the case of careful (or careless) belief. If the analogy were apt, the same inference would hold: control over the care one takes regarding what to believe and over the belief itself is not direct. But there is in fact an important disanalogy between the whistling and belief cases. For belief (that is, the attitude of believing, not the proposition believed) is *not* an action, as whistling is; it can at best be the *result* of an action (the action of bringing it about that one believes something; sometimes the attitude of believing is called an "act" of believing, but this is misleading – "state" is far more appropriate). Let us use the phrase "to form a belief" to express the action in question. Now, as in the whistling case, whether carefully forming a belief constitutes one action or two, one's control over the action(s) is, on the present theory, not direct by hybrid. But in addition – and this is where the disanalogy arises – one's control over the belief itself is not direct but *indirect*.[28]

---

[28] Regarding this issue, consider these remarks in Montmarquet 1999, pp. 843 and 844: "Here what I will try to show is that if ... one's responsibility for one's carelessness is direct, one's responsibility for one's carelessly formed belief is *also* direct ... "; " ... it should be clear that we can speak of an individual as having direct control over his degree of care and, to that extent, direct ... control over his forming the belief that he is then forming"; "My ... conclusion ... is that ... [an agent] may have direct responsibility both for his carelessness and for his carelessly formed belief." The vacillation between talk of a belief and talk of its being formed is plain.

186

It may be that "to form a belief" is sometimes used to express, not the action of bringing it about that one has a certain belief, but the omission that consists in letting it happen that one has a certain belief. But again, on the present theory, one can at best have *indirect* control over such a belief, by way of directly controlling a decision of which the belief is a consequence.

(It may indeed be that "to form a belief" is sometimes used to express simply the coming, or beginning, to have a certain belief. In such a case, there is no necessity that the belief be brought about or allowed to happen. But, if so, then there is no opportunity for anyone to exercise control over it, either directly or indirectly.)

In summary, the central question is: how can I control (whether intentionally or not) my transition from a state of not believing that *p* to a state of believing that *p*? Such control requires that the transition occur either by way of my bringing it about that I believe that *p* or by way of my letting it happen that I believe that *p*. According to the present theory, however I manage to achieve this, in either case my believing that *p* will be a consequence (causal or otherwise) of a decision of mine, and hence something over which I have at best indirect control.

Now, conventional though it may be, the theory of action just sketched is nonetheless controversial. Those who subscribe to it will accept that one cannot have direct control either over the care that one takes regarding what to believe about something or over the belief itself. But those who do not subscribe to it may still resist this conclusion. At this point I could of course try to elaborate the theory and argue for it in turn, but that is an unmanageable task in the present context. It is better to take a different tack. I will now argue that, even if it is allowed that one can have direct control over the care that one takes regarding what to believe about something, still it must be accepted that one cannot have direct control over the belief itself, in precisely the sort of case that particularly concerns Montmarquet.

Montmarquet is concerned in particular with the sort of case in which one's state of (dis)belief is attributable to one's not having a mind that is sensitive to what is true and false. It seems to me that it is just such closed-mindedness that characterizes many people (a great many, I should think) when they engage in wrongdoing, even when (perhaps especially when) their wrongdoing is egregious. Consider Rudolf Höss, for example, who, as commandant at Auschwitz, had over two million people put to death. Or consider William Calley, who led the massacre of civilians at My Lai. Or consider the enormous evil perpetrated by such villains as Hitler, Stalin, Mao, Saddam Hussein... The list is long and gruesome. I see no reason to think that the evidence available to these people was so skewed that they should not be said to have done wrong. But it does seem plausible to think that they paid no heed to this evidence and did not believe that they were doing wrong.[29] And I will now argue that there is good reason to think, regardless of which particular theory of action is in the end to be accepted, that in such cases one's control over one's state of (dis)belief about what it is morally wrong to do can at best be merely indirect.

My argument rests on the following claim: any plausible account of control will deny that we are directly in control of what I have called the results of our non-basic actions.[30] Perhaps, on the theory you prefer, I am in direct control of my raising my hand. Perhaps also, on this theory, my raising my hand is identical with my hand's rising, so that direct control over the former implies direct control over the latter. Perhaps even, on this theory, my raising my hand is identical with my flipping the switch, so that direct control over the former once again implies direct control over the latter. But surely you will agree that I am *not* in direct control of *the switch's going up*.

Let us now apply this observation to the issue at hand. Remember that the central question concerns how I can control my transition from a state of not believing that *p* to a state of believing that *p*. Let us now assume (as is surely typical of the sorts of cases that concern us here) that this transition is not going to happen "on its own" and thus is not something that I can simply let happen. If I am to control it, then, it must be a matter of my controlling my bringing it about that I believe that *p*. How might I bring this belief about? Well, one way might be to adopt the Pascalian strategy, advocated at times by William James, of acting as if I believed that *p*.[31] But notice two things about this sort of case. First, it is clear that, in such a case, my forming the belief that *p* is a non-basic action. Second, such a strategy would seem to require that I attend to the proposition that *p*, which is precisely not what occurs in the cases of inattentiveness that concern Montmarquet. Another strategy might be that which Montmarquet

---

[29] Of course, I cannot be certain that they did not believe this, but it seems likely. Cf. Katz 1993, pp. 19, 26 ff., 66 ff.

[30] Or at least it will deny that we are directly in control of the results of actions that are non-basic in virtue of what Alvin Goldman calls causal generation in Goldman 1970, pp. 22–3. It is only with this type of non-basic action that I will be concerned below.

[31] See James 1968, pp. 719 ff. Cf. Gale 1999, p. 87.

himself advocates. But even if taking such care were in my direct control, *still* we should say that my believing that p is not in my direct control. This is because, in such a case, my bringing it about that I believe that p must be a non-basic action, since I must first change my attitude from one of being "closed" to one of being "open," and it is only *by way of* doing this that I can come to see the truth.

Notice that it would be a mistake to characterize the care that I take in such a case as being a matter of *keeping* an open mind, for this implies that my mind is already open and that all I need to do is maintain such openness. Perhaps, if my mind were open, my believing that p would not be achieved *by* keeping my mind open (just as I would not normally be said to bring it about that I see a certain object by keeping my eyes open), and so perhaps it could be argued that my bringing it about that I believe that p (like my bringing it about that I see the object) would then be a basic action. But the sort of case under consideration here is not like that. Rather than my mind's already being open, so that taking care consists simply in keeping it open, if I am to take care about what I believe I must open my mind. It is only *by way of* doing this that I can bring it about that I believe that p, and thus the latter is a non-basic action (just as my bringing it about that I see the object will be non-basic if I do this by way of opening my eyes). If, then, any plausible account of control will deny that we are directly in control of what I have called the results of our non-basic actions, any such theory will deny that, in the sort of case under discussion, I am directly in control of my believing that p.

I have one final, briefer argument for this same conclusion. It rests on the claim, mentioned earlier, that all basic actions are intentional. (Of course, this too is controversial.) Now, in the sort of case under discussion, in which I do not already believe that p and I am not attending to the proposition that p, my bringing it about that I believe that p will not be something that I do intentionally. (It is one thing to intentionally bring it about that one believes whatever is true; it is quite another to intentionally bring it about, with respect to a particular true proposition that p, that one believes that p.) Hence, in this sort of case, my bringing it about that I believe that p is not a basic action. Once again, then, it follows, from the claim that no one is directly in control of the result of a non-basic action, that I am not directly in control of my believing that p.[32]

---

[32] Cf. Hieronymi 2006 for yet another argument for this same conclusion.

E

I have said that the Origination Thesis implies that culpability for ignorant behavior is rare, and that this conflicts with our common practice of frequently blaming people for such behavior. However, this claim is predicated on the further claim that ignorant behavior is rarely to be traced to a non-ignorant origin (that is, to an item of behavior which the agent believed at the time to be overall morally wrong), and this further claim is itself open to challenge. Thus someone might try to embrace both the Origination Thesis and current practice by maintaining that ignorant behavior frequently has a non-ignorant origin.

I won't try to defend my position here. I leave it to you to judge whether ignorant behavior rarely or frequently has a non-ignorant origin. One of the difficulties in resolving this issue is, of course, a purely empirical one: that of determining how often people engage in behavior that they believe at the time to be overall morally wrong. But another difficulty is conceptual, since it is not clear just what counts as the sort of origin in question. The matter concerns the exact conditions of indirect culpability. According to premise (8), one is indirectly culpable for something only if that thing was a consequence of something else for which one is directly culpable. Even if this is accepted (as I am sure it should be – as I said, I take it to be an analytic truth), it leaves open both what sort of consequence is at issue and whether some other conditions must be satisfied in order for one to be indirectly culpable for something. The fewer restrictions placed on the sort of consequence at issue, the easier it will be to trace ignorant behavior to a non-ignorant origin. Similarly, the fewer other conditions that must be met for indirect culpability to be incurred, the easier once again it will be to trace such behavior to such an origin. I won't try to determine here just what we should say on these questions.[33]

Having said this, let me nonetheless add that culpability for ignorant behavior may be even rarer than the Origination Thesis itself implies. I have argued that all culpability involves a belief on the agent's part that he or she is doing something morally wrong. However, beliefs can be merely dispositional, rather than occurrent. If one believes merely dispositionally

---

[33] My main reason for leaving these questions aside is that I don't think it matters in the end what answers we give to them. This is because I believe that the degree to which one is culpable does not depend at all on what one is indirectly culpable for. I argue for this thesis in Zimmerman 2002b, pp. 560 ff.

that, in doing some act, one is doing wrong, then one need not advert to that act; for to advert to it is to contemplate it, to hold it consciously before one's mind. But while beliefs presumably can be merely dispositional, it is, I suspect, occurrent beliefs about wrongdoing that are, with one possible exception, required for culpability; and such beliefs involve advertence. The reason is this. With one possible exception, if a belief is not occurrent, then one cannot act either with the intention to heed the belief or with the intention not to heed it; if one has no such intention, then one cannot act either deliberately on or deliberately despite the belief; if this is so, then the belief plays no role in the reason for which one performs one's action; and, I am inclined to think, one incurs culpability for one's action only if one's belief concerning wrongdoing plays a role in the reason for which one performs the action. Suppose, for example, that Jill ought to give John some drug but that she doesn't believe this and so doesn't give him the drug; that she fails to believe that she ought to give him the drug because she has given no thought at all to John's treatment; that she has given no thought to his treatment because she has been daydreaming about Jack; and that she believes that it is wrong to daydream about Jack rather than attend to John. But suppose that this belief is merely dispositional. Then it follows that, with one possible exception, this belief played no role in the reason for Jill's failing to give John the drug and hence, I suspect, that she is not culpable for this failure, even though she had the belief.

The one possible exception is this: it may be that routine or habitual actions are performed for reasons to which one does not advert. It may also be that some people engage in deliberate wrongdoing in a routine or habitual, and hence inadvertent, manner. To the extent that this is so, the present considerations concerning advertence do not apply. But to the extent that this is not so, they do apply. So there may be this further restriction on culpability: in cases other than those of routine or habitual actions, one is directly culpable for something only if one adverts to the wrongness of doing it.

F

At the outset of this section I noted that there are a number of ways in which moral ignorance can arise. With respect to Alf, I said that he might not have considered the question whether it was wrong to threaten Brenda; or he might have considered it but come to no conclusion on the matter; or he might have come to the erroneous conclusion that it was not wrong to threaten her. Such an erroneous conclusion might have arisen from non-moral error (misconstrual of some pertinent empirical evidence) or from moral error (either misconstrual of some pertinent evaluative evidence or rejection of the Prospective View). Aristotle is well known for claiming that it is easier to excuse moral ignorance that stems from non-moral error than moral ignorance that stems from moral error, and others have agreed with him.[34] I see no reason to accept this claim. The argument given above applies to all cases of moral ignorance, whether or not they arise from error at all and, if they do, whether they stem from moral or non-moral error.

Aristotle is also well known for drawing a distinction between acting in ignorance and acting from ignorance, and he believes that whether one is culpable for ignorant behavior depends in part on this distinction.[35] It is unclear precisely what the distinction is supposed to consist in. For present purposes, though, the issue is unimportant. Once again, my argument applies to all cases of ignorant behavior, whether performed "in" or "from" ignorance.

It is of course possible to reject my argument outright, without trying to identify some premise in particular as the culprit, simply on the basis that its conclusion conflicts with our common practice of blaming. It might be especially tempting to do this in light of the fact that the Origination Thesis would appear to excuse those who engage in such repulsive behavior as that committed by Hitler, Stalin, Hussein, *et al.* This seems to be the tactic employed by George Sher in a recent article.[36] Such stubbornness would be defensible, if it were the case that rejecting the conclusion is clearly more reasonable than accepting all the premises. As I see it, though, and as I have tried to show in the previous subsections, that is not the case. In the present instance, judiciously "picking one's poison" requires that we revise our practice of blaming.[37]

Perhaps I should also add, as a reminder, that, as noted in the discussion of premise (4) above, ascriptions of culpability constitute just one type of

---

[34] See Aristotle 1941, pp. 964 ff. Cf. Fields 1994.   [35] See Aristotle 1941, pp. 966–7.

[36] Sher 2006, pp. 291 ff. Sher's thesis is that one can be responsible for something that is not in one's control. It may seem that he therefore opposes my premise (4) in particular. However, he makes it clear that the sort of control he has in mind has an epistemic component (it seems akin to what I called intentional control in section 3.5) and that it is with this component that he is particularly concerned. (See Sher 2006, p. 286, including n. 3.) I take Sher's thesis at bottom simply to be a repudiation of the Origination Thesis.

[37] Cf. section 1.6, subsection C.

negative moral evaluation of agents. Thus the unpalatability of being forced, by dint of the foregoing argument, to excuse people for ignorant behavior for which we are accustomed to holding them culpable may be mitigated somewhat by noting that their being inculpable does not preclude their being reprehensible in some other way.[38] Indeed, Hitler, Stalin, and the rest are all surely extremely repugnant, morally; it is not only their behavior that is repulsive. Nonetheless, if such people act in or from ignorance of the fact that they are doing wrong, and if such ignorance cannot be traced to a non-ignorant origin, then, even if repugnant, they are inculpable and, as such, they are not the appropriate objects of (at least some of) the so-called reactive attitudes. In particular, they do not deserve – indeed, they deserve not – to be punished.[39] If, despite this fact, we punish them anyway, then we risk simply piling wrong upon wrong.[40]

4.3 ACCUSES

Ever since J. L. Austin's famous plea for excuses, if not before, the standard account of the distinction between a justification and an excuse has been this: one has a justification for what one has done just in case one did not do overall wrong in doing it; one has an excuse for what one has done just in case one lacks a justification (that is, one did do overall wrong) but is nonetheless not to be blamed – is not culpable – for it.[41] There is an analogue to this concept of an excuse that has strangely escaped the notice

---

[38] See again n. 1 above.

[39] In Arpaly 2003, ch. 3, it is argued that agents can be morally responsible (praiseworthy or blameworthy) for their behavior if they are responsive to considerations that in fact constitute moral reasons to behave or not behave in certain ways, even if they do not conceive of these considerations *as* such reasons – and thus, even if they do not believe that in so responding they are doing moral right or wrong. It may therefore seem that Arpaly denies the conclusion of my argument. Perhaps she does. If so, I'm not sure which premise it is that she would reject or why. However, it may be that Arpaly does not deny my conclusion. Although she talks of "moral responsibility" when discussing praise- and blameworthiness, she explicitly denies (pp. 172–3) that she is concerned with the appropriateness of punishment in particular or with how people should be treated in general. Perhaps, then, she is concerned with a sort of moral reprehensibility other than the culpability with which I am concerned, in which case there is, or may be, no disagreement between us.

[40] I say "risk," since it could happen that punishment of someone who is inculpable is overall morally justified despite his or her inculpability. Deterrence, for example, or incapacitation might provide such justification. But we should surely be skeptical of the assumption that it ever does. Such skepticism need not, of course, be extended to *non*-punitive detention.

[41] Austin 1956–7, pp. 1 ff.

193

of all but a few.[42] There is no common term for this analogue, and so I have coined one: "accuse" (used as a noun, with a hard "s"). One has an accuse just in case one has a justification for what one has done but is nonetheless to be blamed – is culpable – for it.

It may be that some people have overlooked accuses because they have reasoned as follows: the question of whether someone has an excuse arises only when it has been established that that person has done wrong; hence, the question of whether someone is culpable arises only when it has been established that that person has done wrong. But this is clearly fallacious; for one can be blameless in the absence of wrongdoing, even if one cannot properly be said to have an excuse in the absence of wrongdoing.[43] Inculpability is thus compatible both with the presence and with the absence of overall wrongdoing. We should take seriously the possibility that culpability is likewise compatible both with the presence and with the absence of overall wrongdoing.

It may be that the concept of an accuse has no application in certain contexts. Perhaps the law is such a context; perhaps there is some sort of incongruity in the idea of someone's being legally blameworthy (liable to penalty or punishment) without having committed some legal wrong (some offense). But, even if this is so, we should not take the concept to be inapplicable in all contexts. On the contrary, it seems to me that, in the context of morality, the concept is perfectly applicable. My purpose in this section is to argue for the possibility that one be culpable even though one has not done anything overall morally wrong.

As noted in section 4.1, culpability is essentially a matter of how agents are to be assessed or evaluated. Such evaluation is to be distinguished from any form of treatment of the person that gives overt expression to (and thus is founded on) the evaluation, whether this treatment involves simply blaming the person "out loud" or something more serious, such as some sort of official censure or punishment. This evaluation is an evaluation, not of the person *in toto*, but rather of the person with respect to a certain episode in or aspect of his or her life. A person is culpable *for* something, some *particular* thing (an attempt, an act, an omission, or some consequence

---

[42] Among the few: Moore 1912, p. 82; Brandt 1958, pp. 38–9; Parfit 1984, p. 25; Jackson 1986, pp. 362–3; Thomson 1991, p. 295; Haji 1998, p. 146.

[43] It is not at all clear to me that one cannot properly be said to have an excuse in the absence of wrongdoing. On the contrary, it seems likely that one can. (Cf. Zimmerman 1996, pp. 93–5.) But my purpose here is not to challenge the standard account of excuses.

of one of these). This thing, whatever it is, reflects ill on the person, and the person's moral standing is thus diminished to that extent.

As noted in section 1.1, it is the avoidance of overall moral wrongdoing that is the primary concern of the morally conscientious person. Suppose that Carl is such a person. Though conscientious, he may lack confidence in his own ability to discern right from wrong. For this reason, he consults Wanda, whom he believes to be much wiser than he in this regard. He tells Wanda that he can do either *A*, or *B*, or *C*, or *D*, but he's not sure which he ought to do. In her wisdom, Wanda tells him that she thinks he ought to do *A*.

Notice – this is a crucial feature of the case – that both Carl and Wanda recognize that there is a certain "separation," a certain "distance," between act and agent, in the sense that, no matter how well motivated or well intentioned Carl may be, he may nonetheless do overall wrong. (It is precisely in order to avoid this possibility that conscientious people like Carl undertake their conscientious inquiries.) Indeed, the separation is "total," in that the sort of wrongdoing that Carl seeks to avoid is, ultimately, not a function at all of the motive from which or the intention with which he acts. This is not to say that some motive or intention might not be built into the description of some of the acts about which Carl consults Wanda. It could be that *A* is the act of obeying the speed limit out of respect for the law, whereas *B* is the act of obeying the speed limit out of prudence. If Carl is motivated both to do what the law requires and to do what prudence dictates, there seems to be nothing incoherent in Wanda's advising him that he ought to act on the former motive rather than the latter.[44] Nonetheless, there is a sense in which this cannot be Carl's *ultimate* motive when he takes Wanda's advice and does *A*. His ultimate motive has already been established by his conscientiousness; it is the motive of doing his duty, that is, of doing what he is overall morally obligated to do. In taking Wanda's advice – in obeying the speed limit out of respect for the law – Carl is ultimately motivated by duty.[45]

---

[44] Cf. Sverdlik 1996.

[45] It might be thought that Carl's duty is not simply to do *A* but to do it from that sense of duty which in fact motivates his doing it. This is a thesis that is often attributed to Kant. If "duty" is being used univocally, I think this thesis must be mistaken. If being obligated to do *A* implied being obligated to act on the belief that one was obligated to do *A*, an infinite regress of obligation would arise. Such a regress would violate the principle that "ought" implies "can" (concerning which see section 3.5 above). Cf. Ross 1930, pp. 5–6, for a related argument.

195

In virtue of the fact that the sort of wrongdoing at issue is wholly separate from the agent, in the sense just explained, many would call such wrongdoing "objective." As I noted in section 1.6, subsection C, there is indeed a sense in which, even on the Prospective View, obligation and wrongdoing are objective. Nonetheless, as I also noted there, the term "objective" can be used in a variety of ways and is therefore liable to mislead. (It might, for example, suggest that one presupposes the Objective View to be true, and I certainly don't want to suggest that.) So let us simply say here that, given the sort of separation between act and agent currently under discussion, culpability and wrongdoing are *independent* of one another. It is this independence that gives rise not only to the possibility of excuses but also to the possibility of accuses.

On my view, whether someone is culpable for something is intimately tied to whether he (or she) believes that he is doing wrong. (That is: overall moral wrong. As before, this qualification will be implicit throughout this section.) The sort of independence of culpability from wrongdoing that both excuses and accuses represent, then, is, I believe, closely tied to the question whether there is an independence of the belief that one is doing wrong from one's actually doing wrong.

In the last section I gave reasons for thinking that (A) it is possible to do wrong without believing that one is doing wrong. There are similar reasons for thinking that (B) it is possible to believe that one is doing wrong without actually doing wrong. Clearly Claim B cannot be denied on the grounds that it is an analytic truth, involving synonymy, that, if one believes that one is doing wrong, then one is doing wrong; for the consequent of this statement can be entertained while its antecedent is not. However, the contention that this statement expresses an analytic truth that involves analysis cannot be dismissed on the basis that it would be circular, and I know of no other, purely formal reason for rejecting it. Nonetheless, we can say this. In as much as Claim A indicates that doing wrong is to be prised loose, conceptually, from acting in the belief that one is doing wrong, so that the former can occur without the latter, it becomes difficult to see why someone should wish to insist that the latter cannot occur without the former. If one can be mistaken in *failing* to believe that one is doing wrong, why can one not be mistaken (by virtue of an overly sensitive conscience, perhaps, or simply by virtue of a misreading of one's situation) in *believing* that one is doing wrong?

Still, I can imagine someone arguing against Claim B along the following lines: "Rule-consequentialism (of a certain sort) is true. Moreover, it would be better in general if people acted in the belief that they were doing the right thing than if they acted in the belief that they were doing the wrong thing. Hence there is a relevant rule to this effect. Hence it is right to act in the belief that one is doing the right thing and wrong to act in the belief that one is doing the wrong thing." This argument rests on two very questionable assumptions: that rule-consequentialism (of the sort in question) is true, and that it would be better in general if people acted as stipulated. But even if we grant both assumptions, the argument fails to show Claim B to be false. For, even if it is the case that it would be better in general if people acted in the belief that they were doing the right thing, this is at best a *contingent* truth. As long as it does not hold of necessity, Claim B is untouched.

I can also imagine someone arguing against Claim B as follows: "If one acts in the belief that one is doing wrong, then one is thereby showing disrespect to someone, and that is wrong." But even if it is granted (which is again, surely, quite questionable) that it is, of necessity, wrong (that is, overall wrong) to show disrespect to someone, it is surely false that acting in the belief that one is doing wrong involves, of necessity, such disrespect. After all, the action that one takes to be wrong might involve, and one might know it to involve, no victim of disrespect at all. (One might, for example, deliberately destroy some beautiful object to which no one else has or ever will or can have access, believing that one is thereby violating some basic moral rule, but without thereby victimizing, and without believing that one is thereby victimizing, anyone at all.) I suppose that it might be responded that, even in such a case, one is showing disrespect to or for morality as such, and that this is wrong. But, as far as I can tell, this simply constitutes a re-insistence that Claim B is false, rather than a fresh argument against it. Besides, it is apparent that this response fails to recognize that what is at issue is the sort of wrongdoing that is, in the sense described earlier, wholly separate from its agent. When consulting Wanda, Carl might tell her not only that he isn't sure which of *A*, *B*, *C*, and *D* to do, but also that he is currently of the somewhat tentative opinion that his doing *A* would be wrong. He would thereby be indicating both that, if he were to do *A* (without the benefit of Wanda's counsel), he would be acting in the belief that he was doing wrong, and that he recognizes that, in the sense of "wrong" at issue, he might nonetheless *not* in fact be doing wrong. It seems clear, then, that the sort of wrongdoing with which conscientious agents like Carl are concerned is one that requires that we accept Claim B.

I take it that the foregoing remarks suffice to establish the logical independence of doing wrong from believing that one is doing wrong. What is crucial to my purpose is that it be acknowledged that Claim B is true, that is, that it is possible that one believe that one is doing wrong without in fact doing wrong. If it were the case that such a belief is sufficient for culpability, then my case for the possibility of accuses would be complete. And, I believe, the truth is almost that simple – but not quite.

As noted in section 4.1, it is commonly recognized that culpability involves not only a mental but also a metaphysical condition: one must enjoy some kind of freedom of will in order to incur culpability for one's behavior. This is a claim that I accept. (It was crucial to my argument in the last section. See premise (4) of that argument.) Hence a belief that one is doing wrong is *not* sufficient for culpability. Nonetheless, even granting that freedom is a necessary condition of culpability, I can claim that accuses are possible, as long as it is accepted that acting freely in the belief that one is doing wrong is sufficient for being culpable for one's behavior (but not sufficient for actually doing wrong). This, I believe, is precisely what should be accepted.[46] But, of course, there are reasons for thinking that it should be rejected, and I shall now turn to some of these.

A

We may distinguish two groups of cases. In the first group are cases in which, it may seem, one acts freely and in the belief that one is doing wrong, but one is nonetheless *not* culpable for one's behavior; in the second are cases where, it may seem, one acts freely and in the belief that one is doing wrong and one *is* culpable for one's behavior, but one *also* does wrong. If all pertinent cases fall into one or other of these groups, then my plea for accuses must be rejected. I shall consider examples from each group.

---

[46] Or perhaps the claim should be qualified as follows: acting freely in the belief that one is doing wrong, *and* in the belief that some alternative would not be wrong, is sufficient for being culpable for one's behavior. This would rule out someone's incurring culpability simply in virtue of believing (falsely – see n. 9 to chapter 3) that he is in a dilemma.

There are some who would say that a freedom-independent condition of "autonomy" or "authenticity" is also necessary for culpability (See, for example, Haji 1998, chs. 5–7.) I am unpersuaded by this claim, but accepting it would not affect my case for accuses, as long as it is acknowledged that one can act freely *and* autonomously (or authentically – however this is to be understood precisely) in the belief that one is doing wrong, without in fact doing wrong.

For a case that falls into the first group, consider Christine, who acts freely and in the belief that she is doing wrong, but whose action is quite out of character. Normally she walks the strait and narrow; just this once, though, she breaks loose from the shackles of conscience and takes a walk down (what she regards as) some unseemly side-alley. Some would deny that Christine is to blame for her behavior because, they say, culpability has to do with an imputation of fault to one's character,[47] and Christine's character is not in question in this little episode. (Of course, if Christine continued to stray – made a habit of it – then that would be another matter.) But I see no reason to accept this claim. As I explained earlier, the sort of blameworthiness at issue here has to do with how an agent is to be evaluated in light of a certain episode in or aspect of his or her life. This is a judgment of the agent (as reflected in or by this episode or aspect); it is not a judgment of the agent's character. An agent's character can of course itself be a fitting object of moral evaluation, but this is not the same sort of judgment as that involved in evaluating the agent him- or herself. For, while one *has* a character, one *is* not one's character; a judgment of oneself, then, is not identical with a judgment of one's character. Of course, one can be culpable *for* at least some of the character traits that one has; this involves these traits, and to that extent one's character, reflecting ill on oneself. But this simply serves to dramatize the distinction between judging an agent's character and judging the agent in light of his or her character. And surely other things (such as Christine's decision to break loose) can also reflect ill on oneself, whether or not they are representative of one's character. Perhaps there is some sort of mitigation (either in terms of culpability or, as I believe, in terms of some other sort of negative moral evaluation) that is afforded by the fact that one's behavior is out of character rather than in character, but, as long as some degree of culpability is recognized in such cases, it must also be recognized that culpability is not necessarily just a matter of character evaluation.

Consider, next, Sarah, a saintly person who has overly demanding moral standards. She believes that it is her moral obligation to exhaust herself in the service of others, although this is in fact (let us suppose) supererogatory.

---

[47] See, among others, Brandt 1958, pp. 13 ff., and 1959, p. 468; Dahl 1967, p. 420; Fields 1994, pp. 404 ff. On p. 411, Fields seems to suggest that actions that are truly out of character must be in some sense involuntary, but I see no need to accept this. If true, however, this claim would appear to imply that acting in character is required for acting freely, in which case this condition has already been accommodated by my foregoing remarks.

Early one morning her alarm awakes her and, contemplating yet another exhausting day of labor, she collapses back into bed and decides to sleep in an extra hour, feeling guilty about doing so because she believes that this is the wrong thing to do. If acting freely in the belief that one is doing wrong is sufficient for culpability, then this poor woman is to be blamed for her decision to stay in bed. But surely, it may be urged, she is not; hence my account is to be rejected.

In response, I would make four points. First, I am assuming that Sarah is acting freely, in the requisite sense, when she stays in bed. There is undoubtedly an element of weakness of will operating in this sort of case, and, if such weakness were incompatible with the sort of freedom that culpability presupposes, then my account would not imply that she is culpable after all. But it seems to me at best an exaggeration to say that weakness of will eliminates freedom, and so I am willing to concede that Sarah does act freely in this example. Second, however, I am also willing to admit that Sarah is probably admirable in many ways: for her high moral standards, for her sensitivity to and sympathy with the needs of others, for the many fine services that she has rendered to others in the past, and so on. But all of this is quite consistent with her being culpable for her present decision to stay in bed. For, third, we must not downplay the fact that Sarah has indeed, on this one occasion, deliberately and freely decided to do something that she regards as wrong. This, I contend, is sufficient for her being culpable for the decision. The fact that *we* don't regard her behavior as wrong is of no moment; what is important is that *she does* so regard it and has, *despite* this fact, deliberately chosen it. Finally, recall that, in the present sense, one's being culpable simply involves one's being worthy of a certain sort of judgment. Even if (as I believe) being worthy of such a judgment also renders one *deserving* of a certain kind of reaction, it can still be the case that it would be *overall wrong* for someone to evince such a reaction (since one may also deserve, in virtue of something other than one's culpability, *not* to be the object of such a reaction, or the reaction may have some other kind of deleterious consequence). Thus the claim that Sarah is culpable does not imply even that she ought to be blamed "out loud," let alone that she ought to be adversely treated in some more serious manner. And I am quite willing to concede that it may well be wrong to engage in such behavior toward such a saintly person as Sarah.

As an example of a type of case in which one's admirable trait is not linked to one's belief about wrongdoing, consider a parent, Peter, who, moved by sympathy for his child, deliberately refrains from disciplining the child as he thinks he ought. Or consider the case of Huckleberry Finn, who, again moved by sympathy, deliberately refrains from thwarting his slave friend Jim's bid for freedom as he thinks he ought. Surely, it may be said, blaming these people is inappropriate; hence, once again, my account is to be rejected.[48]

In response, I would again point out, first, that one's being culpable for a certain item of behavior is consistent with one's being admirable in certain respects; second, that it is important not to lose sight of the fact that, in these cases, the agent is indeed doing wrong *from his perspective* even if not in fact; and, third, that it might be wrong to *treat* Peter or Huck in some adverse manner, even if it is not inappropriate to blame them in the relevant sense, that is, to *judge* them negatively. I suspect that some may be more inclined to blame Peter than to blame Huckleberry Finn, because they may be more inclined to say that Peter has in fact done the wrong thing. But this is to confuse agent-evaluation with act-evaluation, the very sort of confusion that invocation of the concept of an excuse (and that of an accuse) seeks to avoid. It might also be that some are less inclined to blame Huck because they suspect that he did not believe, deep down, that it was wrong to help Jim to escape. Of course, if this were in fact the case, then my account would not imply that Huck is to blame. But, at least as I understand Mark Twain's intent in telling the story, this was not the case;[49] and so, I would say, Huck is to blame.

B

Let us turn now to a case that falls into the second group mentioned earlier. Here there will be no temptation to say that the agent escapes blame due to the presence of some admirable trait, for no such trait will be exhibited. But here, it may be thought, there is reason to say that the agent has acted wrongly. Consider, for example, a version of Case 10 in which, in light of the evidence available to Brenda, Alf's threat imposed a grave risk of harm on her. Given the Prospective View (and the simplifying assumption that her evidence concerning the actual values at stake was accurate), it follows that Brenda's killing Alf was overall morally justified. But now suppose that, though justified, this killing does not qualify as self-defense since Brenda in fact paid no heed to the evidence and believed that Alf's threat was idle; she killed him merely in order to rid herself of a nuisance,

[48] Cf. Brandt 1958, p. 37, and 1959, p. 359.   [49] Cf. Bennett 1974, pp. 126–7.

believing that it was wrong to do so, thinking that she could take advantage of the situation and escape being charged with murder.[50]

Is Brenda to blame for acting as she did? Many would say so, and my account concurs (on the assumption that she acted freely). But many would also say that Brenda acted wrongly, so that this case does not support the possibility of accuses. Perhaps you are someone who would say this. The claim seems to me untenable. What wrong is it that Brenda is supposed to have done? After all, she thwarted Alf's threat and, given her evidence, this was surely the right thing to do under the circumstances.

But, you may reply, no one wishes to blame Brenda for thwarting Alf's threat. What she is to be blamed for is killing Alf, and that was wrong, even if her thwarting Alf's threat was not.

I agree that it would be misleading to say that Brenda is to blame for thwarting Alf's threat; *that* is not the behavior in virtue of which she incurred culpability. It is indeed for killing Alf that she is to blame, for that is what she took to be wrong. But I deny that this in fact constituted wrongdoing on her part, precisely because her circumstances were such that it was prospectively best for her not only to thwart Alf's threat but also (if this was a distinct action at all) to kill him.

You may reply that Brenda didn't just kill Alf. She murdered him, and murder is wrong by definition. Hence she did do wrong after all.

But that is circular. I agree that she killed Alf and is culpable for this. However, if murder is by definition wrong, I deny that she committed murder. (If "murder" is defined differently, as killing for which the agent is culpable, then of course I have no objection to saying that Brenda committed murder.)

You may contend that Brenda is to blame for *attempting* to kill Alf; in making this attempt, she attempted to do something wrong, and any such attempt is itself wrong.

There are two ways in which to read "it is wrong to attempt to do something wrong." The first is this: if one attempts to do something that is in fact wrong, then one's attempt is also wrong. The second is this: if one attempts to do something that one takes to be wrong, then one's attempt is wrong. Neither reading undermines my case for accuses. The first reading begs the question, since it presupposes that Brenda's killing Alf was wrong. As to the second reading: return to Carl, who has conscientiously consulted Wanda. Suppose again that he has told her not only that he isn't sure which of *A*, *B*, *C*, and *D* to do, but also that he is currently of the somewhat

[50] Cf. n. 53 to chapter 2 and the related discussion of Cases 10B and 10F.

202

tentative opinion that his doing A would be wrong. Suppose that he ought in fact to do A. And suppose, finally, that he cannot do A without attempting to do A. Given all this, we must reject the claim that it is wrong for Carl to attempt to do A, even though he believes A to be wrong. For, given that any act that is a prerequisite of an obligatory act is itself obligatory,[51] it follows that Carl ought to attempt to do A. Hence his attempting to do A is not wrong. Hence it is not in general true that attempting to do what one takes to be wrong is itself wrong, and I see no reason to think that it is true in this particular version of Case 10.

In a final effort to support the thesis that there cannot be culpability without wrongdoing, you may respond by invoking the concept of "perverse" behavior. Let us say that someone who does, or attempts to do, something that he believes to be wrong behaves perversely. Even if Carl's doing A is not wrong, and even if his attempting to do A is not wrong, still, you may claim, his *perversely* doing or attempting to do A is wrong, and that is precisely what he is to blame for. Hence culpability does require wrongdoing after all.

But this can't be right either, for it would imply that Carl is in a moral dilemma, which is surely not the case. Given that (for reasons discussed in the last section) Carl cannot immediately relinquish his belief that doing or attempting to do A would be wrong, he cannot either do or attempt to do A without behaving perversely. If such behavior were wrong, then Carl could not avoid wrongdoing, since his neither doing nor attempting to do A would also be wrong.

I conclude, then, that the possibility of accuses is confirmed rather than refuted by consideration of the sorts of cases just mentioned.

C

Let me address, finally, two objections to my account that do not turn on a consideration of particular cases. The first is this. It may appear that my account collapses the distinction between one's being culpable and one's believing that one is culpable, for the following reason. Suppose that Jill freely performs some act, believing that it is wrong for her to do so. On my account, she is culpable. But, if she believes that it is wrong for her to do

---

[51] Or more precisely: given proposition (3.5′) from chapter 3 (viz., that if P ought to do A and cannot do A without doing B, and P can refrain from doing B, then P ought to do B). As noted in section 3.2, this proposition is implied by the final formulation of the Prospective View.

this act, then she believes that she believes this, and vice versa. Thus, if she is culpable, she believes that she is, and vice versa. But, even if we accept the principle that beliefs and beliefs about beliefs are equivalent in this way (and I won't question it here), this argument is fallacious. On my account, Jill may believe that she is doing wrong, and thus be culpable, without believing that she is culpable; and she may believe that she is culpable without being culpable. This is possible simply because Jill may not herself subscribe to my account. Of course, if Jill does subscribe to my account (and makes the relevant inferences), then (given both the principle about beliefs and the fact that she is not mistaken in believing that she is acting freely) her belief that she is culpable for her action cannot be mistaken, and her being culpable will suffice for her believing that she is. But I cannot see that this poses a problem for the account.

The second objection is this. If the notion of wrongdoing with which I am concerned is, as I have claimed throughout, the notion of that sort of wrongdoing that the conscientious person seeks to avoid, how can it be that culpability is divorced from wrongdoing in the way that I allege; for isn't a conscientious person just as eager to avoid culpability as to avoid wrongdoing? I addressed this objection in section 1.3. Of course, a conscientious person may be eager to avoid culpability, although in some cases I think that this may not be so. (Some conscientious people might regard such concern as sinful self-indulgence.) Moreover, I of course grant that a person who acts conscientiously will succeed in avoiding culpability, even if he doesn't avoid wrongdoing, as long as he is not culpable for the misguided conscience on which he acts. But none of this affects my case for the possibility of accuses. For what it is important to recognize is that the sort of wrongdoing that the conscientious person is eager to avoid is obviously not the sort of wrongdoing that only a conscientious person can commit. Thus, even if it is the case that a conscientious person who avoids wrongdoing will also avoid culpability, that does not imply that everyone who avoids the former will also avoid the latter.

D

There are at least two lessons to be learned from acknowledging the possibility of there being accuses as well as excuses.

The first lesson is this. It has been argued that the principle that "ought" implies "can" entails Frankfurt's principle of alternate possibilities,[52] so that

---

[52] See Frankfurt 1969.

it is a mistake to accept the former but not the latter.[53] (The principle in question is the principle that one is morally responsible for what one has done only if one could have done otherwise. Or, to put it as I did in section 3.5: moral responsibility requires regulative control.) This argument rests on the claim that there cannot be culpability without wrongdoing. If I am correct in denying this claim, the argument collapses. This is significant because there is good reason both to accept the thesis that "ought" implies "can" and to deny the principle of alternate possibilities.[54]

The second lesson is more general and more straightforward. It is simply this: to justify an agent's behavior is not to exculpate the agent. The failure to appreciate this fact can lead and, it seems to me, often does lead to a premature termination of our moral inquiries. We should not think that the discovery that no wrong has been done justifies us in thinking that there are no further moral discoveries to be made.

4.4 A CAUTIONARY CONCLUSION

The fact that the Equivalence Thesis is false shows that it is possible that responsibility and obligation diverge, in that what one is responsible for may not correspond with what one was obligated (not) to do. Our common practice of excusing people for some of their wrongdoing presupposes this fact. However, the Origination Thesis indicates that this practice is too expansive: we frequently blame people for ignorant behavior for which they are not culpable. For that reason, we may regard this thesis as deflationary. My case for accuses, however, is inflationary, in that it implies that our common practice of blaming people only when they have done wrong is too restrictive. There is, then, an unsurprising final, general lesson: we should be skeptical of the accuracy of our everyday judgments regarding the responsibility that people bear for their behavior.

---

[53] See Widerker 1991.
[54] For a defense of the thesis that "ought" implies "can," see sections 3.5 and 3.6 above. For reasons to endorse Frankfurt's rejection of the principle of alternate possibilities, see Zimmerman 2003.

References

Adams, Robert Merrihew 1985. "Involuntary Sins," *Philosophical Review* 94: 3–31.

Alexander, Larry 1993. "Self-Defense, Justification, and Excuse," *Philosophy and Public Affairs* 22: 53–66.

1999. "*Propter Honoris Respectum*: A Unified Excuse of Preemptive Self-Protection," *Notre Dame Law Review* 74: 1,475–1,504.

Anscombe, G.E.M. 1969. *Intention*. Ithaca: Cornell University Press.

Åqvist, Lennart 1967. "Good Samaritans, Contrary-to-Duty Imperatives, and Epistemic Obligations," *Noûs* 1: 361–79.

Aristotle 1941. *The Basic Works of Aristotle*, R. McKeon (ed.). New York: Random House.

Arpaly, Nomy 2003. *Unprincipled Virtue*. Oxford: Oxford University Press.

Austin, J.L. 1956–7. "A Plea for Excuses," *Proceedings of the Aristotelian Society* 57: 1–30.

Bales, R. Eugene 1971. "Act Utilitarianism: Account of Right-making Characteristics or Decision-making Procedure?," *American Philosophical Quarterly* 8: 257–65.

Benbaji, Yitzhak 2005. "Culpable Bystanders, Innocent Threats and the Ethics of Self-Defense," *Canadian Journal of Philosophy* 35: 585–622.

Bennett, Jonathan 1974. "The Conscience of Huckleberry Finn," *Philosophy* 49: 123–34.

Blumenfeld, David 1971. "The Principle of Alternate Possibilities," *Journal of Philosophy* 68: 339–45.

Brand, Myles 1971. "The Language of Not Doing," *American Philosophical Quarterly* 8: 45–53.

Brandt, Richard B. 1958. "Blameworthiness and Obligation," in A.I. Melden (ed.), *Essays in Moral Philosophy* (Seattle: University of Washington Press): 3–39.

1959. *Ethical Theory*. Englewood Cliffs: Prentice-Hall.

Broad, C.D. 1934. *Five Types of Ethical Theory*. London: Kegan Paul, Trench, Trubner.

1946. "Some of the Main Problems in Ethics," *Philosophy* 21: 99–117.

1985. *Ethics*. Dordrecht: Martinus Nijhoff.

Bykvist, Krister 2002. "Alternative Actions and the Spirit of Consequentialism," *Philosophical Studies* 107: 45–68.

Carlson, Erik 1995. *Consequentialism Reconsidered*. Dordrecht: Kluwer.

206

References

1997. "The Intrinsic Value of Non-Basic States of Affairs," *Philosophical Studies* 85: 95–107.

Castañeda, Hector-Neri 1981. "The Paradoxes of Deontic Logic: The Simplest Solution to All of Them in One Fell Swoop," in R. Hilpinen (ed.), *New Studies in Deontic Logic* (Dordrecht: Reidel): 37–85.

Chappell, Timothy 2001. "Option Ranges," *Journal of Applied Philosophy* 18: 107–18.

Chisholm, Roderick M. 1975. "The Intrinsic Value in Disjunctive States of Affairs," *Noûs* 9: 295–308.

1989. *Theory of Knowledge*, 3rd edn. Englewood Cliffs: Prentice-Hall.

Conee, Earl 1989. "Why Moral Dilemmas Are Impossible," *American Philosophical Quarterly* 26: 133–41.

Corrado, Michael 1983. "Trying," *American Philosophical Quarterly* 20: 195–205.

Dahl, Norman 1967. "'Ought' and Blameworthiness," *Journal of Philosophy* 64: 418–28.

Dancy, Jonathan 2002. "Prichard on Duty and Ignorance of Fact," in P. Stratton-Lake (ed.), *Ethical Intuitionism* (Oxford: Clarendon Press, 2002): 229–47.

2004. *Ethics without Principles*. Oxford: Oxford University Press.

Davidson, Donald 1980. *Essays on Actions and Events*. Oxford: Clarendon Press.

Davis, Lawrence H. 1979. *Theory of Action*. Englewood Cliffs: Prentice-Hall.

Davis, Nancy 1984. "Abortion and Self Defense," *Philosophy and Public Affairs* 13: 175–207.

Dennett, Daniel 1984. *Elbow Room*. Cambridge MA: MIT Press.

Ellsberg, Daniel 1961. "Risk, Ambiguity, and the Savage Axioms," in Gärdenfors and Sahlin (eds.) 1988: 245–69.

Ewing, A.C. 1948. *The Definition of Good*. London: Routledge and Kegan Paul.

Feinberg, Joel 1973. *Social Philosophy*. Englewood Cliffs: Prentice-Hall.

Feldman, Fred 1986. *Doing the Best We Can*. Dordrecht: Reidel

1987. "The Paradox of the Knower," *Philosophical Studies* 55: 93–100.

1988. "Concerning the Paradox of Moral Reparation and Other Matters," *Philosophical Studies* 57: 23–39.

1990. "A Simpler Solution to the Paradoxes of Deontic Logic," *Philosophical Perspectives* 4: 309–41.

2006. "Actual Utility, the Objection from Impracticality, and the Move to Expected Utility," *Philosophical Studies* 129: 49–79.

Feldman, Richard 1981. "Fallibilism and Knowing That One Knows," *Philosophical Review* 90: 266–82.

1988. "Having Evidence," in D.F. Austin (ed.), *Philosophical Analysis* (Dordrecht: Kluwer): 83–104.

Fields, Lloyd 1994. "Moral Beliefs and Blameworthiness," *Philosophy* 69: 397–415.

Finkelstein, Claire 2003. "Is Risk a Harm?," *University of Pennsylvania Law Review* 151: 963–1,001.

Fischer, John Martin 1994. *The Metaphysics of Free Will*. Oxford: Blackwell.

1995. "Stories," *Midwest Studies in Philosophy* 20: 1–14.

Fischer, John Martin and Ravizza, Mark 1998. *Responsibility and Control*. Cambridge: Cambridge University Press.

References

Frankena, William K. 1963. "Obligation and Ability," in Max Black (ed.), *Philosophical Analysis* (Englewood Cliffs: Prentice-Hall): 148–65.

Frankfurt, Harry G. 1969. "Alternate Possibilities and Moral Responsibility," *Journal of Philosophy* 66: 829–39.

1988. *The Importance of What We Care About*. Cambridge: Cambridge University Press.

Frazier, Robert L. 1994. "Act Utilitarianism and Decision Procedures," *Utilitas* 6: 43–53.

Gale, Richard M. 1999. "William James and the Willfulness of Belief," *Philosophy and Phenomenological Research* 59: 71–91.

Gärdenfors, Peter and Sahlin, Nils-Eric 1982. "Unreliable Probabilities, Risk Taking, and Decision Making," in Gärdenfors and Sahlin (eds.) 1988: 313–34.

eds. 1988. *Decision, Probability, and Utility*. Cambridge: Cambridge University Press.

Gibbard, Allan 1990. *Wise Choices, Apt Feelings*. Cambridge, MA: Harvard University Press.

Goble, Lou 1993. "The Logic of Obligation, 'Better' and 'Worse'," *Philosophical Studies* 70: 133–63.

1996. "Utilitarian Deontic Logic," *Philosophical Studies* 82: 317–57.

Goldman, Alvin I. 1970. *A Theory of Human Action*. Princeton: Princeton University Press.

Goldman, Holly S. 1976. "Dated Rightness and Moral Imperfection," *Philosophical Review* 85: 449–87.

1978. "Doing the Best One Can," in A.I. Goldman and J. Kim (eds.), *Values and Morals* (Dordrecht: Reidel): 185–214.

Greenspan, Patricia S. 1975. "Conditional Oughts and Hypothetical Imperatives," *Journal of Philosophy* 72: 259–76.

1978. "Oughts and Determinism: A Response to Goldman," *Philosophical Review* 87: 77–83.

Gren, Jonas 2004. *Applying Utilitarianism: The Problem of Practical Action-Guidance*. Gothenburg: Acta Philosophica Gothoburgensia.

Gruzalski, Bart 1981. "Foreseeable Consequence Utilitarianism," *Australasian Journal of Philosophy* 59: 163–76.

Guerrero, Alexander A. 2007. "Don't Know, Don't Kill: Moral Ignorance, Culpability, and Caution," *Philosophical Studies* 136: 59–97.

Haji, Ishtiyaque 1998. *Moral Appraisability*. Oxford: Oxford University Press.

Hare, R.M. 1981. *Moral Thinking*. Oxford: Clarendon Press.

Henderson, G.P. 1966. "'Ought' Implies 'Can'," *Philosophy* 41: 101–12.

Hieronymi, Pamela 2006. "Controlling Attitudes," *Pacific Philosophical Quarterly* 87: 45–74.

Hohfeld, Wesley Newcomb 1919. *Fundamental Legal Conceptions*. New Haven: Yale University Press.

Hornsby, Jennifer 1980. *Actions*. London: Routledge and Kegan Paul.

Howard-Snyder, Frances 1997. "The Rejection of Objective Consequentialism," *Utilitas* 9: 241–8.

2005. "It's the Thought that Counts," *Utilitas* 17: 265–81.

208

References

Huemer, Michael 2007. "Epistemic Possibility," *Synthese* 156: 119–42.

Humberstone, I.L. 1983. "The Background of Circumstances," *Pacific Philosophical Quarterly* 64: 19–34.

Hunt, David 2000. "Moral Responsibility and Unavoidable Action," *Philosophical Studies* 97: 195–227.

Jackson, Frank 1986. "A Probabilistic Approach to Moral Responsibility," in R.B. Marcus *et al.* (eds.), *Logic, Methodology and Philosophy of Science VII* (Amsterdam: Elsevier): 351–65.

1991. "Decision-theoretic Consequentialism and the Nearest and Dearest Objection," *Ethics* 101: 461–82.

Jackson, Frank and Pargetter, Robert 1986. "Oughts, Options, and Actualism," *Philosophical Review* 95: 233–55.

James, William 1968. *The Writings of William James*, J.J. McDermott (ed.). New York: Modern Library.

Kagan, Shelly 1989. *The Limits of Morality*. Oxford: Oxford University Press.

1998. *Normative Ethics*. Boulder, CO: Westview.

Kahneman, Daniel and Tversky, Amos 1979. "Prospect Theory: An Analysis of Decision under Risk," in Gärdenfors and Sahlin (eds.) 1988: 183–214.

Kane, Robert 1996. *The Significance of Free Will*. Oxford: Oxford University Press.

Katz, Fred F. 1993. *Ordinary People and Extraordinary Evil*. Albany: SUNY Press.

Knight, Frank H. 1921. *Risk, Uncertainty and Profit*. Boston: Houghton Mifflin.

Lemmon, E.J. 1962. "Moral Dilemmas," *Philosophical Review* 70: 139–58.

Lemos, Noah 2004. *Common Sense*. Cambridge: Cambridge University Press.

Lemos, Ramon 1980. "Duty and Ignorance," *Southern Journal of Philosophy* 18: 301–12.

Lenman, James 2000. "Consequentialism and Cluelessness," *Philosophy and Public Affairs* 29: 342–70.

Lockhart, Ted 2000. *Moral Uncertainty and Its Consequences*. Oxford: Oxford University Press.

Luce, R. Duncan and Raiffa, Howard 1957. "Individual Decision Making under Uncertainty," in Gärdenfors and Sahlin (eds.) 1988: 48–79.

Ludwig, Kirk 1992. "Impossible Doings," *Philosophical Studies* 65: 257–81.

Marcus, Ruth Barcan 1980. "Moral Dilemmas and Consistency," *Journal of Philosophy* 77: 121–36.

Mason, Elinor 2003. "Consequentialism and the 'Ought Implies Can' Principle," *American Philosophical Quarterly* 40: 319–31.

Mayerfeld, Jamie 1999. *Suffering and Moral Responsibility*. Oxford: Oxford University Press.

McCann, Hugh 1975. "Trying, Paralysis, and Volition," *Review of Metaphysics* 28: 423–42.

McClennen, Edward F. 1983. "Sure-thing Doubts," in Gärdenfors and Sahlin (eds.) 1988: 166–82.

McConnell, Terrance 1988. "Ross on Duty and Ignorance," *History of Philosophy Quarterly* 5: 79–95.

References

McMahan, Jeff 1994. "Self-Defense and the Problem of the Innocent Attacker," *Ethics* 104: 252–90.

2005a. "The Basis of Moral Liability to Defensive Killing," *Philosophical Issues* 15: 386–405.

2005b. "Self-Defense and Culpability," *Law and Philosophy* 24: 751–74.

Mele, Alfred R. 2003. "Agents' Abilities," *Noûs* 37: 447–70.

Mellor, D.H. 2005. *Probability*. London: Routledge.

Milo, Ronald D. 1984. *Immorality*. Princeton: Princeton University Press.

Montague, Phillip 1981. "Self-Defense and Choosing between Lives," *Philosophical Studies* 40: 207–19.

2004. "Blameworthiness, Vice, and the Objectivity of Morals," *Pacific Philosophical Quarterly* 85: 68–84.

Montmarquet, James 1993. *Epistemic Virtue and Doxastic Responsibility*. Lanham, MD: Rowman and Littlefield.

1995. "Culpable Ignorance and Excuses," *Philosophical Studies* 80: 41–9.

1999. "Zimmerman on Culpable Ignorance," *Ethics* 109: 842–5.

Moore, G.E. 1903. *Principia Ethica*. Cambridge: Cambridge University Press.

1912. *Ethics*. Oxford: Oxford University Press.

Moore, Robert E. 1979. "Refraining," *Philosophical Studies* 36: 407–24.

Nagel, Thomas 1976. "Moral Luck," *Proceedings of the Aristotelian Society*, suppl. vol. 1: 137–51.

Norcross, Alastair 1990. "Consequentialism and the Unforeseeable Future," *Analysis* 50: 253–6.

Nowell Smith, P.H. 1960. "Ifs and Cans," *Theoria* 32: 85–101.

Oddie, Graham and Menzies, Peter 1992. "An Objectivist's Guide to Subjective Value," *Ethics* 102: 512–33.

Oldfield, Edward 1977. "An Approach to a Theory of Intrinsic Value," *Philosophical Studies* 32: 233–49.

O'Shaughnessy, Brian 1973. "Trying (as the Mental Pineal Gland)," *Journal of Philosophy* 70: 365–86.

Otsuka, Michael 1994. "Killing the Innocent in Self-Defense," *Philosophy and Public Affairs* 23: 74–94.

1998. "Incompatibilism and the Avoidability of Blame," *Ethics* 108: 685–701.

Øverland, Gerhard 2005. "Self-Defence among Innocent People," *Journal of Moral Philosophy* 2: 127–46.

Owen, David G. (ed.) 1995. *Philosophical Foundations of Tort Law*. Oxford: Clarendon Press.

Parfit, Derek 1984. *Reasons and Persons*. Oxford: Clarendon Press.

Pereboom, Derk 2000. "Alternative Possibilities and Causal Histories," *Philosophical Perspectives* 14: 119–37.

Prichard, H.A. 1932. "Duty and Ignorance of Fact," in H.A. Prichard, *Moral Obligation* (Oxford: Clarendon Press, 1949): 18–39.

Quinn, Warren S. 1974. "Theories of Intrinsic Value," *American Philosophical Quarterly* 11: 123–32.

Regan, Donald 1980. *Utilitarianism and Co-operation*. Oxford: Clarendon Press.

Rescher, Nicholas 1983. *Risk*. Lanham, MD: University Press of America.

References

Richman, Robert J. 1983. *God, Free Will, and Morality*. Dordrecht: Reidel.
Rivera López, Eduardo, 2006. "Is It Possible to Be Fully Excused for a Wrong Action?," *Philosophy and Phenomenological Research* 73: 124–42.
Robinson, Richard 1971. "Ought and Ought Not," *Philosophy* 46: 193–202.
Rodin, David 2002. *War and Self-Defense*. Oxford: Clarendon Press.
Ross, W.D. 1930. *The Right and the Good*. Oxford: Clarendon Press.
    1939. *Foundations of Ethics*. Oxford: Clarendon Press.
Rumfitt, Ian 2003. "Savoir Faire," *Journal of Philosophy* 100: 158–66.
Russell, Bertrand 1966. *Philosophical Essays*. London: George Allen & Unwin.
Savage, Leonard J. 1953. "Allais' Paradox," in Gärdenfors and Sahlin (eds.) 1988: 163–5.
Schlick, Moritz 1966. "When Is a Man Responsible?," in B. Berofsky (ed.), *Free Will and Determinism* (New York: Harper and Row): 54–63.
Schlossberger, Eugene 1992. *Moral Responsibility and Persons*. Philadelphia: Temple University Press.
Schroeder, Christopher H. 1995. "Causation, Compensation, and Moral Responsibility," in Owen (ed.) 1995: 347–61.
Sher, George 2006. "Out of Control," *Ethics* 116: 285–301.
Sinnott-Armstrong, Walter 1988. *Moral Dilemmas*. Oxford: Blackwell.
Slote, Michael 1989. *Beyond Optimizing*. Cambridge, MA: Harvard University Press.
Smart, J.J.C. 1973. "An Outline of a System of Utilitarian Ethics," in J.J.C. Smart and B. Williams, *Utilitariansim: For and Against* (Cambridge: Cambridge University Press): 3–74.
Smith, Holly 1983. "Culpable Ignorance," *Philosophical Review* 92: 543–71.
    1991. "Varieties of Moral Worth and Moral Credit," *Ethics* 101: 279–303.
Smith, Michael 2006. "Moore on the Right, the Good, and Uncertainty," in T. Horgan and M. Timmons (eds.), *Metaethics after Moore* (Oxford: Oxford University Press): 133–48.
    in press. "Consequentialism and the Nearest and Dearest Objection," in I. Ravenscroft (ed.), *Minds, Ethics, and Conditionals* (Oxford: Oxford University Press).
Snowdon, Paul 2003. "Knowing How and Knowing That: A Distinction Reconsidered," *Proceedings of the Aristotelian Society* 104: 1–29.
Sobel, Jordan Howard 1976. "Utilitarianism and Past and Future Mistakes," *Noûs* 10: 195–219.
Sosa, David 1993. "Consequences of Consequentialism," *Mind* 102: 101–22.
Stanley, Jason and Williamson, Timothy 2001. "Knowing How," *Journal of Philosophy* 98: 411–44.
Stocker, Michael 1971. "'Ought' and 'Can'," *Australasian Journal of Philosophy* 49: 303–16.
Strasser, Mark 1989. "Actual versus Probable Utilitarianism," *Southern Journal of Philosophy* 27: 585–97.
Strawson, Galen 1986. *Freedom and Belief*. Oxford: Clarendon Press.
Strawson, P.F. 1962. "Freedom and Resentment," *Proceedings of the British Academy* 48: 187–211.

References

Sverdlik, Steven 1993. "Pure Negligence," *American Philosophical Quarterly* 30: 137–49.

1996. "Motive and Rightness," *Ethics* 106: 327–49.

Thomason, Richmond H. 1981. "Deontic Logic and the Role of Freedom in Moral Deliberation," in R. Hilpinen (ed.), *New Studies in Deontic Logic* (Dordrecht: Reidel): 177–86.

Thomson, Judith Jarvis 1986. *Rights, Restitution, and Risk.* Cambridge, MA: Harvard University Press.

1990. *The Realm of Rights.* Cambridge, MA: Harvard University Press.

1991. "Self-Defense," *Philosophy and Public Affairs* 20: 283–310.

2001. *Goodness and Advice.* Princeton: Princeton University Press.

Timmons, Mark 2002. *Moral Theory.* Lanham, MD: Rowman and Littlefield.

Uniacke, Suzanne 1994. *Permissible Killing.* Cambridge: Cambridge University Press.

van Fraassen, Bas 1973. "Values and the Heart's Command," *Journal of Philosophy* 70: 5–19.

van Inwagen, Peter 1983. *An Essay on Free Will.* Oxford: Clarendon Press.

von Wright, Georg Henrik 1971. *Explanation and Understanding.* Ithaca: Cornell University Press.

Vorobej, Mark 2000. "Prosaic Possibilism," *Philosophical Studies* 97: 131–6.

Waldron, Jeremy 1995. "Moments of Carelessness and Massive Loss," in Owen (ed.) 1995: 387–408.

Wallace, R. Jay 1994. *Responsibility and the Moral Sentiments.* Cambridge, MA: Harvard University Press.

Weirich, Paul 2001. "Risk's Place in Decision Rules," *Synthese* 126: 427–41.

White, Alan R. 1975. *Modal Thinking.* Oxford: Blackwell.

Widerker, David 1991. "Frankfurt on 'Ought Implies Can' and Alternative Possibilities," *Analysis* 51: 222–4.

1995. "Libertarianism and Frankfurt's Attack on the Principle of Alternative Possibilities," *Philosophical Review* 104: 247–61.

Wiland, Eric 2005. "Monkeys, Typewriters, and Objective Consequentialism," *Ratio* 18: 352–60.

Williams, Bernard 1973. "Ethical Consistency," in Bernard Williams, *Problems of the Self* (Cambridge: Cambridge University Press): 166–86.

1981. *Moral Luck.* Cambridge: Cambridge University Press.

Wolf, Susan 1980. "Asymmetrical Freedom," *Journal of Philosophy* 77: 151–66.

1982. "Moral Saints," *Journal of Philosophy* 79: 419–39.

1987. "Sanity and the Metaphysics of Responsibility," in F. Schoeman (ed.), *Responsibility, Character, and the Emotions* (Cambridge: Cambridge University Press): 46–62.

Zagzebski, Linda 2000. "Does Libertarian Freedom Require Alternate Possibilities?," *Philosophical Perspectives* 14: 231–48.

Zimmerman, Michael J. 1984. *An Essay on Human Action.* New York: Peter Lang.

1988. *An Essay on Moral Responsibility.* Totowa: Rowman and Littlefield.

1994. "Rights, Compensation, and Culpability," *Law and Philosophy* 13: 419–50.

1995. "Responsibility Regarding the Unthinkable," *Midwest Studies in Philosophy* 20: 204–23.

References

1996. *The Concept of Moral Obligation*. Cambridge: Cambridge University Press.

1997a. "Moral Responsibility and Ignorance," *Ethics* 107: 410–26.

1997b. "A Plea for Accuses," *American Philosophical Quarterly* 34: 229–43.

2001. *The Nature of Intrinsic Value*. Lanham, MD: Rowman and Littlefield.

2002a. "Controlling Ignorance: A Bitter Truth," *Journal of Social Philosophy* 32: 483–90.

2002b. "Taking Luck Seriously," *Journal of Philosophy* 99: 554–76.

2003. "The Moral Significance of Alternate Possibilities," in D. Widerker and M. McKenna (eds.), *Moral Responsibility and Alternative Possibilities* (Aldershot: Ashgate): 301–25.

2004. "Another Plea for Excuses," *American Philosophical Quarterly* 41: 259–66.

2006a. "Is Moral Obligation Objective or Subjective?," *Utilitas* 18: 329–61.

2006b. "Moral Luck: A Partial Map," *Canadian Journal of Philosophy* 36: 585–608.

2006c. "On the Fulfillment of Moral Obligation," *Ethical Theory and Moral Practice* 9: 577–97.

2006d. "The Relevance of Risk to Wrongdoing," in K. McDaniel, *et al.* (eds.), *The Good, the Right, Life and Death* (Aldershot: Ashgate Press, 2006): 151–70.

2006e. "Risk, Rights, and Restitution," *Philosophical Studies* 128: 285–311.

2006f. "Shifts in Moral Obligation," *Harvard Review of Philosophy* 14: 62–79.

2007. "The Good and the Right," *Utilitas*, 19: 326–53.

Index of names

Adams, Robert Merrihew, 179
Alexander, Larry, 111
Anscombe, G.E.M., 90
Åqvist, Lennart, 122
Aristotle, 172, 192
Arpaly, Nomy, 193
Austin, J.L., 193

Bales, R. Eugene, 66
Benbaji, Yitzhak, 114
Bennett, Jonathan, 201
Blumenfeld, David, 148
Brand, Myles, 134
Brandt, Richard B., 16, 18, 179, 194, 199, 201
Broad, C.D., 12, 16, 93
Bykvist, Krister, 125

Carlson, Erik, 25, 125
Castañeda, Hector-Neri, 31
Chappell, Timothy, 66
Chisholm, Roderick M., 25, 36, 41
Conee, Earl, 67
Corrado, Michael, 135

Dahl, Norman, 199
Dancy, Jonathan, 13, 51, 68, 73
Davidson, Donald, 12, 90, 135, 185
Davis, Lawrence H., 134
Davis, Nancy, 114
Dennett, Daniel, 170

Ellsberg, Daniel, 55
Ewing, A.C., 15, 70

Feinberg, Joel, 4, 86
Feldman, Fred, 31, 60, 70, 71, 119, 122, 124, 128, 158
Feldman, Richard, 36, 39, 41
Fields, Lloyd, 192, 199
Finkelstein, Claire, 81

Fischer, John Martin, x, 148, 180
Frankena, William K., 14
Frankfurt, Harry G., 148, 172, 181, 204
Frazier, Robert L., 66

Gale, Richard M., 188
Gärdenfors, Peter, 55
Gibbard, Allan, 28
Goble, Lou, 119, 121, 123, 124, 127
Goldman, Alvin I., 24, 91, 188
Goldman, Holly S., 119, 128
    see also Smith, Holly
Greenspan, Patricia S., 61, 119
Gren, Jonas, 66, 70
Gruzalski, Bart, 32
Guerrero, Alexander A., 178

Haji, Ishtiyaque, 148, 194, 198
Hare, R.M., 66
Henderson, G.P., 152
Hieronymi, Pamela, 189
Hohfeld, Wesley Newcomb, 78
Hornsby, Jennifer, 135
Howard-Snyder, Frances, 133, 138
Huemer, Michael, 37
Humberstone, I.L., 119
Hunt, David, 148

Jackson, Frank, ix–xi, xii, 6, 17, 18, 26, 27, 29, 31, 33, 35, 39, 42, 46, 49, 59, 70, 71, 89, 93, 95, 104, 119, 121, 123, 170, 194
James, William, 188

Kagan, Shelly, 18, 73
Kahneman, Daniel, 21, 54
Kane, Robert, 148
Kant, Immanuel, 195
Katz, Fred E., 188
Knight, Frank H., 21

214

Index of names

Lemmon, E.J., 122
Lemos, Noah, 45
Lemos, Ramon, 133
Lenman, James, 66
Lockhart, Ted, 65
Luce, R. Duncan, 21
Ludwig, Kirk, 135

Marcus, Ruth Barcan, 122
Mason, Elinor, 24
Mayerfeld, Jamie, 51
McCann, Hugh, 135
McClennen, Edward F., 54
McConnell, Terrance, 9, 13
McMahan, Jeff, 102, 103, 112
Mele, Alfred R., 24
Mellor, D.H., 34, 36, 37
Menzies, Peter, 31
Milo, Ronald D., 179
Montague, Phillip, 93, 102
Montmarquet, James, 177, 183–8
Moore, G.E., 2–3, 17–18, 20, 27, 39, 45, 48, 50, 118, 132, 170, 194
Moore, Robert E., 134

Nagel, Thomas, 173
Norcross, Alastair, 66
Nowell Smith, P.H., 132, 149

Oddie, Graham, 31
Oldfield, Edward, 25
O'Shaughnessy, Brian, 135
Otsuka, Michael, 117, 148
Øverland, Gerhard, 114

Parfit, Derek, 170, 194
Pargetter, Robert, 119, 121, 123
Pereboom, Derk, 148
Prichard, H.A., xi, 8, 11

Quinn, Warren S., 25

Raiffa, Howard, 21
Ravizza, Mark, 148, 180
Regan, Donald, x
Rescher, Nicholas, 21–3, 52
Richman, Robert J., 152
Rivera López, Eduardo, 171
Robinson, Richard, 152
Rodin, David, 113, 116, 117
Ross, W.D., xi, 1, 8–14, 17, 28, 32, 44, 73–7, 87–91, 96, 135, 144, 184, 195

Rumfitt, Ian, 133
Russell, Bertrand, 18, 55

Sahlin, Nils-Eric, 55
Savage, Leonard J., 53, 54
Schlick, Moritz, 170
Schlossberger, Eugene, 179–81
Schroeder, Christopher H., 84
Sher, George, 192
Sinnott-Armstrong, Walter, 152
Slote, Michael, 5
Smart, J.J.C., 170
Smith, Holly, 176
    see also Goldman, Holly S.
Smith, Michael, 39
Snowdon, Paul, 133
Sobel, Jordan Howard, 119
Sosa, David, 26
Stanley, Jason, 133
Stocker, Michael, 152
Strasser, Mark, 70
Strawson, Galen, 173
Strawson, P.F., 180
Sverdlik, Steven, 177, 195

Thomason, Richmond H., 119
Thomson, Judith Jarvis, 1, 32, 47–8, 80–3, 93, 101, 102, 114, 116, 194
Timmons, Mark, 170
Tversky, Amos, 21, 54
Twain, Mark, 180, 201

Uniacke, Suzanne, 113, 116

van Fraassen, Bas, 122
van Inwagen, Peter, 148, 180
von Wright, Georg Henrik, 183, 184
Vorobej, Mark, 125

Waldron, Jeremy, 84
Wallace, R. Jay, 171, 180
Weirich, Paul, 55
White, Alan R., 152
Widerker, David, 148, 205
Wiland, Eric, 24
Williams, Bernard, 31, 122, 173
Williamson, Timothy, 133
Wolf, Susan, 16, 181

Zagzebski, Linda, 148

215

Index of subjects

accuses, 104, 109, 171–2, 193–205
action,
  basic *vs.* non-basic, 133, 184–6, 188–9
  courses of, 127–47, 151–68
  habitual, 191
  intentional, 24–6, 48, 91–2, 107, 118,
    132–8, 145, 185–6, 189, 191, 195
  results of, 183, 184–5, 186, 188, 189
acts, individuation of, 90, 129, 186, 188, 202
Actualism, 118–27
Allais's paradox, 53–4
alternatives, 130, 141, 147, 158, 169, 170
  see also options
Attempt Thesis, 11, 135
attempts, 11, 134–8, 145–6, 150, 182, 184,
  194, 202–3

blameworthiness, 9–10, 15–18, 30, 35,
  48–9, 60, 103–4, 157, 169–71,
  175–83, 190–205

"can,"
  see control
carefulness and carelessness, 183–6, 189
Case 1, 6, 8, 11
Case 2, 17–18, 46–8, 49, 137, 170
Case 3, 17–21, 23–40, 49, 52, 57–9, 70–1,
  85, 93, 98, 104
Case 4, 53
Case 5, 55
Case 6, 55
Case 7, 68
Case 8, 89, 138, 145
Case 9, 92, 94–5
Case 10, 97–9, 107–8, 117, 120, 174,
  201, 203
  Case 10A, 100, 104–6, 107–9, 111, 116
  Case 10B, 108–9, 112, 115, 116, 202
  Case 10C, 110, 111–12, 113, 115, 117

Case 10E, 106–9, 111, 113, 116
Case 10F, 109, 112, 115, 116, 202
Case 10G, 110–13, 115, 117
Case 10H, 113
Case 11, 120, 124, 136, 140
Case 12, 124, 137
Case 13, 124–5, 126, 132, 134, 135–6, 149
Case 14, 125, 126, 132, 136, 150
character, 180–1, 199
closed-mindedness, 187–9
compensation, 83–5, 95
conscientiousness, 2, 7, 14–16, 18, 20, 27–8,
  33, 35, 43, 45, 49, 57–61, 62–5,
  67–8, 70, 93, 195–6, 199, 202–4
consequentialism, 2–3, 5, 19, 25, 33, 58, 72,
  75, 76, 99, 129, 196
control, 2, 11–14, 23, 42, 72, 92, 112, 113,
  116, 119–20, 122, 129, 146–53, 172,
  175, 178–80, 181
  coincidental *vs.* intentional, 24, 91, 133,
    149–51, 172, 178, 185, 187
  complete *vs.* partial, 12–14, 150–1, 178
  direct *vs.* indirect, 12–13, 150–1, 154,
    175, 178, 182, 183–9
  immediate *vs.* remote, 128, 150–68, 178
  regulative *vs.* guidance, 148–50, 178,
    180, 205
Correlativity Thesis, 78–80, 85, 86–7, 88,
  92, 93–4, 96, 100, 102, 107, 111,
  117, 143
culpability,
  direct *vs.* indirect, 175–8, 182–3, 190, 191
  see also blameworthiness

decision procedures, 65–6
desert, 84, 181–2, 193, 200

endangerment, 97, 106–7, 110
Equivalence Thesis, 171, 205

evidence, 6–8, 17–20, 24, 30–1, 34–46,
    47–52, 54–60, 65–6, 69–70, 72, 77,
    86–8, 92–116, 124, 126, 137, 144,
    153, 157, 158, 164, 169–70, 173,
    174, 188, 192, 201
excuses, 10, 48, 103, 112, 157, 171–93, 196,
    201, 204–5
    vs. justifications, 171, 193, 205

fidelity, 75, 79, 85, 87–97, 144, 151–68
Figure 3.1, 154, 155, 158, 164
Figure 3.2, 159, 160
Figure 3.3, 160
Figure 3.4, 165
Figure 4.1, 182, 184
freedom of will or action, 148, 172, 179–80,
    181, 185, 198, 200–2, 203
    see also control

Good Samaritan Paradox, 121

harm, 20–3, 73, 80–3, 97–100, 104–11,
    113–14, 116, 144
Harm Thesis, 80, 81
High-Risk Thesis, 81, 83

incapacitation, 156–7, 162–4
inheritance principles, 47–8, 82, 131–2
intentional action,
    see action, intentional
interests, 92, 94, 112

justifications, 104–5, 111–13
    see also excuses, vs. justifications

know-how,
    see control, coincidental *vs.* intentional

laudability,
    see praiseworthiness
luck, 9, 29–30, 84, 106, 115–16, 173

Means Principle for Rights, 81, 82
moral dilemmas,
    see obligation, conflicts of
moral evaluation, types of, 172, 179–82,
    193, 194, 199–201
motives, 195

Objective View,
    see obligation, Objective View of

obligation,
    associative *vs.* non-associative, 79–80, 87,
        88, 96–7, 109, 116, 143, 164
    cancellation of, 164
    conditional *vs.* unconditional, 61–4, 118,
        124, 129, 135, 138–46, 151, 165
    conflicts of, 29, 61, 66–8, 94, 122, 203
    direct *vs.* indirect, 90–1, 119, 135, 138,
        144–6, 162
    extinction of, 163, 165
    fulfillment of, 123, 153–6, 158, 161, 163,
        166–8, 171
    immediate *vs.* remote, 128, 151–68
    infringement of, 155, 157, 158, 161,
        166–8
    knowledge of, 10, 14, 43–5, 57–71, 173
    levels of, 61–4, 68, 77, 119, 141–3, 146,
        164–5
    Objective View of, 2–6, 8–10, 17–33,
        41–2, 45–6, 48–51, 57–9, 65, 68–9,
        71, 74–7, 87–8, 90–1, 92, 98–100,
        103–6, 112, 116, 118–19, 126–7,
        144, 157, 169, 178, 196
        first formulation, 2, 72, 119
        second formulation, 76, 77
    orders of, 60–8
    overriding of, 80, 101, 111, 154,
        164–6, 171
    prima facie, 73–80, 83, 100, 111, 118–19,
        142–4, 146, 151, 153, 171
    Prospective View of,
        first formulation, 6
        second formulation, 19
        third formulation, 33, 49
        fourth formulation, 39
        fifth formulation, 42, 49–50, 51
        sixth formulation, 56, 72, 126
        seventh formulation, 78, 87, 118,
            126, 142
        eighth formulation, 128
        final formulations, 135, 139, 141, 142,
            143, 145, 146
    recurrence of, 94, 164
    restoration of, 155, 165
    shifts in, 119, 123, 151–68
    Subjective View of, 5–6, 8–16, 27, 33–5,
        42–3, 45–6, 49–51, 72, 74, 87–8, 90,
        118, 127, 157, 169, 174
    subsidiary,
        see obligation, levels of
    supersession of, 163–6

obligation, (cont.)
termination of, 164
violation of,
see obligation, infringement of
omission, 172, 175, 185–6, 194
Optionality, Principle of, 146–53
options, 2, 23–6, 72, 119–20, 147
Origination Thesis, 176, 190, 192, 205
"ought," ambiguity of, 1, 6–7, 15, 27, 31, 60–8, 93

Possibilism, 118–68
praiseworthiness, 16, 169, 171, 180, 181, 193
probability, 6, 18–20, 22–3, 25, 33–42, 46, 51–5, 57, 69–70, 88–9, 106, 111, 126–7, 129, 134, 143
see also evidence
promising,
see fidelity
Prospective View,
see obligation, Prospective View of
punishment and reward, 180–2, 193–4

regret, 28
reparation, 75
responsibility, 29, 115, 147, 148, 169–205
see also blameworthiness; praiseworthiness
"responsibility," ambiguity of, 30, 169–71
reward,
see punishment and reward
rightness and doing right, 1, 2, 5, 8–9, 28, 45, 58–9, 72, 76–8, 90, 111, 119, 133–4, 139, 141, 142–3, 146, 170, 180, 195, 197, 202
rights, 73, 78–117, 144
conditional *vs.* unconditional, 102
forfeiture of, 102–17, 164
human, 113–15
infringement of, 80, 81, 83, 86, 93, 95, 99, 100–2, 107–8, 116, 117, 156
involuntary loss of, 111, 113–17
overriding of, 83
to life, 100–17, 144
violation of,
see rights, infringement of
waiver of, 101, 112, 116, 117, 161, 164
rights theory, 4, 34

risk, 19–24, 26–7, 28–30, 33, 37, 51, 52, 55, 72, 80–7, 93, 97, 99, 106–11, 114, 126, 132, 134, 136, 174, 201
see also wrongness and wrongdoing, risk of
Risk Thesis, 81–7
first formulation, 81
second formulation, 85
third formulation, 87
Russian roulette, 81, 93

self-defense, 73, 97–117, 201
self-imposed impossibility, 146, 152–5
Subjective View,
see obligation, Subjective View of
suitability, moral, 74–8, 87, 89, 92–4, 142–4, 153, 165
supererogation, 55–6, 57, 199–200

uncertainty, doxastic *vs.* epistemic, ix, 170

value,
actual, 19–20, 22–3, 26–31, 33, 37–40, 45–6, 49, 52–3, 58, 64–6, 70, 74, 77–8, 88, 94, 97–114, 124, 129, 153, 158, 169, 174, 201
expectable, 38–42, 43, 46, 48–56, 74, 126
expected, 19–28, 32–3, 35, 37–40, 49, 52, 65, 129, 136–8
prospective, 18–19, 21–2, 23, 33, 51–9, 64–5, 69–71, 72, 77, 89–96, 108–10, 118, 124, 126, 129, 130–1, 133–8, 139, 153, 159–60, 165, 174, 202
virtue theory, 4, 5, 33, 58, 72, 76, 99, 129

Wrongdoing,
First Principle of, 155, 158, 160
Second Principle of, 160–3, 166
Third Principle of, 166
Fourth Principle of, 167
Fifth Principle of, 167
wrongness and wrongdoing, 1–2, 5, 7, 10, 14–18, 20, 29, 35, 46, 48–50, 54, 72, 75–9, 81, 85, 97–114, 116, 119, 122, 133–4, 139, 141, 142–3, 146, 153–8, 160–8, 170–1
beliefs about, 173–205
risk of, 20, 57–71
sanctioning of, 122–4

Made in the USA
Lexington, KY
03 June 2013